Siegel's

CIVIL PROCEDURE

Essay and Multiple-Choice Questions and Answers

BRIAN N. SIEGEL
J.D., Columbia Law School
and
LAZAR EMANUEL
J.D., Harvard Law School

ASPEN

PUBLISHERS

111 Eighth Avenue, New York, NY 10011
www.aspenpublishers.com

Printed in the United States of America.
2 3 4 5 6 7 8 9 0
ISBN 0-7355-5684-9

This book is intended as a general review of a legal subject. It is not intended as a source of advice for the solution of legal matters or problems. For advice on legal matters, the reader should consult an attorney.

About Aspen Publishers

Aspen Publishers, headquartered in New York City, is a leading information provider for attorneys, business professionals, and law students. Written by preeminent authorities, our products consist of analytical and practical information covering both U.S. and international topics. We publish in the full range of formats, including updated manuals, books, periodicals, CDs, and online products.

Our proprietary content is complemented by 2,500 legal databases, containing over 11 million documents, available through our Loislaw division. Aspen Publishers also offers a wide range of topical legal and business databases linked to Loislaw's primary material. Our mission is to provide accurate, timely, and authoritative content in easily accessible formats, supported by unmatched customer care.

To order any Aspen Publishers title, go to *www.aspenpublishers.com* or call 1-800-638-8437.

To reinstate your manual update service, call 1-800-638-8437.

For more information on Loislaw products, go to *www.loislaw.com* or call 1-800-364-2512.

For Customer Care issues, e-mail *CustomerCare@aspenpublishers.com*; call 1-800-234-1660; or fax 1-800-901-9075.

Aspen Publishers
a Wolters Kluwer business

Acknowledgment

The authors gratefully acknowledge the assistance of the California Committee of Bar Examiners, which provided access to questions upon which many of the questions in this book are based.

Introduction

Although law school grades are a significant factor in obtaining a summer internship or entry position at a law firm, no formalized preparation for finals is offered at most law schools. For the most part, students are expected to fend for themselves in learning how to take a law school exam. Ironically, law school exams ordinarily bear little correspondence to the teaching methods used by professors during the school year. Professors require you to spend most of your time briefing cases. Although many claim this is "great preparation" for issue-spotting on exams, it really isn't. Because, in briefing cases, you are made to focus on one or two principles of law at a time, you don't get practice in relating one issue to another or in developing a picture of an entire problem or the entire course. When exams finally come, you're forced to make an abrupt 180-degree turn. Suddenly, you are asked to recognize, define, and discuss a variety of issues buried within a single multi-issue fact pattern. In most schools, you are then asked to select among a number of possible answers, all of which look inviting but only one of which is right.

The comprehensive course outline you've created so diligently, and with such pain, means little if you're unable to apply its contents on your final exams. There is a vast difference between reading opinions in which the legal principles are clearly stated, and applying those same principles to hypothetical essay exams and multiple-choice questions.

The purpose of this book is to help you bridge the gap between memorizing a rule of law and **understanding how to use it** in an exam. After an initial overview describing the exam writing process, you see a large number of hypotheticals which test your ability to write analytical essays and to pick the right answers to multiple-choice questions. **Read them—all of them!** Then review the suggested answers which follow. You'll find that the key to superior grades lies in applying your knowledge through questions and answers, not through rote memory.

GOOD LUCK !

Table of Contents

Multiple-Choice Questions

Multiple-Choice Answers

Tables and Index

Preparing Effectively for Essay Examinations[1]

To achieve superior scores on essay exams, a law student must (1) learn and understand "blackletter" principles and rules of law for each subject; (2) analyze how those principles of law arise within a test fact pattern; and (3) write clearly and succinctly a short discussion of each principle and how it relates to the facts. One of the most common misconceptions about law school is that you must memorize each word on every page of your casebooks or outlines to do well on exams. The reality is that you can commit an entire casebook to memory and still do poorly on an exam. Our review of hundreds of student answers has shown us that most students can recite the rules. The students who do *best* on exams are able to analyze how the rules they have memorized relate to the facts in the questions, and how to communicate their analysis to the grader. The following pages cover what you need to know to achieve superior scores on your law school essay exams.

The "ERC" Process

To study effectively for law school exams you must be able to "*ERC*" (*E*lementize, *R*ecognize, and *C*onceptualize) each legal principle covered in your casebooks and course outlines. *Elementizing* means reducing each legal theory and rule you learn to a concise, straightforward statement of its essential elements. Without knowledge of these elements, it's difficult to see all the issues as they arise.

For example, if you are asked, "What is self-defense?", it is *not* enough to say, "self-defense is permitted when, if someone is about to hit you, you can prevent him from doing it." This layperson description would leave a grader wondering if you had actually attended law school. An accurate statement of the self-defense principle would go something like this: "When one reasonably believes she is in imminent danger of an offensive touching, she may assert whatever force she reasonably believes necessary under the circumstances to prevent the offensive touching from occurring." This formulation correctly shows that there are four separate, distinct elements which must be satisfied before the defense of self-defense can be successfully asserted: (1) the actor must have a *reasonable belief* that (2) the touching which she seeks to prevent is *offensive*, and that (3) the offensive touching is *imminent*, and

---

1 To illustrate the principles of effective exam preparation, we have used examples from Torts and Constitutional Law. However, these principles apply to all subjects. One of the most difficult tasks faced by law students is learning how to apply principles from one area of the law to another. We leave it to you, the reader, to think of comparable examples for the subject-matter of this book.

(4) she must use no greater force than she ***reasonably believes necessary under the circumstances*** to prevent the offensive touching from occurring.

Recognizing means perceiving or anticipating which words or ideas within a legal principle are likely to be the source of issues, and how those issues are likely to arise within a given hypothetical fact pattern. With respect to the self-defense concept, there are four ***potential*** issues. Did the actor reasonably believe the other person was about to make an offensive contact with her? Was the contact imminent? Would the contact have been offensive? Did she use only such force as she reasonably believed necessary to prevent the imminent, offensive touching?

Conceptualizing means imagining situations in which each of the elements of a rule of law can give rise to factual issues. ***Unless you can imagine or construct an application of each element of a rule, you don't truly understand the legal principles behind the rule!*** In our opinion, the inability to conjure up hypothetical fact patterns or stories involving particular rules of law foretells a likelihood that you will miss issues involving those rules on an exam. It's ***crucial*** (1) to ***recognize*** that issues result from the interaction of facts with the words defining a rule of law; and (2) to develop the ability to ***conceptualize*** or ***imagine*** fact patterns using the words or concepts within the rule.

For example, a set of facts illustrating the "reasonable belief" element of the self-defense rule might be the following:

> One evening, A and B had an argument at a bar. A screamed at B, "I'm going to get a knife and stab you!" A then ran out of the bar. B, who was armed with a concealed pistol, left the bar about 15 minutes later. As B was walking home, he heard someone running toward him from behind. B drew his pistol, turned, and shot the person advancing toward him (who was only about ten feet away when the shooting occurred). When B walked over to his victim, he realized that the person he had shot was dead and was not A, but another individual who had simply decided to take an evening jog. There would certainly be an issue whether B had a reasonable belief that the person who was running behind him was A. In the subsequent wrongful-death action, the victim's estate would contend that the earlier threat by A was not enough to give B a reasonable belief that the person running behind him was A. B could contend in rebuttal that given the prior altercation at the bar, A's threat, the darkness, and the fact that the incident occurred soon after A's threat, his belief that A was about to attack him was "reasonable."

An illustration of how the word "imminent" might generate an issue is the following:

> X and Y had been feuding for some time. One afternoon, X suddenly attacked Y with a hunting knife. However, Y was able to wrest the knife

> away from X. At that point, X retreated about four feet away from Y and screamed: "You were lucky this time, but next time I'll have a gun and you'll be finished." Y, having good reason to believe that X would subsequently carry out his threats (after all, X had just attempted to kill Y), immediately thrust the knife into X's chest, killing him. While Y certainly had a reasonable belief that X would attempt to kill him the ***next time*** the two met, Y would probably ***not*** be able to assert the self-defense privilege because the element of "imminency" was absent.

A fact pattern illustrating the actor's right to use only that force which is reasonably necessary under the circumstances might be the following:

> D rolled up a newspaper and was about to strike E on the shoulder with it. As D pulled back his arm for the purpose of delivering the blow, E drew a knife and plunged it into D's chest. While E had every reason to believe that D was about to deliver an offensive impact on him, E probably could not successfully assert the self-defense privilege because the force he utilized in response was greater than reasonably necessary under the circumstances to prevent the impact. E could simply have deflected D's blow or punched D away. The use of a knife constituted a degree of force by E which was ***not*** reasonable, given the minor injury which he would have suffered from the newspaper's impact.

"Mental games" such as these must be played with every element of every rule you learn.

Issue-Spotting

One of the keys to doing well on an essay examination is issue-spotting. In fact, issue-spotting is ***the*** most important skill you will learn in law school. If you recognize a legal issue, you can always find the applicable rule of law (if there is any) by researching the issue. But if you fail to see the issues, you won't learn the steps that lead to success or failure on exams or, for that matter, in the practice of law. It is important to remember that (1) an issue is a question to be decided by the judge or jury; and (2) a question is "in issue" when it can be disputed or argued about at trial. The bottom line is that *if you don't spot an issue, you can't raise it or discuss it.*

The key to issue-spotting is to learn to approach a problem in the same way as an attorney does. Let's assume you've been admitted to practice and a client enters your office with a legal problem. He will recite his facts to you and give you any documents that may be pertinent. He will then want to know if he can sue (or be sued, if your client seeks to avoid liability). To answer your client's questions intelligently, you will have to decide the following: (1) what principles or rules can possibly be asserted by your client; (2) what defense or defenses can possibly be raised to these principles; (3) what issues may arise if these defenses are asserted; (4) what arguments can each side make to persuade the fact-finder to resolve the issue in his favor; and (5) finally, what will the *likely* outcome of each issue be. *All the issues which can possibly arise at trial will be relevant to your answers.*

How to Discuss an Issue

Keep in mind that *rules of law are the guides to issues* (i.e., an issue arises where there is a question whether the facts do, or do not, satisfy an element of a rule); a rule of law *cannot dispose of an issue* unless the rule can reasonably be *applied to the facts.*

A good way to learn how to discuss an issue is to study the following mini-hypothetical and the two student responses which follow it.

Mini-Hypothetical

A and B were involved in making a movie which was being filmed at a local bar. The script called for A to appear to throw a bottle (which was actually a rubber prop) at B. The fluorescent lighting at the bar had been altered for the movie—the usual subdued blue lights had been replaced with rather bright white lights. The cameraperson had stationed herself just to the left of the swinging doors which served as the main entrance to the bar. As the scene was unfolding, C, a regular patron of the bar, unwittingly walked into it. The guard who was usually stationed immediately outside the bar had momentarily left his post to visit the restroom. As C pushed the barroom doors inward, the left door panel knocked the camera to the ground with a resounding crash. The first (and only) thing C saw was A (about 5 feet from C), who was getting ready to throw the bottle at B, who was at the other end of the bar (about 15 feet from A). Without hesitation, C pushed A to the ground and punched him in the face. Plastic surgery was required to restore A's profile to its Hollywood-handsome pre-altercation look.

Discuss A's right against C.

Pertinent Principles of Law:

1. Under the rule defining the prevention-of-crime privilege, if one sees that someone is about to commit what she reasonably believes to be a felony or misdemeanor involving a breach of the peace, she may exercise whatever degree of force is reasonably necessary under the circumstances to prevent that person from committing the crime.

2. Under the defense-of-others privilege, where one reasonably believes that someone is about to cause an offensive contact upon a third party, she may use whatever force is reasonably necessary under the circumstances to prevent the contact. Some jurisdictions, however, limit this privilege to situations in which the actor and the third party are related.

First Student Answer

Did C commit an assault and battery upon A?

An assault occurs when the defendant intentionally causes the plaintiff to be reasonably in apprehension of an imminent, offensive touching. The facts state that C punched A to the ground. Thus, a battery would have occurred at this point. We are also told that C punched A in the face. It is reasonable to assume that A saw the punch being thrown at him, and therefore A felt in imminent danger of an offensive touching. Based upon the facts, C has committed an assault and battery upon A.

Were C's actions justifiable under the defense-of-others privilege?

C could successfully assert the defense-of-others and prevention-of-crime privileges. When C opened the bar doors, A appeared to be throwing the bottle at B. Although the "bottle" was actually a prop, C had no way of knowing this fact. Also, it was necessary for C to punch A in the face to assure that A could not get back up, retrieve the bottle, and again throw it at B. While the plastic surgery required by A is unfortunate, C could not be successfully charged with assault and battery.

Second Student Answer

Assault and Battery:

C committed an assault (causing A to be reasonably in apprehension of an imminent, offensive contact) when A saw that C's punch was about to hit him, and battery (causing an offensive contact upon A) when (1) C knocked A to the ground, and (2) C punched A.

Defense-of-Others/Prevention-of-Crime Defenses:

C would undoubtedly assert the privileges of defense-of-others (when defendant reasonably believed the plaintiff was about to make an offensive contact upon a third party, he was entitled to use whatever force was reasonably necessary to prevent the contact); and prevention-of-crime defense (when one reasonably believes another is about to commit a felony or misdemeanor involving a breach of the peace, he may exercise whatever force is reasonably necessary to prevent that person from committing a crime).

A could contend that C was not reasonable in believing that A was about to cause harm to B because the enhanced lighting at the bar and camera crash should have indicated to C, a regular customer, that a movie was being filmed. However, C could probably successfully contend in rebuttal that his belief was reasonable in light of the facts that (1) he had not seen the camera when he attacked A, and (2) instantaneous action was required (he did not have time to notice the enhanced lighting around the bar).

A might also contend that the justification was forfeited because the degree of force used by C was not reasonable, since C did not have to punch A in the face after A had already been pushed to the ground (i.e., the danger to B was no longer present). However, C could argue in rebuttal that it was necessary to knockout A (an individual with apparently violent propensities) while the opportunity existed, rather than risk a drawn-out scuffle in which A might prevail. The facts do not indicate how big A and C were; but assuming C was not significantly larger than A, C's contention will probably be successful. If, however, C was significantly larger than A, the punch may have been excessive (since C could presumably have simply held A down).

Critique

Let's examine the First Student Answer first. It mistakenly treats as an "issue" the assault and battery committed by C upon A. While the actions creating these torts must be mentioned in the facts to provide a foundation for a discussion of the applicable privileges, there was no need to discuss them further because they were not the issue the examiners were testing for.

The structure of the initial paragraph of First Student Answer is also incorrect. After an assault is defined in the first sentence, the second sentence abruptly describes the facts necessary to constitute the commission of a battery. The third sentence then sets forth the elements of a battery. The fourth sentence completes the discussion of assault by describing the facts pertaining to that tort. The two-sentence break between the original mention of assault and the facts which constitute assault is confusing; the facts which call for the application of a rule should be mentioned *immediately* after the rule is stated.

A more serious error, however, occurs in the second paragraph of the First Student Answer. While there is an allusion to the correct principle of law (prevention of crime), the **rule is not stated**. As a consequence, the grader can only guess why the student thinks the facts set forth in the subsequent sentences are significant. A grader reading this answer could not be certain whether the student recognized that the issues revolved around the **reasonable belief** and **necessary force** elements of the prevention-of-crime privilege. Superior exam-writing requires that the pertinent facts be **tied** directly and clearly to the operative rule.

The Second Student Answer is very much better than the First Answer. It disposes of C's assault and battery upon A in a few words (yet tells the grader that the writer knows these torts are present). More importantly, the grader can easily see the issues which would arise if the prevention-of crime privilege were asserted (i.e., "whether C's belief that A was about to commit a crime against B was reasonable" and "whether C used unnecessary force in punching A after A had been knocked to the ground"). Finally, it also utilizes all the facts by indicating how an attorney would assert those facts which are most advantageous to her client.

Structuring Your Answer

Graders will give high marks to a clearly written, well-structured answer. Each issue you discuss should follow a specific and consistent structure which a grader can easily follow.

The Second Student Answer basically utilizes the **I-R-A-A-O format** with respect to each issue. In this format, the **I** stands for the word **Issue**; the **R** for **Rule of law**; the initial **A** for the words **one side's Argument**; the second **A** for **the other party's rebuttal Argument**; and the **O** for your **Opinion as to how the issue would be resolved**. The **I-R-A-A-O** format emphasizes the importance of (1) discussing **both** sides of an issue, and (2) communicating to the grader that where an issue arises, an attorney can only advise her client as to the **probable** decision on that issue.

A somewhat different format for analyzing each issue is the **I-R-A-C format**. Here, the **I** stands for **Issue;** the **R** for **Rule of law;** the **A** for **Application of the facts to the rule of law;** and the **C** for **Conclusion. I-R-A-C** is a legitimate approach to the discussion of a particular issue, within the time constraints imposed by the question. The **I-R-A-C format** must be applied to each issue in the question; it is not the solution to the entire answer. If there are six issues in a question, for example, you should offer six separate, independent **I-R-A-C** analyses.

We believe that the **I-R-A-C** approach is preferable to the **I-R-A-A-O** formula. However, either can be used to analyze and organize essay exam answers. Whatever format you choose, however, you should be consistent throughout the exam and remember the following rules:

First, *analyze all of the relevant facts.* Facts have significance in a particular case *only as they come under the applicable rules of law.* The facts presented must be analyzed and examined to see if they do or do not satisfy one element or another of the applicable rules, and the essential facts and rules must be stated and argued in your analysis.

Second, you must communicate to the grader the *precise rule of law* controlling the facts. In their eagerness to commence their arguments, students sometimes fail to state the applicable rule of law first. Remember, the *R* in either format stands for *Rule of Law.* Defining the rule of law *before* an analysis of the facts is essential in order to allow the grader to follow your reasoning.

Third, it is important to treat *each side of an issue with equal detail.* If a hypothetical describes how an elderly man was killed when he ventured upon the land of a huge power company to obtain a better view of a nuclear reactor, your sympathies might understandably fall on the side of the old man. The grader will nevertheless expect you to see and make every possible argument for the other side. Don't permit your personal viewpoint to affect your answer! A good lawyer never does! When discussing an issue, always state the arguments for each side.

Finally, don't forget to *state your opinion or conclusion* on each issue. Keep in mind, however, that your opinion or conclusion is probably the *least* important part of an exam answer. Why? Because your professor knows that no attorney can tell her client exactly how a judge or jury will decide a particular issue. By definition, an issue is a legal dispute which can go either way. An attorney, therefore, can offer her client only her best opinion about the likelihood of victory or defeat on an issue. Since the decision on any issue lies with the judge or jury, no attorney can ever be absolutely certain of the resolution.

Discuss All Possible Issues

As we've noted, a student should draw *some* type of conclusion or opinion for each issue raised. Whatever your conclusion on a particular issue, it is essential to anticipate and discuss *all of the issues* which would arise if the question were actually tried in court.

Let's assume that a negligence hypothetical involves issues pertaining to duty, breach of duty, proximate causation, and contributory negligence. If the defendant prevails on any one of these issues, he will avoid liability. Nevertheless, even if you feel strongly that the defendant owed no duty to the plaintiff, you *must* go on to discuss all of the other potential issues as well (breach of duty, proximate causation, and contributory negligence). If you were to terminate your answer after a discussion of the duty element only, you'd receive an inferior grade.

Why should you have to discuss every possible issue if you are relatively certain that the outcome of a particular issue would be dispositive of the entire case? Because at the commencement of litigation, neither party can be *absolutely positive* about which issues he will prevail upon at trial. We can state with confidence that every attorney with some degree of experience has won issues he thought he would lose, and has lost issues on which victory was assured. Since one can never be absolutely certain how a factual issue will be resolved by the fact-finder, a good attorney (and exam-writer) will consider *all* possible issues.

To understand the importance of discussing all of the potential issues, you should reflect on what you will do in the actual practice of law. If you represent the defendant, for example, it is your job to raise every possible defense. If there are five potential defenses, and your pleadings only rely on three of them (because you're sure you will win on all three), and the plaintiff is somehow successful on all three issues, your client may well sue you for malpractice. Your client's contention would be that you should be liable because if you had only raised the two additional issues, you might have prevailed on at least one of them, and therefore liability would have been avoided. It is an attorney's duty to raise *all* legitimate issues. A similar philosophy should be followed when taking essay exams.

What exactly do you say when you've resolved the initial issue in favor of the defendant, and discussion of any additional issues would seem to be moot? The answer is simple. You begin the discussion of the next issue with something like, "Assuming, however, the plaintiff prevailed on the foregoing issue, the next issue would be . . ." The grader will understand and appreciate what you have done.

The corollary to the importance of raising all potential issues is that you should avoid discussion of obvious non-issues. Raising non-issues is detrimental in three ways: first, you waste a lot of precious time; second, you usually receive absolutely no points for discussing a point which the grader deems extraneous; and third, it suggests to the grader that you lack the ability to distinguish the significant from the irrelevant. The best guideline for avoiding the discussion of a non-issue is to ask yourself, "Would I, as an attorney, feel comfortable about raising that particular issue or objection in front of a judge"?

Delineate the Transition from One Issue to the Next

It's a good idea to make it easy for the grader to see the issues you've found. One way to accomplish this is to cover no more than one issue per paragraph. Another way is to underline each issue statement. Provided time permits, we recommend that you use both techniques. The essay answers in this book contain numerous illustrations of these suggestions.

One frequent student error is to write two separate paragraphs in which all of the arguments for one side are made in the initial paragraph, and all of the rebuttal arguments by the other side are made in the next paragraph. This is *a bad idea*. It obliges the grader to reconstruct the exam answer in his mind several times to determine whether all possible issues have been discussed by both sides. It will also cause you to state the same rule of law more than once. A better-organized answer presents a given argument by one side and follows that immediately in the same paragraph with the other side's rebuttal to that argument.

Understanding the "Call" of a Question

The statement *at the end of* an essay question or of the fact pattern in a multiple-choice question is sometimes referred to as the "call" of the question. It usually asks you to do something specific like "discuss," "discuss the rights of the parties," "what are X's rights?" "advise X," "the best grounds on which to find the statute unconstitutional are:," "D can be convicted of:," "how should the estate be distributed?," etc. The call of the question should be read carefully because it tells you exactly what you're expected to do. If a question asks, "what are X's rights against Y?" or "X is liable to Y for: . . ." you don't have to spend a lot of time on Y's rights against Z. You will usually receive absolutely no credit for discussing issues or facts that are not required by the call. On the other hand, if the call of an essay question is simply "discuss" or "discuss the rights of the parties," then *all* foreseeable issues must be covered by your answer.

Students are often led astray by an essay question's call. For example, if you are asked for "X's rights against Y" or to "advise X," you may think you may limit yourself to X's viewpoint with respect to the issues. This is *not correct!* You cannot resolve one party's rights against another party without considering the issues which would arise (and the arguments which the other side would assert) if litigation occurred. In short, although the call of the question may appear to focus on the rights of one of the parties to the litigation, a superior answer will cover all the issues and arguments which that person might *encounter* (not just the arguments she would *make*) in attempting to pursue her rights against the other side.

The Importance of Analyzing the Question Carefully Before Writing

The overriding *time pressure* of an essay exam is probably a major reason why many students fail to analyze a question carefully before writing. Five minutes into the allocated time for a particular question, you may notice that the person next to you is writing furiously. This thought then flashes through your mind, "Oh, my goodness, he's putting down more words on the paper than I am, and therefore he's bound to get a better grade." It can be stated *unequivocally* that there is no necessary correlation between the number of words on your exam paper and the grade you'll receive. Students who begin their answer after only five minutes of analysis have probably seen only the most obvious issues, and missed many, if not most, of the subtle ones. They are also likely to be less well-organized.

Opinions differ as to how much time you should spend analyzing and outlining a question before you actually write the answer. We believe that you should spend at least 12 to 18 minutes analyzing, organizing, and outlining a one-hour question before writing your answer. This will usually provide sufficient time to analyze and organize the question thoroughly *and* enough time to write a relatively complete answer. Remember that each word of the question must be scrutinized to determine if it (1) suggests an issue under the operative rules of law, or (2) can be used in making an argument for the resolution of an issue. Since you can't receive points for an issue you don't spot, it is usually wise to read a question *twice* before starting your outline.

When to Make an Assumption

The instructions for a question may tell you to *assume* facts which are necessary to the answer. Even when these instructions are *not* given, you may be obliged to make certain assumptions about missing facts in order to write a thorough answer. Assumptions should be made only when you are told or when you, as the attorney for one of the parties described in the question, would be obliged to solicit additional information from your client. On the other hand, assumptions should *never be used to change or alter the question*. Don't ever write something like "if the facts in the question were . . . , instead of . . . , then . . . would result." If you do this, you are wasting time on facts which are extraneous to the problem before you. Professors want you to deal with *their* fact patterns, not your own.

Students sometimes try to "write around" information they think is missing. They assume that their professor has failed to include every piece of data necessary for a thorough answer. This is generally *wrong*. The professor may have omitted some facts deliberately to see if the student *can figure out what to do* under the circumstances. In some instances, the professor may have omitted them inadvertently (even law professors are sometimes human).

The way to deal with the omission of essential information is to describe (1) what fact (or facts) appear to be missing, and (2) why that information is important. As an example, go back to the "movie shoot" hypothetical we discussed above. In that fact pattern, there was no mention of the relative strength of A and C. This fact could be extremely important. If C weighed 240 pounds and was built like a professional football linebacker, while A tipped the scales at a mere 160 pounds, punching A in the face after he had been pushed to the ground would probably constitute unnecessary force (thereby causing C to forfeit the prevention-of-crime privilege). If the physiques of the parties were reversed, however, C's punch to A's face would probably constitute reasonable behavior. Under the facts, C had to deal the "knockout" blow while the opportunity presented itself. The last sentences of the Second Student Answer above show that the student understood these subtleties and correctly supplied the essential missing facts and assumptions.

Assumptions should be made in a manner which keeps the other issues open (i.e., they lead to a discussion of all other possible issues). Don't assume facts which would virtually dispose of the entire hypothetical in a few sentences. For example, suppose that A called B a "convicted felon" (a statement which is inherently defamatory, i.e., a defamatory statement is one which tends to subject the plaintiff to hatred, contempt, or ridicule). If A's statement is true, he has a complete defense to B's action for defamation. If the facts don't tell whether A's statement was true or not, it would *not* be wise to write something like, "We'll assume that A's statement about B is accurate, and therefore B cannot successfully sue A for defamation." So facile an approach would rarely be appreciated by the grader. The proper way to handle this situation would be to state, "If we assume that A's statement about B is not correct, A cannot raise the defense of truth." You've communicated to the grader that you recognize the need to assume an essential fact and that you've assumed it in a way that enables you to proceed to discuss all other issues.

Case Names

A law student is ordinarily *not* expected to recall case names on an exam. The professor knows that you have read several hundred cases for each course, and that you would have to be a memory expert to have all of the names at your fingertips. If you confront a fact pattern which seems similar to a case which you have reviewed (but you cannot recall its name), just write something like, "One case we've read held that . . ." or "It has been held that. . . . " In this manner, you have informed the grader that you are relying on a case which contained a fact pattern similar to the question at issue.

The only exception to this rule is in the case of a landmark decision (e.g., *Roe v. Wade*). Landmark opinions are usually those which change or alter established law.[2] These cases are usually easy to identify, because you will probably have spent an entire class period discussing each of them. *Palsgraf v. Long Island Rail Road* is a prime example of a landmark case in Torts. In these special cases, you may be expected to remember the case by name, as well as the proposition of law which it stands for. However, this represents a very limited exception to the general rule which counsels against wasting precious time trying to memorize and reproduce case names.

How to Handle Time Pressures

What do you do when there are five minutes left in the exam and you have only written down two-thirds of your answer? One thing *not* to do is write something like, "No time left!" or "Not enough time!" This gets you nothing but the satisfaction of knowing you have communicated your personal frustrations to the grader. Another thing *not* to do is insert in the exam booklet the outline you may have made on a piece of scrap paper. Professors will rarely look at these.

First of all, it is not necessarily a bad thing to be pressed for time. The person who finishes five minutes early has very possibly missed some important issues. The more proficient you become in knowing what is expected of you on an exam, the greater the difficulty you may experience in staying within the time limits. Second, remember that (at least to some extent) you're graded against your classmates' answers and they're under exactly the same time pressure as you. In short, don't panic if you can't write the "perfect" answer in the allotted time. Nobody does!

The best hedge against misuse of time is to **review as many old exams as possible**. These exercises will give you a familiarity with the process of organizing and writing an exam answer, which, in turn, should result in an enhanced ability to stay within the time boundaries. If you nevertheless find that you have about 15 minutes of writing to do and five minutes to do

---

2 In Constitutional Law and Criminal Procedure, many cases will qualify as "landmark" cases. Students studying these subjects should try to associate case names with the corresponding holdings and reproduce both in their exam answers.

it in, write a paragraph which summarizes the remaining issues or arguments you would discuss if time permitted. As long as you've indicated that you're aware of the remaining legal issues, you'll probably receive some credit for them. Your analytical and argumentative skills will already be apparent to the grader by virtue of the issues that you have previously discussed.

Write Legibly

Make sure your answer is legible. Students should **not** assume that their professors will be willing to take their papers to the local pharmacist to have them deciphered. Remember, your professor may have 75 to 150 separate exams to grade. If your answer is difficult to read, you will rarely be given the benefit of the doubt. On the other hand, a legible, well-organized paper creates a very positive mental impact upon the grader.

Many schools allow students to type their exams. If you type your exam, you'll probably be in a room with a lot of other people who are typing theirs. Some schools may have programs that allow you to type on your laptop or on a school laptop. If it's your own laptop, the school will provide software that blocks you from accessing any other programs or information on your hard drive while you type the exam. Computer-typing is not widely available, however, so if you type you will more than likely be typing on a typewriter. If the constant clack-clack-clack of typewriters keeps you from concentrating, you shouldn't type. If you do write your exam on a typewriter, be sure to leave at least one blank line between typewritten lines, so that handwritten changes and insertions in your answers can be made easily.

If you decide against typing, your answer will probably be written in a "bluebook." It is usually a good idea to write only on the odd numbered pages (i.e., 1, 3, 5, etc.). You may also want to leave a blank line between each written line. These things will usually make the answer easier to read. If you discover that you have left out a word or phrase, you can insert it into the proper place by means of a caret sign ($\wedge$). If you feel that you've omitted an entire issue, you can write it on the facing blank page. A symbol can be used to indicate where the additional portion of the answer should be inserted. While it's not ideal to have your answer take on the appearance of a road map, reference to an adjoining page by means of a symbol is much better than trying to squeeze six lines into one, and the symbol will help to indicate to the grader where the same symbol appears in another part of your answer.

The Importance of Reviewing Prior Exams

As we've mentioned, it is *extremely important to review old exams*. The transition from blackletter law to essay exam can be a difficult experience if the process has not been practiced. Although this book provides a large number of essay and multiple-choice questions, ***don't stop here***! Most law schools have recent tests on file in the library, by course. We strongly suggest that you make a copy of every old exam you can obtain (especially those given by your professors) at the beginning of each semester. The demand for these documents usually increases dramatically as "finals time" draws closer.

The exams for each course should be scrutinized *throughout the semester*. They should be reviewed as you complete each chapter in your casebook. Generally, the order of exam questions follows the sequence of the materials in your casebook. Thus, the first question on a law school test may involve the initial three chapters of the casebook; the second question may pertain to the fourth and fifth chapters; etc. In any event, ***don't wait*** until the semester is nearly over to begin reviewing old exams.

Keep in mind that no one is born with the ability to analyze questions and write superior answers to law school exams. Like any other skill, it is developed and perfected only through application. If you don't take the time to analyze numerous examinations from prior years, this evolutionary process just won't occur. Don't just ***think about*** the answers to past exam questions; take the time to ***write the answers down***. It's also wise to look back at an answer a day or two after you've written it. You will invariably see (1) ways in which the organization could have been improved, and (2) arguments you missed.

As you practice spotting issues on past exams, you will see how rules of law become the sources of issues on finals. As we've already noted, if you don't ***understand*** how rules of law translate into issues, you won't be able to achieve superior grades on your exams. Reviewing exams from prior years should also reveal that certain issues tend to be lumped together in the same question. For instance, where a fact pattern involves a false statement made by one person about another, three potential theories of liability are often present—defamation, invasion of privacy (false, public light), and intentional infliction of severe emotional distress. You will need to see if any or all of these legal remedies apply to the facts.

Finally, one of the best means of evaluating if you understand a subject (or a particular area within a subject) is to attempt to create a hypothetical exam for that subject. Your exam should contain as many issues as possible.

If you can write an issue-packed exam, you probably know that subject well. If you can't, then you probably haven't yet acquired an adequate understanding of how the principles of law in that subject can spawn issues.

As Always, a Caveat

The suggestions and advice offered in this book represent the product of many years of experience in the field of legal education. We are confident that the techniques and concepts described in these pages will help you prepare for, and succeed, at your exams. Nevertheless, particular professors sometimes have a preference for exam-writing techniques which are not stressed in this book. Some instructors expect at least a nominal reference to the *prima facie* elements of all pertinent legal theories (even though one or more of those principles is *not* placed into issue). Other professors want their students to emphasize public policy considerations in the arguments they make on a particular issue. Because this book is intended for nation-wide consumption, these individualized preferences have *not* been stressed. The best way to find out whether your professor has a penchant for a particular writing approach is to ask her to provide you with a model answer to a previous exam. If a model answer is not available, speak to upper-class students who received a superior grade in that professor's class.

One final point. While the principles cited in the answers to the questions in this book have been drawn from commonly used sources (i.e., case-books, hornbooks, etc.), it is conceivable that they may be inconsistent with those taught by your professor. In instances where a conflict exists between our formulation of a legal principle and the one which is taught by your professor, *follow the latter!* Since your grades are determined by your professors, their views should always supplant the views expressed in this book.

Essay Exam Questions

Question 1

APOW owns and operates a nuclear power plant. For one hour ___
three successive days, the plant emitted heavy radiation over the surrounding area, which has a population of 10,000. Several individuals injured by
the radiation emitted on the third day brought a class action for "damages"
in an appropriate federal district court against APOW on behalf of all those
injured on one or more of the three days. After describing the relevant facts,
the complaint alleged only that APOW was responsible for "wrongful
conduct." Jurisdiction was based properly and exclusively on diversity of
citizenship.

1. APOW moved to dismiss the complaint for failure to state a claim
   upon which relief could be granted. The motion was denied.

2. APOW then opposed plaintiffs' motion to certify the class, arguing
   that there was no common issue and that plaintiffs' claims were not
   typical of the class. Certification was granted.

3. During discovery, plaintiffs requested that APOW produce a memorandum concerning possible legal liability for nuclear power accidents,
   prepared by APOW's legal staff prior to the accident, but following
   minor accidents at another company's nuclear power plant. APOW
   objected. The state in which the action was brought had abolished its
   own work product doctrine a year earlier. The court held that the
   memorandum could be discovered.

Were the court's rulings correct? Discuss.

Question 2

Owner was the driver and Rider a passenger in Owner's expensive auto when it collided on a State X highway with a pickup truck driven by Trucker, a citizen of adjoining State Y. Both vehicles were damaged. Owner, Rider, and Trucker were injured.

Owner, a citizen of State X, sued Trucker in a federal district court in State X, claiming $80,000 in property damage to his auto. In his answer, Trucker denied negligence and asserted contributory negligence. After a nonjury trial, the court expressly found that Trucker was not negligent. Judgment was entered for Trucker and has become final.

Subsequently, Rider commenced a $400,000 personal injury suit against Owner in an appropriate State X court. State X has adopted the Federal Rules of Civil Procedure. Prior to trial, Owner timely moved that the suit be dismissed on the ground that Trucker was an indispensable party and had not been made a defendant. After a hearing, the court denied Owner's motion.

Before trial, Trucker timely petitioned to intervene as a plaintiff, and the court granted the petition over Owner's objection.

Trucker's complaint in intervention sought $200,000 for personal injury and property damage against Owner, who counterclaimed for $150,000 in personal injury damages. Rider was permitted to assert a $400,000 cross-complaint against Trucker, over Trucker's objection.

None of the claims asserted is barred by a statute of limitations.

1. In the State X court action, did the court correctly rule that
    a. Trucker was not an indispensable party?
    b. Trucker could intervene?
    c. Rider could cross-complain against Trucker?

Discuss.

2. In the State X court action, what effect, if any, should the federal district court action have on
    a. Rider's claim against Owner?
    b. Rider's cross-complaint against Trucker?
    c. Trucker's claim against Owner?
    d. Owner's counterclaim against Trucker?

Discuss.

Question 3

Seler, a citizen of State S, and Byer, a citizen of State B, met in State B and signed a written contract by which Seler agreed to sell Whiteacre, located in State W, to Byer. The contract provided that the purchase price of Whiteacre was $85,000. Seler returned to State S and sent Byer a deed conveying good title to Whiteacre.

Byer did not send Seler any money, but brought an action against Seler for reformation of the contract to correct an alleged error in the contract price. Byer alleged that the agreed price was $37,500, and that the $85,000 figure in the contract was a typographical error. The action was brought in a federal district court in State B. Subject matter jurisdiction was based on diversity. Personal jurisdiction over Seler was based on service of process under State B's long-arm statute.

A. Seler moved to dismiss the action, alleging lack of personal and subject matter jurisdiction. The motion was denied.

B. Seler then filed an answer asserting that the written contract accurately stated the agreed price. In addition, he counterclaimed for the $85,000 purchase price set forth in the contract and demanded a jury trial. Byer answered the counterclaim and moved to strike the demand for jury trial. The motion was denied.

C. Seler then served Byer with interrogatories demanding responses to the following questions: "(1) Have you had Whiteacre appraised? (2) If so, state by whom, state the appraised value or values, and attach copies of all written reports received from all appraisers." Over Byer's timely objections to the interrogatories, the court ordered disclosure only of the identity of appraisers and the property's appraised values.

D. At trial, Byer testified that the agreed price was $37,500 and that the $85,000 figure in the written contract was a typographical error. An appraiser testified on behalf of Byer that the value of Whiteacre when the contract was signed was, at most, $42,200. Byer rested his case. Seler testified that the agreed price was $85,000, and judgment was entered accordingly. Byer promptly moved for judgment notwithstanding the verdict (JNOV is now called "judgment as a matter of law") or, in the alternative, for a new trial. The court granted the motion for JNOV. No other motions were made during or after trial.

1. Did the court rule correctly on the motion to dismiss? Discuss.
2. Did the court rule correctly on the motion to strike the demand for a jury trial? Discuss.

3. Did the court rule correctly on the objection to the interrogatories? Discuss.

4. Was the evidence admitted at trial such that the court was correct in granting the motion for JNOV? Discuss.

5. What procedural argument or arguments should Seler have made in opposition to the motion for JNOV? Discuss.

Question 4

Daw had just spent five days of vacation in State X and was on his way home to State A when his car collided with a vehicle driven by Paul. The collision occurred in State Y, ten miles beyond the State X border.

Paul, a citizen of State X, filed an action against Daw in a State X state court. Paul alleged that he had suffered $700 in property damage when his car was struck by Daw's car. Daw was served at his home in State A and moved to quash service of process on the ground that the court lacked personal jurisdiction over him. The motion was denied.

Daw then filed an answer that denied negligence on his part and alleged contributory negligence.

Paul served interrogatories on Daw that requested the substance of a conversation that Daw had with his wife and his attorney's investigator soon after the accident. When Daw refused to answer those interrogatories, Paul moved to compel answers, and the court granted the motion. A $700 default judgment was entered against Daw when he refused to comply with the discovery order. State X follows the Federal Rules of Civil Procedure with regard to discovery sanctions. Daw did not appeal the judgment, which then became final.

Paul filed a complaint against Daw in the U.S. district court in State X for $78,000 for personal injuries arising out of the accident. In his answer, Daw denied negligence and alleged contributory negligence. He also counterclaimed for damages for personal injuries resulting from the accident.

Both Paul and Daw moved for summary judgment based on *res judicata* and collateral estoppel.

1. Was the State X court correct in denying Daw's motion to quash? Discuss.

2. Was the State X court correct in granting a default judgment against Daw? Discuss.

3. How should the U.S. district court rule on

   a. Paul's motion for summary judgment on his complaint and on Daw's counterclaim? Discuss.

   b. Daw's motion for summary judgment on Paul's complaint? Discuss.

Question 5

Two years ago, Worker was injured by a defectively constructed machine while he was working in an industrial plant in State A. The machine had been manufactured by Macco, a State B corporation. While Worker was being treated for his injuries in Hospital in State A, Doctor, Worker's physician, prescribed medicine to which Worker was allergic. Worker's condition worsened gradually after that, but it was not clear whether his decline was due to the medicine or his injuries.

Worker sued Hospital in a state court in State A for negligence. Hospital's defenses were that (1) it was not responsible for the acts of Doctor since she was an independent contractor, (2) Doctor had not been negligent, and (3) Worker's present condition was caused by his injury, not the medicine. The trial court, sitting without a jury, found that Doctor had not acted negligently and that Doctor was not an agent of Hospital. The court made no finding on the cause of Worker's worsened condition. Judgment was entered for Hospital. No appeal was taken.

One month ago, Worker died and Worker's widow, Paula, who had lived in State A for five years, returned to her original home in State C. As executrix of her husband's estate duly qualified in State C, she has now filed suit in a state court in State C against Macco for the wrongful death of her husband. She has also filed suit against Doctor in a state court in State A for the damages she sustained as a result of the death of her husband. None of these suits is barred by a statute of limitations.

Macco sells its machinery in 40 states and maintains an office in State C. During the past ten years, Macco has sold its products in State C. Its annual sales volume in that state is between $400,000 and $500,000. The machine that injured Worker was originally sold to a corporation in State A, which sold it to Worker's employer.

A statute in State C provides: "The courts of this state may exercise jurisdiction over a person and property to the full extent permitted by the Constitution of the United States."

1. Assuming appropriate objection by Macco, may State C exercise jurisdiction over Macco in Paula's suit as executrix? Discuss.

2. What effect, if any, does Worker's suit in State A have on
   a. Paula's action in State C against Macco? Discuss.
   b. Paula's action in State A against Doctor? Discuss.

Question 6

Paul, a citizen of State X, brought suit against Dave, a citizen of State Y, in the U.S. district court in State Y for property damage caused to Paul's car when Dave's car ran into it in State Y. Jurisdiction was based on diversity of citizenship. The action was filed two weeks before the expiration of the period of State Y's one-year statute of limitations for negligent torts.

One month later, Paul filed an amended complaint that added a claim for personal injury arising out of the car accident. Dave moved to dismiss the personal injury claim. Because State Y had no rule allowing an amendment to relate back to the time of the original pleading under any circumstances, the district court granted Dave's motion, holding that the personal injury claim was barred by the State Y statute of limitations.

Dave next filed a third-party complaint impleading Insco, which he alleged was his auto insurer. Dave claimed Insco owed him the duty to defend against Paul's suit and to reimburse him for any loss. Insco, a State Y corporation, moved to dismiss the third-party complaint on the following grounds: (a) the third-party complaint was not authorized under the Federal Rules of Civil Procedure, (b) the district court lacked subject matter jurisdiction, and (c) the insurance policy had been fraudulently obtained. The district court dismissed Dave's third-party complaint.

At trial, over objection, the district court admitted the testimony of Dave's witness, Wit. Wit had not been listed by Dave in the pretrial order prepared pursuant to the Federal Rules of Civil Procedure. Though Dave could not demonstrate a valid reason why he had not included Wit in the pretrial order, the district court was of the view that no prejudice had resulted to Paul since he had been aware of Wit's existence.

Did the district court err in

1. granting Dave's motion to dismiss the personal injury claim? Discuss.
2. dismissing Dave's third-party complaint impleading Insco? Discuss.
3. admitting the testimony of Wit? Discuss.

Question 7

On March 15, 1987, Pat brought suit against Truco, a corporation, as sole defendant, in the U.S. district court in State Red. The State Red statute of limitations for personal injury claims caused by negligence is two years.

The complaint alleged (1) that Pat "resided" in State Red at the time of the events complained of and had become a "resident" of State White on March 1, 1987; (2) that Truco was a citizen of State Red; and (3) that on March 20, 1986, in State Red, Dan, a citizen of State Red and an employee of defendant Truco, negligently drove a motor vehicle, striking Pat and causing various personal injuries. The complaint sought a damage judgment against Truco for $100,000. Truco moved to dismiss the complaint on the following grounds: (1) lack of subject matter jurisdiction, and (2) failure of the complaint to join Dan as a defendant.

After its motions were denied, Truco's answer denied all of the allegations of Pat's complaint except that its citizenship is in State Red and that Dan was negligent.

At the pretrial conference, Pat and Truco stipulated that (1) plaintiff's actual damages were $85,000, and (2) Truco would be liable to Pat if Dan was an employee of Truco.

At trial on February 1, 1990, undisputed testimony admitted into evidence established that Pat was a citizen of State White at the time the complaint was filed, and that on March 20, 1986, when the accident occurred in State Red, Dan was driving a car owned by Truco with defendant's permission, but was *not* employed by Truco.

After each party rested, (1) Truco moved for a judgment as a matter of law, based on the stipulation and evidence introduced at trial; and (2) Pat moved for (a) permission to amend her complaint to insert a claim based upon a statute of State Red imposing liability upon the owner of a motor vehicle for the negligence of a driver operating the vehicle with the owner's permission, and (b) a judgment as a matter of law in her favor against Truco on the complaint as amended, for $85,000.

How should the court have decided

1. Truco's initial two motions to dismiss?
2. Truco's motion for a judgment as a matter of law?
3. Pat's post-trial motions?

Discuss.

Question 8

Albert is a touring professional golfer domiciled in State Red. Par Golf Clubs is incorporated and has its central administrative office in State Red, but its major manufacturing facility is located in State Green. Par pays Albert $25,000 per year for Albert's endorsement of a set of golf clubs that it manufactures in State Red and sells through independent retailers in every state. Albert uses these clubs in the tournaments in which he plays throughout the United States. Whenever he is interviewed, he specifically endorses the clubs.

Harold lives in State White. He is a weekend golfer. While at a golf tournament in State Red, he heard Albert's endorsement of the Par Golf Clubs and purchased a set from a golf shop in State Red.

While in State White, Harold was using one of the clubs for the first time. As a result of a metallurgical defect, the head of the club flew off the shaft and seriously injured Frances and Robert, both of whom are residents of State Green and were on a golfing holiday with Harold in State White.

Frances sued Par and Albert in a state court in State White. Par was sued as the manufacturer and Albert as the endorser of a defective product. Frances's complaint was based on theories of negligence and strict liability in tort. Two copies of the summons and complaint were personally delivered to Albert, who was "served personally and also on behalf of Par." At the time, Albert was physically present and playing in a tournament in State White. A copy of the complaint and summons was also personally delivered to the president of Par while he was on vacation in Hawaii. State White statutes authorize such service in actions for injuries received within the state.

1. Assuming all appropriate objections are properly made, may State White take jurisdiction over Albert and Par? Discuss.
2. Was Par validly served? Discuss.
3. Assuming Albert and Par desire to remove Frances's case to the U.S. district court in State Red, what arguments should Frances make in opposition? Discuss.
4. Assuming a final judgment on the merits is obtained in *Frances v. Albert and Par Golf Clubs, Inc.*, in a subsequent action by Robert in State Green, what use may Robert make of the judgment? What use may Par and Albert make of the judgment? Discuss.

Question 9

Pete, a citizen of State X, saw an advertisement in a newspaper published in adjoining State Y, but distributed also in State X. It described a new chemical process just developed by Devco, a State Z corporation, which has its principal office in State Z. The advertisement claimed the new process would revolutionize the industrial dye industry and urged readers to purchase stock in Devco. Pete wrote Devco requesting more information about the new process. Devco sent Pete promotional brochures that directed persons interested in buying Devco stock to consult Bull, a stockbroker.

Bull is a State X citizen, but his brokerage office is in State Y. Most of Bull's business has been selling Devco stock, for which Devco has paid him a commission. Devco did no business in either State X or State Y. Pete purchased 20,000 shares of Devco stock through Bull. Pete is the only Devco shareholder who is domiciled in State X. Shortly after Pete purchased his stock, it was found that the new chemical process developed by Devco had no commercial value. As a result, the value of Pete's Devco stock declined.

Pete sued Devco in the U.S. district court in State X, alleging jurisdiction based on diversity of citizenship. The complaint purported to state a claim for relief based solely on common law fraud and contained a demand for a jury trial.

Devco then moved for dismissal of the complaint on the ground that the court lacked personal jurisdiction over it. Under State X law, a court has jurisdiction over a foreign corporation only if it is doing business in the state. The motion was denied, the court holding that it had jurisdiction to the full extent permitted by Fourteenth Amendment due process.

Devco moved to have Bull joined as a party-defendant. The motion was granted. Bull then moved for dismissal of the action against him on the ground that the district court in State X lacked subject matter jurisdiction. The motion was granted.

Devco answered the complaint and moved to strike Pete's demand for jury trial on the ground that factual issues in the case involved very complex scientific matters beyond the intellectual capabilities of the average juror, and therefore it had no adequate remedy at law. The district court struck Pete's jury trial demand and set the case for a bench trial.

1. Did the district court in State X have personal jurisdiction over Devco? Discuss.

2. Did the district court in State X have subject matter jurisdiction over the action against Bull? Discuss.

3. Assuming the district court in State X had subject matter jurisdiction over the claim against Bull, was the court correct in ordering Bull joined as a party-defendant? Discuss.

4. Did the district court err in striking Pete's demand for a jury trial? Discuss.

Question 10

Valco is a corporation incorporated in State B. Its principal office and sole manufacturing plant is in State A. It manufactures pressure valves for compressed air tanks. It purchases from Mity, a corporation, the "collars" affixed to the pressure valves, which are used to attach the valve to the air tank. Mity is incorporated and has its sole place of business in State A.

The Valco pressure valve on a piece of machinery owned by Peter and Quincy and used by them in State C exploded. Peter and Quincy were seriously injured. At all times, Peter was a citizen of State C. At the time of the explosion, Quincy was a citizen of State A, but after the accident he moved to State B, where he is now domiciled.

Peter and Quincy wish to assert claims against Valco and Mity on the theory that the valve exploded because of a defective collar. Valco has informed Peter and Quincy that it will claim that a written notice recalling the valves had been sent to them and to all other users of this model valve, and that Peter and Quincy ignored the notice.

1. If Peter, as sole plaintiff, institutes an action against Valco, as sole defendant, in the U.S. district court in State C, may Valco object to the failure by Peter to join Mity as a defendant? May Valco bring Mity into the case as a defendant, and, if so, how? Discuss.

2. If Peter and Quincy institute an action against Valco and Mity in the U.S. district court in State C for $100,000 damages each, what issues may be raised as to joinder of parties plaintiff, joinder of parties defendant, joinder of causes of action, jurisdiction over the defendants, and jurisdiction over the subject matter? How should the trial court rule on each issue? Discuss.

3. If an action by Peter, as sole plaintiff, against Valco and Mity is commenced and tried in the U.S. district court in State A, should the trial court apply State A law, State C law, or federal law on the issues of (a) whether plaintiff must plead freedom from contributory fault, and (b) who has the burden of persuasion on the issue of contributory fault? Discuss.

Question 11

Don Pickles was a teenage comedian. In early September, Merv Griffey, a talent agent, took Don under his wing, and in two months made Don a star. In early December, Merv told Don that he had booked him to give a performance at the Palladium in California on New Year's Eve. Don immediately advised Merv that he had a verbal agreement with Ms. Bigbucks, a prominent New York attorney, to play at the latter's New Year's Eve party (where Don had previously performed). Merv advised Don to "cancel out" Bigbucks since "verbal contracts are unenforceable," which Don immediately did via telegram. Don and Merv both lived in Chicago, Illinois.

Two weeks later, when in Massachusetts en route to New Jersey to visit his girlfriend, Don stopped at a roadside restaurant. As he exited his car, he was served with a summons and complaint in an action filed by Bigbucks against Don and the Palladium Corporation in the U.S. district court for Massachusetts. The complaint alleged that Don was liable for breach of contract and that the Palladium Corporation was liable in the amount of $75,000 for inducing breach of the Don-Bigbucks agreement. Bigbucks asked for an injunction precluding Don from playing at the Palladium because her remedy at law was inadequate. Bigbucks premised this assertion on the grounds that Bigbucks had already invited many of her major clients to the party and would "lose face" if Don played somewhere else. The Palladium is located in California, owned by Palladium Corporation, a New York corporation (where its board of directors meets monthly). Palladium Corporation was served by delivering a copy of the summons and complaint to the president's personal secretary at its corporate offices in New York.

Don answered by denying all but the jurisdictional allegations of Bigbucks's complaint (i.e., he admitted that he was an Illinois citizen). Don also filed a third-party complaint against Merv for misadvising him as to his legal obligations to Bigbucks. Palladium Corporation filed an answer denying Bigbucks's allegations and a third-party complaint against Merv, claiming that Merv never advised them of an outstanding contract for Don's services. Palladium Corporation also filed a motion to transfer pursuant to 28 U.S.C. §§1404 and 1406, asking that the matter be transferred to the appropriate U.S. district court in California, but this motion was denied.

Before Merv was served with Don's third-party complaint, Don called him and complained about being "in the middle of a federal case." Don advised Merv that unless the latter "got him out of this mess, he was going to find another agent." Don also advised Merv to "come see him right away" in Boston, Massachusetts. Immediately after Merv arrived at the airport, Don asked Merv if the Palladium show was going to be cancelled. When Merv said "No," Don motioned to a process server who handed Merv the third-party complaint and summons. The Palladium Corporation served Merv by mailing a certified letter containing a copy of the summons and complaint to his office in Chicago. Merv's secretary signed for it and later gave the documents to him. This type of service was permissible under Massachusetts law. Merv responded to the third-party complaints by making the appropriate motions to dismiss them. When these motions were denied, he filed an answer denying liability to both Don and the Palladium Corporation.

The trial judge determined that she would hear the request for injunctive relief first (as was permissible under Massachusetts law) since this was the "lynchpin" issue. At trial, Don raised the defense of minority against Bigbucks's action, even though he had not stated it as an affirmative defense in this answer. The court, upon objection by Bigbucks, held that this defense was at variance with the pleading and could not now be raised. The court also held that Bigbucks was entitled to the relief she sought from Don. The jury decided that (1) Bigbucks was entitled to recover on her claim against the Palladium Corporation, and (2) Don and the Palladium Corporation were entitled to prevail on their third-party claims against Merv.

Discuss the issues that could be raised on appeal.

Question 12

Ped is a citizen of State A. Driver is a citizen of State D. Health is a corporation incorporated in State H. Its sole place of business is a hospital in State A. Ped was injured when struck by a motor vehicle operated by Driver in State A and hospitalized in the Health hospital. His injuries were allegedly aggravated as a result of Health's negligence.

Ped sued Driver and Health in a State A court, claiming damages in the sum of $100,000 and alleging that he was uncertain which defendant was responsible for which portion of his damages.

Upon Health's timely petition, the case was removed to the U.S. district court in State A. Thereafter, Ped moved to have the case remanded to the applicable state court in State A. Ped's motion was granted.

After remand, Health demurred on the grounds of improper joinder of several causes of action. The demurrer was overruled.

Both Health and Driver filed answers denying liability and damages. Ped then filed timely request for admissions asking that each defendant admit liability, reserving for trial only the issue of damages. Both defendants filed timely objections on the grounds that the requests called for legal conclusions. The objections were sustained.

Following a jury trial, a verdict was returned in favor of Ped and against both defendants in the sum of $43,652.89. Ped moved for a new trial on the issue of damages and, in the alternative, on all issues. He supported his motion by the affidavits of five jurors who stated that: (1) immediately after entering the jury room, the jurors took a ballot on the issue of whether Ped should recover and the vote was 12 to 0 in favor of Ped and against both defendants; (2) each juror then wrote down his or her idea of the amount of the recovery; the figures were totaled, divided by 12, and the result was $43,652.89; and (3) all jurors then agreed that their verdict would be $43,652.89. Based upon defendants' objections, the court refused to consider the affidavits and denied Ped's motion for a new trial.

Discuss the correctness of the court's rulings, setting forth the arguments that might reasonably be made in support of and in opposition to each of the following:

1. Ped's motion to remand
2. Health's demurrer
3. Ped's request for admissions
4. Ped's motion for a new trial

Question 13

Abel, an African American citizen of State Red, attempted to rent an apartment in a building in State Red owned by Cozy Nook, Inc., a State Red corporation. Abel's offer to rent was refused, and the apartment was rented to Dod for a term of two years.

Abel then obtained housing in State White, and sued Cozy Nook in a State White court of general jurisdiction, alleging a racially motivated denial of housing in violation of a federal statute. The complaint prayed for money damages and a mandatory injunction requiring defendant to give plaintiff possession of the apartment plaintiff had offered to rent or a similar apartment in the same building. Cozy Nook maintained a bank account in State White at Bank, but had no other business dealings in that state. This account was attached by Abel after notice and a hearing attended by Cozy Nook's president. Pursuant to State White law, the president of Cozy Nook was also personally served in State White with notice of the summons and complaint in the main action.

The federal statute authorized actions to be brought in "appropriate state or local courts of general jurisdiction," as well as federal court. The statute has been construed by the U.S. Supreme Court to require trial by jury in federal court suits. State White law does not provide for a jury trial in such cases.

Cozy Nook:

1. Moved to dismiss the action on the grounds that
    a. Dod was not a party;
    b. the court lacked jurisdiction over the person;
    c. proper service had not been accomplished;
    d. State White was an inconvenient forum; and
2. Made a timely demand for jury trial if the action was not dismissed.

How should the court rule on each ground set forth in the motion to dismiss and on the demand for jury trial?

Discuss.

Question 14

Tinselware, Inc., an Arizona corporation, sells widgets only in Phoenix, Arizona. Maureen, an employee of Tinselware, initiated telephone negotiations with Don, hoping he would purchase widgets for resale in California. Don, domiciled in San Francisco, responded to Maureen's telephone call by driving to Phoenix.

While in Phoenix, Don bought 75,000 widgets at $1 each. After returning to California, he discovered that the widgets did not function properly. He filed a breach of contract action against Tinselware in the U.S. district court in San Francisco.

Summons and complaint were hand delivered to Maureen in Arizona, on behalf of Tinselware, Inc. Don then mailed a copy of the summons and complaint to the president of Tinselware (a permissible means of service of process under California law).

Tinselware successfully moved to have the action dismissed because of (1) lack of subject matter and personal jurisdiction, and (2) lack of proper service. If Tinselware's motions had been denied, it would have attempted to have the action transferred to the U.S. district court in Nevada so that each party could travel an approximately equal distance to attend trial. Don then filed a new complaint against Maureen in the U.S. district court in San Francisco. However, the applicable statute of limitations had run after dismissal of the first suit and prior to refiling the second suit, so his action was dismissed.

1. Was the court's dismissal of the original action on each of the grounds stated correct?

2. Could the court have transferred the action to a federal district court in Nevada?

3. Was the dismissal of Don's action against Maureen correct?

Question 15

Defendant airliner, carrying passengers and cargo from Boston to Philadelphia, skidded off the runway during takeoff, causing minor injuries to all the passengers. There were 40 passengers aboard from various states. Pete was one of the passengers. Pete is domiciled in Arizona, but owns several apartment houses in Los Angeles (which is in the Central District of California).

Pete files a diversity class action against Defendant in U.S. District Court for the Central District of California. Pete seeks an $80,000 recovery for his minor personal injuries and to recover for injuries suffered by each of the other passengers. There is some nonconclusive indication that Doeing Company's engine may have malfunctioned during takeoff, causing the accident. Doeing Company is a Delaware corporation with its principal place of business in Massachusetts.

Defendant is incorporated in Massachusetts. However, the majority of its flights originate and land on the West Coast, and Defendant's main booking terminal and reservation center is in Arizona. Defendant would prefer to defend in Massachusetts, where the crash occurred and where it believes juries are less liberal.

Defendant made the following motions:

1. that the court lacks subject matter jurisdiction;
2. that a class action is not appropriate;
3. that venue is not proper; and
4. that if venue is proper, the action should be transferred to the appropriate federal district court in Massachusetts.

Defendant has also impleaded the Doeing Company.

Discuss the likely outcome of Defendant's motions and its impleader action.

Question 16

Paul sued Doe in the appropriate U.S. district court in State X for personal injuries, including a broken leg, allegedly caused by Doe's negligent operation of a motor vehicle in State X. Suit was filed January 2, 1990. The injuries were alleged to have been, and in fact were, received on March 1, 1989. Thereafter the following took place:

On July 1, 1990, Paul filed a motion for leave to file an amended complaint, setting forth that in the previous month, while doing exercises prescribed by his doctor to strengthen the leg that was broken, he fell and suffered a fracture of the other leg, for which he claimed additional damages of $10,000. The court denied the motion. A one-year statute of limitations is applicable to all actions in State X.

On July 25, 1990, Doe filed an answer denying liability and alleging, as a further and separate defense, that on February 20, 1990, in consideration of the sum of $10,000 paid to Paul by Doe, Paul had executed a release of all claims he had against Doe. Paul then asked for and was granted leave to file a second amended complaint adding a count for rescission of the release on the grounds of fraud. Doe filed an appropriate answer to the second amended complaint, denying any fraud.

Doe applied for an order requiring Paul to submit to a physical examination and to furnish copies of all of his medical and hospital reports since the date of the accident and for one year prior thereto. The court issued the order over Paul's objection that the matters were privileged and not relevant.

Paul timely demanded a jury trial. Doe thereafter moved that the issues raised by the second amended complaint be tried first by the court (without a jury). Doe's motion was granted.

Discuss the correctness of the court's ruling on each of the following:

1. Paul's motion for leave to file his first amended complaint
2. Paul's motion for leave to file his second amended complaint
3. Doe's application for an order for a physical examination and copies of his medical reports
4. Doe's motion for an initial trial before the court (without a jury) on the issues raised by the second amended complaint

Question 17

Smith, a citizen of State X, was an employee of Zonco, a corporation that was incorporated and had its principal place of business in State X. A truck owned by Zonco, while driven by Smith, struck Patricia, a citizen of State Y. Patricia was injured and sued Zonco for $150,000 in the U.S. district court in State X, alleging that Zonco and Smith were negligent. Smith was not made a party-defendant.

Zonco made a motion to dismiss the complaint for failure to join Smith. The motion was overruled. Thereafter, Zonco answered, denying the negligence of either Zonco or Smith, and further denying that Patricia was injured.

Patricia then served Zonco with a notice to produce a written statement made and signed by a co-worker of Smith who was riding with Smith at the time of the accident. The statement had been obtained by an adjuster for Zonco's insurance carrier. Zonco refused to produce the statement, and the court sustained that refusal.

Patricia took the deposition of Smith at which Smith testified under oath that (1) Patricia was crossing the intersection in the pedestrian crosswalk with the green light, and (2) the truck driven by Smith ran into Patricia because the brakes failed. Patricia filed the deposition with a motion for summary judgment on the issue of liability, reserving for the jury only the question of damages. The motion was denied.

The action was tried before a jury. At the conclusion of the evidence, Zonco moved for a judgment as a matter of law. There was uncontradicted testimony introduced at trial that Smith was employed by Zonco and that Patricia had suffered a severe, painful injury as a consequence of the accident, and that her special damages for medical and hospital bills and loss of earnings were $80,000. The jury returned a verdict in the sum of $85,000. Zonco moved for a judgment notwithstanding the verdict. This motion was denied. Patricia moved for a new trial solely on the issue of damages. The trial judge ordered that the motion should be granted, unless Zonco consented to an increase in the judgment to $95,000.

Discuss the arguments that might reasonably have been made to the trial court in support of, and in opposition to, the court's rulings on

1. Zonco's motion to dismiss for failure to join Smith;
2. Patricia's notice to produce;
3. Patricia's motion for summary judgment;
4. Zonco's motion for judgment notwithstanding the verdict; and
5. Patricia's motion for a new trial.

Question 18

On January 25, 2001, Paul (an inventor) sued Dumbo, Inc. (a manufacturer of video games) in the U.S. district court in Ohio. Paul is a citizen of that state. Dumbo is incorporated in Delaware. Its principal place of business is in Pennsylvania. However, it maintains a warehouse in Ohio from which it sells its products directly to local retailers and makes approximately 5 percent of its gross sales.

Paul's complaint contends that he invented a new video game called Enemy Attack, which Dumbo produced and sold in violation of Paul's common law copyright rights. Paul sought damages of $100,000 and an injunction prohibiting Dumbo from making any further sales of the game. Pursuant to Ohio law, service of process was made upon Dumbo by personally serving each member of its board of directors.

On February 10, Dumbo filed an FRCP 12(b) motion to dismiss Paul's complaint on the grounds that (1) it failed to state a claim upon which relief could be granted, (2) the court lacked personal jurisdiction over it, and (3) service of process was improper because it was not accomplished pursuant to the FRCP. The initial contention was supported by a Points and Authorities that asserted that no case had, as yet, extended common law copyright rights to video games. Dumbo's motion was denied.

On February 20, Dumbo answered Paul's complaint, contending that, while it had entered into an agreement with Paul for the rights to distribute the Enemy Attack video game, it had been sued by Susan on the grounds that Paul had "stolen" the game from her. As a result, Dumbo had been obliged to pay Susan $80,000 for the rights to Enemy Attack after its attorneys determined her action was probably meritorious. Additionally, Dumbo claimed it had "loaned" Paul a computer and numerous electronic components, which he said were necessary to create the game; but Paul had sold these items to other persons. In addition to its answer, Dumbo's answer contained a counterclaim, demanding reimbursement of the $80,000 paid to Susan and an additional $10,000 (reflecting the alleged value of the materials delivered to Paul). Dumbo's answer and counterclaim were served on Paul's attorney on February 23.

On March 14, Dumbo requested the clerk of the court to enter a default on its counterclaim. The clerk did so. On March 16, Dumbo asked for a judgment on the default in the amount of $90,000 (as per its counterclaim), and the judgment was so entered.

On April 20, Dumbo moved for a judgment on the pleadings with respect to Paul's claim, contending that (1) by failing to answer its affirmative defense of material breach, Paul had admitted the assertions contained therein; and (2) by reason of the default judgment that had now become final, Paul was barred from denying Dumbo's defense that Paul materially breached their agreement. Paul replied that (1) the default judgment was prematurely entered and is therefore invalid; and (2) pursuant to FRCP 60(b), Paul should be relieved of the default judgment because a summer clerk, to whom Paul's attorney had given the answer and counterclaim for the purpose of making copies, had accidentally misplaced the item in the copying room. As a result, Paul's attorney failed to note on her calendar the date when a response to Dumbo's counterclaim was made.

Discuss the court's rulings on Dumbo's FRCP 12(b) motion and the likely outcome of

1. Dumbo's motion for judgment on the pleadings; and
2. Paul's motion to be relieved from Dumbo's default judgment.

Question 19

Salco is a corporation, incorporated and having its principal place of business in State A. Its sole business is the sale of products by mail order. It advertises its products in national magazines. None of these magazines is published in State B. Salco employs no agents or salespeople in State B.

Poe, a citizen of State B, commenced a class action in a competent State B court against Salco for fraud and misrepresentation in the sale of certain hi-tech alarm clocks to him and other citizens of State B. He alleged that 300 such clocks were sold to citizens of State B, and that he and each such person was damaged in the sum of $250. He asked for actual damages in the amount of $75,000, and punitive damages in the sum of $25 million. In accordance with State B law, process was served on Salco by sending a copy of the complaint and summons by registered mail, return receipt requested, to the president of Salco at the company's principal place of business in State A.

Salco filed a petition for removal from the State B court to the U.S. district court in State B. After removal, Salco filed a FRCP 12(b) motion to dismiss the matter. The motion was denied. Poe then filed a motion to remand to the State B court on the ground that the complaint did not state a claim within the jurisdiction of the U.S. district court.

The motion was denied. Salco then moved for a more definite statement. This motion was also denied. The action then proceeded to trial. Judgment on the merits was rendered in favor of Salco.

After the judgment was final, Jones, a citizen of State B, filed an action in a State B court against Salco, based on the same claims of fraud and misrepresentation in the sale to him of one of the 300 alarm clocks. Salco filed a motion to dismiss upon the ground that the judgment in *Poe v. Salco* was a bar to the action by Jones. The motion was granted.

1. Was the U.S. district court correct in its rulings on
    a. the FRCP 12(b) motion to dismiss the case?
    b. the motion to remand in *Poe v. Salco* on the ground that the complaint did not state a claim within the jurisdiction of the U.S. district court?
    c. the motion for a more definite statement?
2. Was the State B court correct in its ruling on the motion to dismiss in *Jones v. Salco* on the ground that the prior judgment was a bar?

Question 20

Paula, a citizen of the State of Calvada, purchased a box of breakfast cereal produced by Krispy at a grocery store in Calvada. As part of a promotional campaign by Krispy, there was a certificate in the box that stated that by sending "the certificate and $1 to Glassco, A Street, Central City, State of Black, USA," the sender would receive by return mail six cocktail glasses. Paula sent in the certificate and $1 and thereafter received the glasses. While she was washing them for the first time, one shattered in her hand, cutting the tendons and permanently injuring Paula.

Paula sued Glassco for $100,000 in a Calvada state court, basing jurisdiction on a Calvada statute giving its courts jurisdiction over "any person who commits a tortious act in this state with respect to any cause of action arising out of such act." The statute further provided that in such cases, process could be served on a foreign corporation by mailing a copy of the summons and complaint by registered mail, return receipt requested, to the corporation at its "place of business outside of the state." Glassco was incorporated in and had its principal place of business in State White.

Copies of the summons and complaint were mailed by registered mail, return receipt requested, addressed to "Glassco, A Street, Central City, State of Black, USA" and were returned with the notation "not accepted by addressee."

After the statutory time for appearance had expired, the default of Glassco was entered and the case heard as a default matter. Other than medical testimony, the only evidence received was Paula's testimony concerning the manner in which she obtained the glasses and the fact that while she was carefully washing one glass it shattered in her hand. Judgment was in Paula's favor for $25,000.

1. Is the Calvada verdict a valid judgment? Discuss.
2. Assuming that it is a valid judgment, may Glassco nevertheless have it set aside, and, if so, on what grounds? Discuss.
3. Assuming that the judgment is set aside and a new trial is held, is Paula likely to prevail if the only evidence offered by her is the same as that presented at the hearing at which the default judgment was rendered? Discuss.

Question 21

Peter is a citizen of State Red. Stanford James is a citizen of State White. On August 20, 1990, in State White, Peter was injured when the car he was driving collided with a car owned and driven by Stanford James. The applicable statute of limitations in both States Red and White is two years.

On August 16, 2002, Peter filed suit in the U.S. district court for State Red to recover for personal injuries he received in the collision. The complaint set forth the correct date and place of the collision, but erroneously named the defendant as James Stanford.

On August 30, 2002, while Stanford James was in State Red at the invitation of Peter to discuss the settlement of Peter's claim, he was personally served with the summons and complaint. Thereafter the following occurred:

Stanford James filed a Rule 12(b) motion to dismiss the action, or, in the alternative, to transfer the action to the U.S. district court in State White. Both motions were denied.

Peter then moved to amend his complaint to name Stanford James as defendant in place of James Stanford. The motion was granted.

Stanford James then filed an answer that, among other matters, alleged that Peter's claim was barred by the statute of limitations. Stanford James then moved for judgment on the pleadings on that ground. The motion was granted.

Assuming all appropriate grounds were urged in support of and in opposition to each of the motions mentioned, was the trial court correct in its rulings on

1. Stanford James's Rule 12(b) motion? Discuss.
2. Stanford James's motion to transfer? Discuss.
3. Peter's motion to amend the complaint? Discuss.
4. Stanford James's motion for judgment on the pleadings? Discuss.

Question 22

While visiting Austin, Texas, Paul was arrested outside of Silley's Department Store, an exclusive men's clothing store. As he was departing, Mary Poppins, the cashier at Silley's, shouted "Stop thief!" Bill Joe Bobb, a police officer who responded to Mary's shout, tackled Paul and applied a chokehold, allegedly causing Paul serious, permanent injuries.

Both Poppins and Bobb are citizens of Texas. Bobb lives in Austin. Paul is a citizen of Oklahoma. Bobb owns a 5 percent limited partnership interest in an eight-unit apartment house in Oklahoma. The limited partnership was formed in Texas and is operated by a general partner who is domiciled in Texas. As a limited partner, Bobb has no say in how limited partnership assets are operated. Silley's does a mail order business from its department store, and 14 percent of its mail order sales are to persons in Oklahoma (this represents 3 percent of Silley's total business). Silley's is a Texas corporation with its principal place of business in Texas.

Question 1:

Paul sued Bobb and Silley's in the U.S. district court in Oklahoma. He claimed they committed false imprisonment and were each liable to him for $85,000. Silley's and Bobb do *not* desire to stand trial in Oklahoma. Describe their procedural alternatives. Assume the Texas and Oklahoma long-arm statutes give their courts all requisites of personal jurisdiction consistent with due process.

Assumption 1 (applicable to questions 2 and 3 only):

Assume Paul did not commence an action in Oklahoma, but moved to Nebraska, where he sued Bobb under a federal civil rights statute and for assault and battery. Assume he also sued Mary and Silley's for false arrest (a tort in Nebraska).

Question 2:

Can Paul join all of these parties in a single action? (Assume personal jurisdiction is satisfied.)

Question 3:

Would the U.S. district court in Nebraska have subject matter jurisdiction over Paul's claim?

Assumption 2 (applicable to questions 4, 5, and 6):

Assume that Paul commenced an action against both Bobb and the Austin, Texas, Police Department (the "ATPD") in the U.S. district court in Texas. Paul's claim against the latter is that it is vicariously liable for the conduct of Bobb (conduct that violated a federal civil rights statute). The ATPD, however, construes the applicable U.S. statute as precluding vicarious liability unless the Department authorized the chokehold complained of by the plaintiff. Bobb has claimed that, pursuant to his union's contract with the ATPD, the latter entity must pay legal fees incurred by him in his defense. The ATPD, however, asserts that this obligation does not arise if the conduct is alleged to be unconstitutional.

Question 4:

How can the ATPD raise its claim that it is not vicariously liable for Bobb's conduct?

Question 5:

Can Bobb assert a claim against the ATPD in the present action (*Paul v. Bobb & ATPD*)?

Question 6:

Numerous police departments around the country are concerned that if Paul's alleged federal claim is successful, similar actions will be pursued against them. As a consequence, they desire to intervene upon the side of the ATPD. Will they be permitted to do so?

Question 23

Pam, a patient injured in a nursing home fire, brought a suit for $77,000 against the home's operators, D Inc., in U.S. district court in State X, where the nursing home in which P resides is located. Jurisdiction was properly based on diversity of citizenship because even though P resides in State X, her domicile is actually in State Y. Under the law of State X, the failure of a nursing home to install smoke detectors in each patient's room is considered negligence per se. P alleged D's failure to install the device; D's answer denied all allegations in the complaint.

P promptly moved for summary judgment as to liability, attaching her own sworn affidavit stating that no smoke detector had been installed in her room. D's attorney responded with a memorandum asserting, "My client stands by its Answer in this case." The court denied the motion.

P then initiated discovery. She first served an interrogatory on D asking whether it had installed a smoke detector in P's room. The appropriate corporate official responded, "No."

P also requested D to produce for inspection its fire investigator's report, hoping that the investigator's early investigation of the since-demolished home showed no smoke detectors present. D refused to comply with the discovery request. P moved to compel production, and the court ordered D to produce the report for inspection and also held D in contempt of court for refusing the discovery request.

At trial, Mac, D's maintenance director, testified that smoke detectors had been installed in P's room; P's motion to disallow M's testimony as inconsistent with the interrogatory answer was denied.

Was the district court correct in its ruling

1. on P's motion for summary judgment as to liability?
2. on P's motion to compel production of the fire investigator's report?
3. holding D in contempt for refusing P's discovery request?
4. on P's motion to disallow M's testimony concerning the installation of a smoke detector in P's room?

Discuss.

Question 24

Borrow, a resident of State A, obtained a $12,000 car loan from Finco. Finco is incorporated and has its principal place of business in State A. When Borrow began making installment repayments against the loan, she was dismayed to learn that her required monthly payments were in an amount greater than she had expected.

Borrow brought suit against Finco in a state court in State A, asserting a claim under the federal Truth-in-Lending Act ("TLA"). TLA specifically requires lenders to disclose to a borrower in a consumer loan transaction the amount of the monthly loan payment. TLA further provides that a borrower whose rights under TLA have been violated may bring an action against the lender in a U.S. district court, or in any other court of competent jurisdiction.

Finco filed its answer denying liability and asserting a counterclaim against Borrow under state law for recovery of the full amount owed on the loan. Finco then timely removed the suit to the U.S. district court for the district of State A. In the district court, Borrow moved to remand the action. The motion was denied.

Shortly thereafter Borrow moved to amend her complaint to (1) add an additional defendant, Dealer, the company that had sold her the car, (2) allege that Dealer violated State A's Consumer Protection Law ("CPL") by providing her erroneous information about the terms of her loan, and (3) allege that Dealer's CPL violation had resulted in $20,000 in damages. Dealer is incorporated in State A and conducts all of its business there. The district court denied the motion to amend on the ground that the court lacked subject matter jurisdiction over Borrow's claim against Dealer.

Borrow next moved for partial summary judgment that, if granted, would preclude Finco from denying that its lending agreement violated TLA. In support of this motion, Borrow offered uncontradicted evidence that in previous lawsuits brought by other borrowers in federal court, final judgments had been entered against Finco on holdings that, under circumstances identical with those in the present lawsuit, Finco's failure to make the required loan payment disclosure violated TLA. Borrow's motion was denied.

Were the district court's rulings correct as to

1. Borrow's motion to remand?

2. Borrow's motion to amend her complaint?

3. Borrow's motion for partial summary judgment?

Discuss.

Question 25

On March 1 of last year, Paul, a citizen of State X, was involved in a three-car accident in State Y with Dave and Al, both of whom are State Y citizens. Wilma, Paul's wife, was a passenger in his car. Immediately after the accident, Wilma obtained signed statements from two witnesses. Later, Paul employed Len, a lawyer, to study the statements and advise him. Len made some handwritten notes on the statements and placed them in his files.

On February 15 of this year, Paul filed a complaint against Dave in the U.S. district court for State Y. All allegations of the complaint and the prayer for relief are set forth below:

1. Plaintiff is a citizen of State X. Defendant is a citizen of State Y. The amount in controversy, exclusive of interest and costs, exceeds $75,000.

2. On March 1 of last year, Defendant negligently operated his automobile and collided with Plaintiff's automobile.

3. As a result, Plaintiff suffered personal injuries, pain of body and mind, and incurred medical expenses in the sum of $25,000.

Wherefore, Plaintiff prays for a judgment against Defendant of $250,000.

Dave timely answered Paul's complaint as follows:

Defendant neither admits nor denies the allegations of Plaintiff's complaint, but demands strict proof of each and every allegation.

Paul did not amend his complaint, but moved for judgment on the pleadings. Dave countered with his own motion for judgment on the pleadings. The district court denied both motions.

On May 1 of this year, Paul successfully moved to amend his complaint, adding Al as an additional defendant. After being properly served with a copy of the amended complaint, Al moved to dismiss on the ground that the applicable one-year statute of limitations for personal injury actions had expired at the time the amendment was filed and before he had notice of Paul's action. A statute of State Y provides:

If an action is filed within the limitations period provided by law, a new defendant added after the running of that period shall not be entitled to dismissal on the ground that the period has run, if the claim against the new defendant arises out of the same occurrence as the original claim.

In the belief that this statute was controlling, the district court denied Al's motion.

Thereafter, Al served an interrogatory on Paul asking whether Paul took "the statements of any witnesses to the accident" and requesting the submission of "copies of any such statements." Paul asserted that the interrogatory was "objectionable on grounds of work product" and refused to provide any answer or produce any documents. Al moved for an order compelling (1) an answer to the interrogatory, and (2) the production of the requested documents. The motion was granted.

Did the court rule correctly on

1. the motions for judgment on the pleadings?
2. Al's motion to dismiss?
3. Al's motion to compel an answer to his interrogatory and the production of documents?

Discuss.

Question 26

Danielle was flying her small airplane through the dark of night from her home in State X to a resort in State Y. Before she could reach her destination, she made a forced landing on a highway in State Z and hit a truck driven by Price, a resident of State Y. The truck was demolished, and Price sustained personal injuries resulting in medical expenses in excess of $75,000. Although a State Z statute requires the use of headlights after sunset, the trucks headlights were not on at the time of the accident, and Danielle did not see the truck.

Price sued Danielle in the U.S. district court of State Z, basing jurisdiction on diversity of citizenship. The complaint stated in relevant part, "Defendant negligently failed to operate her plane in a safe manner including, specifically, failure to use carburetor heat, causing her engine to fail and causing her to crash into Plaintiff."

Danielle filed an answer denying negligence on her part. Neither the complaint nor the answer made any allegations of contributory negligence or the lack thereof.

Prior to trial, Danielle filed a timely motion requesting that the owner of the truck, Trucko, be made a party on the ground that Trucko is indispensable to the full and final resolution of the dispute. Trucko is incorporated in State X. Trucko conducts no business in State Z, but its trucks occasionally, though not regularly, use State Z highways on trips between State X and State Y. The court denied the motion on the grounds that it had no jurisdiction over Trucko and that, even if it had jurisdiction, service of process would be difficult.

Price moved for an examination of Danielle by a physician to determine whether Danielle's eyesight, hearing, and physical dexterity were adequate for piloting an airplane. Over Danielle's opposition, the motion was granted.

At a pretrial conference, the court entered an order stating that the case would be tried on the issue of Danielle's negligence. The issue of contributory negligence was not discussed.

At the trial, Danielle introduced evidence without objection, showing that the engine failed without any known cause, that this presented a sudden emergency, and that Danielle could not see Price's truck because its headlights were off.

Over Price's timely objections, the court instructed the jury that it could consider the issue of possible contributory negligence on the part of Price.

Was the court correct in

1. denying Danielle's motion to make Trucko a party and allowing the case to go forward without the presence of Trucko?
2. granting Price's motion for a physical examination of Danielle?
3. allowing the jury to consider the issue of contributory negligence?

Discuss.

Question 27

In 1985, the town of Paz entered into a waste management contract with Daz, Inc., by which Paz agreed to build a wastewater treatment plant and to make the plant available to Daz for the treatment of wastewater. Under the contract, Daz agreed to pay the operating costs of the facility for the first ten years and thereafter to pay a "reasonable" user charge for the continuing use of the facility. In 1995, the Environmental Protection Agency ("EPA") informed Paz that the Clean Water Act ("CWA"), a federal statute, required Paz to implement a user charge system whereby each user of the plant must pay a proportionate share of the cost of operating and maintaining the entire wastewater treatment system based upon that user's contribution to the total waste flow. The EPA also advised Paz that the user charge system currently applied to Daz was inconsistent with the user charge system required by the CWA. In general, the CWA creates a federal regulatory scheme designed to promote clean water for the benefit of the public. The provisions of the CWA are enforceable by the EPA. The statute includes no private enforcement mechanism.

Paz filed a lawsuit against Daz in a U.S. district court seeking to force Daz to comply with the EPA/CWA mandated user charge system. Paz alleged that the lawsuit came within the court's federal question jurisdiction. The essence of Paz's claim is that the waste management contract between Paz and Daz requires Daz to pay any user charges mandated by state or federal law. Since the CWA mandated the imposition of specific type of user charge, Daz was contractually obligated to pay that charge. Daz has filed a motion to dismiss under FRCP 12(b)(1). How should the court rule? Explain.

Question 28

Abe is a commercial real estate developer. He entered into a contract with Bob under which Bob agreed to construct a strip mall on property owned by Abe. As part of the contract, Carl was named as a surety, i.e., an insurer, for Bob's performance under the contract. After the commencement of the construction, a dispute arose between Abe and Bob in which Abe claimed that Bob was in default under the contract. Bob claimed that Donna, Abe's agent, was preventing Bob from completing the project. Abe and Carl are citizens of California. Bob and Donna are citizens of Arizona. Abe has sued Bob in a U.S. district court claiming breach of contract. He seeks damages of over $100,000. In answering the following questions, be certain to address the applicable FRCP and any pertinent jurisdictional statutes.

1. May Bob implead Carl? Explain.

2. Assuming for purposes of this subpart that Bob is allowed to implead Carl, may Carl file a claim against Abe related to the construction project? Explain.

3. Assuming for purposes of this subpart that Bob is allowed to implead Carl, may Carl file a claim against Abe unrelated to the construction project? Explain.

4. Assuming for purposes of this subpart that Bob is allowed to implead Carl, may Abe file a claim against Carl related to the construction project? Explain.

5. If Bob does not attempt to implead Carl, may Carl intervene? Explain.

6. May Bob file a counterclaim against Abe, joining Donna as a defendant on that counterclaim, asserting that Abe and Donna have undermined Bob's ability to complete the construction project? Explain (as to both Abe and Donna).

7. Assuming that Bob does not file a counterclaim against Abe and Donna, may Donna intervene, claiming that Bob's performance under the contract amounts to tortuous interference with Donna's ability to perform as Abe's agent on the construction project? Explain. (Assume that Donna has stated a claim on which relief can be granted.)

8. Assuming for purposes of this subpart that Donna is allowed to intervene as a plaintiff, may Abe file a claim against Donna related to the underlying dispute between Abe and Bob? Explain.

Question 29

Delmore, a citizen of California, entered into a contract with the city of Industry, California, to perform repair work on Industrial Blvd., the city's main thoroughfare. The contract required Delmore to provide a payment bond to ensure that he would pay all subcontractors and suppliers for the project. Pursuant to this requirement, Delmore obtained a payment bond from Surety, Inc., a New York corporation. Thereafter, Delmore subcontracted with Patricia, also a citizen of California, for certain labor, material, supplies and services for the Industrial Blvd. project. Patricia performed her obligations under the subcontract. Pursuant to the subcontract, Delmore owes Patricia $100,000. However, he refuses to pay her based on a preexisting debt owed to him by Patricia. Patricia has filed two suits. The first was filed in a California state court against Delmore claiming breach of contract and seeking $100,000 in damages. The second was filed in a U.S. district court sitting in California against Surety seeking to enforce the payment bond in that same amount. In the federal action, Surety has filed a motion to dismiss under FRCP 12(b)(7), claiming that Delmore is a person who should be joined in the federal proceeding and without whom the federal court cannot proceed. How should the federal district court rule on Surety's motion?

Question 30

A and B entered into a long-term delivery contract under which B was obligated to deliver certain goods to A on July 1 of each year from 1999 until 2009. For the first two years of the agreement (1999-2000), B performed as required, but in 2001, B failed to make the required delivery until mid-December of that year. A sued B in a State X court claiming breach of contract and seeking damages for the failure to make the 2001 delivery in a timely fashion. B defended on the ground that there was an intervening act of God (a 100-year flood) and that the contract was procured by A through fraud. B also claimed that the contract allowed him to make the delivery either on July 1 or within four months of that date. All issues were fully litigated. The court found that there had been no 100-year flood, that there was no fraud, and that the contract permitted B to ship the goods within four months of the July 1 date. Judgment was entered for A, the court finding that B failed to make the shipment within four months of July 1, 2001. In 2002, B again failed to meet the July 1 delivery date, but did make a delivery on August 30 of that year. A again sued B in a State X court seeking damages for breach of contract.

1. Is A bound by the finding in the first proceeding that the contract allowed B to make the delivery within four months of July 1?

2. If B raises a defense of claim preclusion, how should the court rule? Does it matter whether the breach at issue in the first proceeding was considered material?

3. Since the court in the first proceeding made several findings, is B bound by the finding of no fraud? Explain?

4. Suppose in the first case that the court found for B despite the fact that B had not shipped within four months of July 1, concluding both that there was a 100-year flood and that the contract was procured through fraud. Would A be precluded from bringing the second suit?

5. Suppose that while making the August 30, 2002, delivery, B's driver, D, negligently damaged A's loading dock. A files a negligence suit against D. Judgment, however, is for D. If A now attempts to sue B for damages to the loading dock, may B rely on the prior judgment in favor of D as bar to that suit?

6. Same facts as subpart 5, except that the judgment in the *A v. D* proceeding was against D and in favor of A. Would B be bound by that judgment?

*Essay Exam
Answers*

Answer to Question 1

Did the court properly deny APOW's motion to dismiss?

For a complaint to be sufficient under FRCP 8(a), it must contain: (1) a short, plain statement of the grounds for subject matter jurisdiction; (2) a short, plain statement of the claim showing that the pleader is entitled to relief; and (3) a description of the relief demanded by the plaintiff. The facts indicate that subject matter jurisdiction was "properly" based on diversity of citizenship, and so it must be assumed that each member of the class suffered harm in excess of $75,000. APOW ("D") probably contended that the facts described in the complaint (that emissions from the plant had injured people) are not sufficient to put it on notice of the nature of the action against it. However, plaintiffs would argue in rebuttal that the allegations were sufficient to satisfy the liberal standards of notice pleading and that D should have recognized that numerous possible legal theories (strict liability, nuisance, negligence and trespass) that could be inferred from those allegations. Therefore, D was on proper notice of the claims against it, which is all that the rule requires.

D probably also argued that the damages or relief claimed by plaintiffs is not clearly described (from the given facts, this assertion appears to be well taken). Plaintiffs would contend in rebuttal, however, that by their prayer for "damages," they intended to recover whatever losses or injuries were proven at trial. Given the liberal standards of notice pleading, a court would probably accept this interpretation. In short, D's motion was properly denied.

Was the grant of certification proper?

For a class action to be maintained, (1) there must be common questions of law or fact, and (2) the representative's claim must be typical of the class represented. D probably argued that since the plaintiffs were injured on the third day of the emissions, their claims are not representative of persons harmed on the first and second days. Also, each plaintiff may have been injured to a different extent and possibly in a different manner (if different types of emissions were involved). If so, there would be no common factual issues. However, if it is likely that the emissions were all from the same source (i.e., a malfunctioning valve), certification was probably proper. The types of claims for all three days would be identical and the question of D's liability would be common to the entire class. In such instance, the representative's claims would be typical of the class (at least until it can be established that each day's emissions were from a different source).

Was the memorandum discoverable?

The discoverability of the memo depends initially on the FRCP. If it would be discoverable under the FRCP, no conflict with state law would exist (since the state has no work product doctrine). If it would *not* be discoverable under the FRCP, the federal court must determine if application of the federal rule would be consistent with the standards of the Rules Enabling Act (REA).

Under FRCP 26(b)(3), a party may discover documents prepared in anticipation of litigation or for trial by another party or her counsel, only upon showing a substantial need for the items and that they (or their "substantial equivalent") cannot otherwise be obtained without undue hardship. Plaintiffs probably contended that the memo involved was not within this privilege because it was not prepared in anticipation of litigation (i.e., there is no indication that anyone was threatening suit against D over minor accidents at *another* company's plant). The rule, however, has not been so narrowly construed. D could successfully argue that (1) the memo was created to assist D in responding to claims which would inevitably be made when similar "incidents" occurred at a D plant; (2) there was no reason why plaintiffs could not recreate the memo by doing their own research; and (3) to the extent that the memo contained the lawyer's impressions or conclusions, it would absolutely be nondiscoverable. Since D's position is consistent with the standards of FRCP 26(b)(3), the memo would *not* be discoverable under the FRCP.

Assuming the memo was *not* discoverable under the FRCP, plaintiffs might have contended that, under the *Erie doctrine,* where state substantive law conflicts with the FRCP, the latter is superseded by the former. The FRCP are not, however, limited by the *Erie* doctrine. D, therefore, would have argued that *Hanna v. Plumer* held that where a provision of the FRCP was validly enacted, it is controlling when in conflict with any state rule. The measure of that validity is provided by the REA, under which a federal rule must be rationally classifiable as procedural and may not abridge, enlarge, or modify a substantive right. Rule 26(b)(3) is rationally classifiable as procedural since it regulates the manner in which information is exchanged between parties to a federal lawsuit. Next, although state law creates a "right" to discovery of this material, that right arises only in the context of litigation and therefore cannot be properly characterized as substantive. In other words, this state rule does not regulate primary human activity. As a consequence, FRCP 26(b)(3) does not abridge, enlarge, or modify a state substantive right.

Plaintiffs could contend that the state legislature has a strong desire to permit discovery of any relevant unprivileged information because it abolishes the work product rule. Thus, the FRCP provision is in conflict with a substantive rule of law (and therefore the memo should be discoverable). However, since (1) discovery has always been associated with the procedural aspects of trial, (2) there is no state enactment that expressly makes work product discoverable, and (3) plaintiffs chose to litigate in a federal court (which would normally apply the FRCP), the court's decision permitting discovery of the memorandum was probably incorrect.

Answer to Question 2

Was Trucker ("T") a party who ought to be joined in the State X action?

Under FRCP 19(a), a person ought to be joined in a pending action when it is feasible to do so and when (1) complete relief cannot be given to the existing parties if he is not joined, (2) the absentee's interests will be substantially prejudiced if he is not joined, or (3) the parties already subject to the action might be exposed to inconsistent judgments or double liability if he is not joined. We can assume feasibility since nothing in the facts suggests to the contrary. As to whether T ought to be joined, complete relief can be given to the existing parties in his absence — i.e., Rider ("R") can obtain a judgment for the full amount of his injuries from Owner ("O"). Also, T's interests are not likely to be prejudiced if he is not joined since nothing in the *R v. O* proceeding would seem to impair T's interests in any legal or practical way.

O might contend, however, that since he and T were joint tortfeasors, he could be liable for the entire judgment if T were not joined (whereas if T were joined, and they were deemed to be joint tortfeasors, O would have a right of contribution against T). Thus, the failure to join T exposes O to excessive liability. However, an absent party's status as a joint torfeasor is never, standing alone, a sufficient basis on which to require joinder of that party under Rule 19(a).

Was the State X court correct in granting T's motion to intervene?

Under FRCP 24(a), a party has a right to intervene when the disposition of an action may, as a practical matter, impair his interests and these interests are **not** likely to be adequately represented by the existing parties. T would probably **not** come within this standard because his interests would not appear to be affected by the *R v. O* litigation. Since R's conduct with respect to the accident was different from T's, whether R won or lost would have no effect on a possible subsequent lawsuit by T against O.

However, under FRCP 24(b), one may be permitted to intervene where there is a common question of law or fact between (1) the existing action, and (2) the claim or defense sought to be asserted by the intervenor. A trial court arguably could determine that R and T share a common claim with respect to the transaction (i.e., that O operated his vehicle in a negligent manner). Thus, the trial court's decision to permit T to intervene was probably correct.

Was the State X court correct in permitting R to cross-claim against T?

Under FRCP 13(g), a party may assert a cross-claim against a co-party if his action arises out of the occurrence that is the subject of the original action. Since both R and T are co-party plaintiffs and since R's claim against T arises out of the collision between O and T, it appears that the court was correct in permitting R to cross-claim against T. Some courts, however, have interpreted Rule 13(g) as permitting cross-claims between co-plaintiffs only when those co-plaintiffs have been joined as co-parties to a counter-claim filed by a defendant. Under this approach, R would not be entitled to cross-claim against T.

What is the effect of the federal action on R's action against O?

The federal action would have no effect on R's state court action against O, since the fact that T was not negligent vis-à-vis O would *not* imply that O had failed to act reasonably with respect to R. T's negligence is simply not the same issue as O's negligence or lack thereof.

What is the effect of the federal action on R's cross-claim against T?

Under *res judicata* principles, where there has been a prior, final judgment between the parties or their privies with respect to the cause of action being asserted in a subsequent lawsuit, the latter action is barred. However, O and R do not appear to be in privity with each other. O was not R's legal representative (sometimes called "procedural privy"), nor was there any type of legal relationship between O and R (sometimes called "substantive privy"). Thus, the prior federal lawsuit would have no effect upon R's cross-complaint against T since R, as a nonparty and as someone who was not in privity with a party, cannot be bound by that judgment consistent with principles of due process.

What is the effect of the federal action upon T's claim against O in the federal district court?

Under FRCP 13(a), a party must assert a counterclaim that she has against the opposing party if it (1) arises out of the occurrence that is the basis of the latter's claim against the former, and (2) there is no need for the presence of third parties over whom the court cannot acquire jurisdiction. If this is not done, the claim is barred. Since (1) T's claim for personal injury damages arose out of the collision between O and T (which was the basis for the former's state court action against the latter), and (2) R's presence was not necessary to T's claim against O, T's claim against O will be treated as having been a compulsory counterclaim in the previous lawsuit and will be barred.

What is the effect of the federal action upon O's counterclaim against T?

Under the *res judicata* principles described above, O's counterclaim against T for personal injuries would be barred by the earlier federal court decision that T had no liability to O. O therefore would be precluded from reasserting that claim.

Answer to Question 3

The motion to dismiss based on subject matter and personal jurisdiction:

For a U.S. district court to be competent, there must be diversity of citizenship (no plaintiff and no defendant may be citizens of the same state) and the amount in controversy must exceed $75,000. One part of the diversity requirement is satisfied since Seler ("S") and Byer ("B") are citizens of different states. The amount in controversy requirement, however, is not satisfied. S would argue that the amount in controversy alleged by B is only $47,500, i.e., the amount of the alleged error in the contract. This argument is correct since the disputed amount between the parties is precisely this amount. However, B might contend that in an action for equitable relief most courts will measure the amount in controversy by the greater of the amount either the plaintiff stands to gain or the defendant stands to lose. While this legal position is well taken, here the amount the plaintiff stands to gain and the defendant stands to lose is identical for both parties, namely, $47,500. Regardless of who prevails, one party will gain and the other party will lose $47,500. Hence the amount in controversy is not satisfied under these facts.

For a court to take personal jurisdiction over an out-of-state defendant: (1) there must be a long-arm statute that permits it to do so (since the facts are silent, we'll assume that State B's long-arm statute gave its courts all personal jurisdiction consistent with due process), and (2) the defendant must have sufficient minimum contacts with the forum so as not to offend traditional notions of fair play and substantial justice. B would contend that since the contract was signed in State B, S has sufficient minimum contacts with that jurisdiction. In support of that position, B would argue that S's contacts with the forum state were purposeful and that the claim arose out of those contacts. S would argue in response that an isolated appearance in one state for the purpose of concluding a business transaction pertaining to property in another state is *not* constitutionally adequate to create personal jurisdiction. S is likely correct. To satisfy the minimum contacts test, S's contacts would have to be of a quantity and quality that would make the exercise of jurisdiction reasonable. In the absence of some showing of a continuing relationship between S and State B with respect to this particular transaction, that standard would not be satisfied. Thus, the district court erred in denying S's motion to dismiss for lack of personal jurisdiction.

S's demand for a jury trial:

Pursuant to FRCP 38(a) and the Seventh Amendment, each party is entitled to a jury trial with respect to legal issues. While reformation has traditionally been recognized as an equitable (rather than legal) claim, S could have contended that the reformation question is inextricably associated with the legal issue of whether B breached the contract by refusing to pay S $85,000 for Whiteacre. Since *Beacon Theatres, Inc. v. Westover* said legal claims must be tried prior to equitable ones, S's demand for a jury trial probably should *not* have been denied.

Disclosure of the appraisers' identities and the appraisals:

Pursuant to FRCP 34, documents and other tangible things must be obtained by a request to produce. Since S demanded the appraisal reports within the context of interrogatories, B was arguably not required to comply. On the other hand, given the liberality of the federal rules, S's interrogatories could be treated as requests for production, thus requiring B's compliance. Indeed, interrogatories and requests for production are often served together. The court's ruling, although perhaps technically correct, is suspect under the liberal standards of the federal rules.

B probably objected to the other information requested on the ground that it was irrelevant (appraisal reports would not necessarily indicate the price the parties agreed to) and, possibly, that it represented B's work product.

The first objection probably would *not* be successful because a party may ordinarily obtain disclosure of any information that is reasonably calculated to lead to the discovery of admissible evidence. FRCP 26(b)(1). If the appraisals were made *prior to* the commencement of the action, they would tend to show the fair market value of Whiteacre, and therefore the probable purchase price agreed upon by the parties.

If B's appraisals showed that the land was worth $85,000, it is unlikely that S would have sold it to him for $37,500. Conversely, if the land was worth $37,500, it would tend to corroborate that a mistake had been made (i.e., B probably would not have agreed to pay $85,000 for Whiteacre). If the appraisals were made *after* the litigation had commenced, they would still be admissible (to the extent they did not contain advice or suggestions to B's attorney) because S would have the right to know the nature of the evidence that B intended to present, so that he might counter it.

The second objection will *not* be successful with respect to any expert B expects to call at trial. Under FRCP 26(a)(2), an expert who may be called to testify must prepare a report containing (1) the expert's opinions and the basis for them, (2) the data considered by the expert, (3) any exhibits the expert will use, (4) the expert's qualifications, (5) the compensation she is receiving, and (6) a list of other cases in which she has testified within the prior four years. Thus, while B would not have to hand over work product documents, B would have to provide the information requested by S concerning the identity of testifying witnesses and their opinions within 90 days of the trial, or the court would have to exclude B from using this evidence at trial. FRCP 37(c)(1).

However, B's second objection probably will succeed with respect to any appraisers B has retained in anticipation of litigation, but who will not testify in the action. The federal rules allow discovery of such experts only upon a showing of *exceptional circumstances*. FRCP 26(b)(4)(B). Since S could retain its own appraisers, the court should not have allowed S to discover the opinions of these experts.

Thus, the court ruled correctly with respect to B's objections concerning the opinion of witnesses B expected to use at trial, but was in error to the extent the order encompassed nontestifying experts.

Evidence submitted with respect to the JNOV motion:

A jury's determination of a factual issue should not be disturbed, unless there was an insufficient evidentiary basis for it. B probably contended that the preponderance of the evidence favored him since he had introduced expert testimony that the land was worth only $42,200. Nevertheless, based upon the demeanor of the witnesses, the jury could have believed S while disbelieving the testimony of B and his appraiser. Additionally, the jury might have believed that even though Whiteacre was worth only $42,200, B may have exercised poor business judgment and entered into the transaction anyway. Thus, the court was probably *not* correct in granting B's JNOV (now called "judgment as a matter of law").

Procedural arguments:

Pursuant to FRCP 50(b), a party seeking a JNOV *must* have made a motion for a judgment as a matter of law at the close of all evidence. Since the facts do not indicate that such a motion was made, S should have contended that the JNOV was not properly granted.

Answer to Question 4

Motion to quash:

The State X court was **not** correct in denying Daw's motion to quash. For a court to exercise personal jurisdiction over an out-of-state defendant, the latter must have sufficient minimum contacts with the forum so as not to offend traditional notions of fair play and substantial justice. There seems to be little question that Daw ("D") did **not** have sufficient minimum contacts with State X since (1) the accident did not occur in that state, (2) D owns no property there, and (3) D visited the jurisdiction only for a short period of time.

The fact that D filed an answer after the motion to quash was denied is irrelevant and does not constitute a waiver of his personal jurisdiction argument in a majority of jurisdictions. Once a trial court denies a motion to quash, finding that personal jurisdiction has been established, in most states the defendant is free to defend on the merits without waiving the right to challenge the trial court's ruling on appeal. In some states, however, the defendant is required to file a writ of mandate against the trial court in order to challenge that court's denial of the motion to quash. In such jurisdictions, then, D would have waived any further objection to the trial court's jurisdiction.

Default judgment against D:

Whether the State X court was correct in granting a default judgment depends upon the resolution of two issues: (1) Whether D properly refused to answer the interrogatory, and (2) if he should have answered, whether a default judgment was an excessive sanction.

Was D's conversation with the investigator and his wife privileged?

D probably contended that the conversation was not admissible because "confidential" communications to one's spouse and to one's attorney are ordinarily privileged. P probably asserted that (1) the statement to D's wife was not confidential since it was made in front of the investigator, (2) the statement to the investigator was not confidential because it was made in front of D's wife, and (3) the investigator was not D's attorney. However, D should have been able to successfully argue in rebuttal that both conversations were "confidential" since (1) the statements were made in front of persons whom D reasonably believed would retain his statements in confidence, and (2) the attorney-client privilege ordinarily extends to "essential" personnel of the attorney, such as the investigator.

Assuming the statement was not privileged, is summary judgment an appropriate sanction?

Under FRCP 37(b)(2)(C), if a party refuses to obey a court order after being directed to do so, the court may make such order as is "just" (including the right to render a default judgment against the disobedient party). However, it could be contended by D that the order was not just in this instance since the failure by D to respond to this inquiry didn't materially hinder the ability of P to present his case. Also, even if D had advised his wife and the investigator that he was at fault, he might have been incorrect (not being an attorney, he would not be capable of making this determination, even if he believed he could). Thus, regardless of how damaging D's statements might appear, they would not necessarily be dispositive of the case. The court probably should *not* have rendered a default judgment.

How should the district court rule?

P's summary judgment:

P's summary judgment motion may have been premised on the doctrine of *res judicata.* That doctrine bars the assertion of claims that have previously gone to judgment — claim preclusion — and of issues that have been previously litigated and decided — issue preclusion. Under the principles of intersystem preclusion and the Full Faith and Credit statute, the federal court will be required to apply the law of preclusion that would be followed by a state court sitting in State X.

Claim preclusion applies only when a prior claim has been asserted. Therefore, P has no argument based on claim preclusion since D raised no claims in the prior lawsuit. Summary judgment on this basis therefore would be inappropriate.

On the other hand, most state courts follow the federal model with respect to counterclaims and require that a defendant assert all counterclaims that he may have against a plaintiff when those counterclaims are transactionally related to the plaintiff's claims against him. If a defendant fails to assert a transactionally related counterclaim in the initial proceeding, he will be barred from later asserting that claim in any other proceeding, the counterclaim being deemed compulsory in the first proceeding. If State X follows this majority rule, D will be barred in this second proceeding from asserting any claim against P arising out of the accident that was the subject of the first proceeding. The federal court in the second proceeding will honor that state rule under the compulsion of the *Erie doctrine* since allowing D to proceed with his counterclaim under such circumstances would be outcome determinative at the forum shopping stage, the federal forum being available to adjudicate D's claim while the state forum would not. Thus, if State X has a "transactional" compulsory counterclaim rule, summary judgment in favor of P on D's counterclaim would be appropriate.

P might also rely on issue preclusion as a basis for summary judgment on his own claim against D, specifically on the issue of D's negligence. Again, the federal court would be required to apply the law of State X. Under universally accepted principles of issue preclusion, the issue must have been actually litigated in the prior proceeding. However, the issue of D's negligence was never "actually litigated" (i.e., P was granted a default judgment in the context of sanctions). Therefore, issue preclusion would not be available under these circumstances. Thus, P's summary judgment motion relying on issue preclusion should be denied.

D's summary judgment on P's complaint:

D's motion for summary judgment would seek to apply the doctrine of claim preclusion against P. Again, under the standards of intersystem preclusion, the federal court will follow the law of State X in determining whether the doctrine applies. Under the majority rule, the doctrine of claim preclusion requires a plaintiff to file all transactionally related claims he has against the D in a single proceeding. Once the initial proceeding goes to final judgment, all rights of action arising out of the transaction that was the subject of that proceeding are subject to preclusion. If P prevails in the first proceeding, any unasserted rights of action are "merged" into the judgment. If P loses in that proceeding, any unasserted rights of action are "barred." In this case, since P's personal injury claims arise out of the same set of facts (i.e., the same transaction) as P's property damage claims, and since the property damage proceeding has gone to final judgment, P would now be precluded from asserting those personal injury claims in any other proceeding against D. Accordingly, D would be entitled to summary judgment.

On the other hand, if State X is a minority jurisdiction that follows the "primary rights" definition of a claim, summary judgment would be inappropriate. Under the primary rights approach, a claim is defined by the interest the claim is designed to protect. Interests in property and interests involving personal injuries are deemed separate primary rights. In essence, a party is allowed to split her cause of action, filing separate lawsuits to vindicate different primary rights. Under this theory, P would be allowed to file a second proceedings to vindicate his primary right to be free from personal injury.

Answer to Question 5

May State C assert personal jurisdiction over Macco ("M")?

We'll assume that (1) the lawsuit was properly filed and served, and (2) the State C court is competent to hear this matter.

A State C court may exercise "specific" personal jurisdiction over M only if the standards of the minimum contacts test are satisfied. Paula ("P"), therefore, would have the burden of establishing that M purposely availed itself of the opportunity of doing business in State C and that P's cause of action arose out of those purposeful contacts. If P satisfies these elements, the assertion of jurisdiction would be presumptively reasonable, and M would have the heavy burden of rebutting that presumption. Alternatively, P could attempt to demonstrate that State C could exercise "general" jurisdiction over M on the theory that M's contacts with the state are so continuous and systematic that M should be subjected to personal jurisdiction even over claims unrelated to those contacts. The standards for general jurisdiction are quite high and require a relationship with the state that is tantamount to that of a citizen of the state.

It would be difficult for P to satisfy either of these tests. As to specific jurisdiction, while M clearly has purposeful contacts with State C — an office in the state and up to $500,000 in annual business over a ten-year period — none of those contacts appears to be related to P's wrongful death claim, which arose in State A. P, therefore, could not satisfy the second element of the test. As to general jurisdiction, M's contacts are not sufficient to establish the type of relationship with the state that would satisfy the applicable standards. Unless M's contacts with State C represent essentially the sum total of M's business, or at the very least, a substantial portion thereof, the assertion of general jurisdiction over it would be quite unlikely.

Effect of Worker ("W")'s prior lawsuit on P's action against M:

Since the initial proceeding was in a State A court, the Full Faith and Credit Clause will require the State C court to apply the principles of preclusion that would be applied by a State A court. This intersystem preclusion principle will have little importance in the immediate case, however, since under universally accepted principles of preclusion, the prior judgment will have no effect on P's action against M.

Under *res judicata* principles, where there has been a final, valid judgment on the merits between the parties (or their privies) with respect to a claim that is being asserted in a subsequent lawsuit, the latter action is barred under the doctrine of claim preclusion. Similarly, issues that have been litigated, decided, and were essential to a prior proceeding against the same parties (or their privies) will be precluded from relitigation under the doctrine of issue preclusion. Neither doctrine is satisfied here. As to claim preclusion, two elements are lacking. First, this suit does not involve the same parties. Although P, as executrix, will be treated as having been in privity with W, M was not a party to the prior proceeding nor in privity with any party to that proceeding. Second, the claims asserted in these suits are not the same claims. The first suit involves the negligence of Doctor ("D") and the responsibility of Hospital ("H") for that negligence; the second suit involves the liability of M for the accident.

As to issue preclusion, the only issues litigated, decided, and essential in the first proceeding pertained to the negligence of D and the liability of H for the actions of D. Neither issue is relevant to the second proceeding. Hence, issue preclusion would not apply.

Effect of W's prior lawsuit upon P's action against Doctor:

First, P could not successfully assert claim or issue preclusion against D for the simple reason that D was not a party to the first proceeding nor in privity with anyone who was a party to that proceeding. In fact, there was a specific finding that D was not H's agent. Therefore, under principles of due process, D will not be bound by the judgment or rulings in that proceeding.

On the other hand, D might be able to assert issue preclusion against P. While P was not a party to that proceeding, as explained above, as the executrix of W's estate, she will be treated as being in privity with W in the first proceeding. Hence, she is bound by that proceeding. The question is whether D, a nonparty and nonprivy, can benefit from that proceeding. The concept of mutuality prohibits assertion of issue preclusion by a person who would not be bound by the first proceeding. D clearly falls into that latter category. Hence, if State A adheres to the principle of mutuality, a State C court, under the principles of intersystem preclusion described above, would not permit D to assert issue preclusion against P. On the other hand, most jurisdictions have now abandoned the mutuality requirement for defensive assertions of issue preclusion. If State A falls into that category, then State C will be required to allow D to assert issue preclusion against P even though D is not himself bound by the prior judgment.

Assuming State A has abandoned the mutuality requirement, under the doctrine of issue preclusion, where a particular issue has been actually litigated in a prior action, a court may preclude it from being relitigated where that issue was essential to the outcome of the earlier case. D could contend that the issue of his D's negligence was actually litigated, decided, and essential to the previous judgment.

P could argue that the findings by the State A court were "alternative" findings, either of which standing alone would support the judgment. As such, neither finding should be treated as "essential" to the prior judgment. Courts have adopted three approaches to such alternative findings. First, some courts hold that unless both findings are appealed and then affirmed on appeal, neither finding will be treated as essential. Under this approach, since there was no appeal of the State A proceeding, neither finding would be binding on P in a subsequent lawsuit. Next, some courts have held that so long as the issue was thoroughly and carefully addressed in the initial proceeding, it will be treated as binding in all subsequent proceedings. Under this approach, P would be bound by the finding that D was not negligent if that question was thoroughly and carefully addressed in the prior proceeding. Finally, a few courts follow the principle that both alternative findings are binding regardless of care with which either finding was made. Under this approach, P would be bound by the finding that D was not negligent. Hence, the result here will depend on the rule adopted by State A, which, under principles of intersystem preclusion, must now be applied by State C.

Answer to Question 6

Did the court err in granting Dave ("D")'s motion to dismiss?

FRCP 15(c) allows relation back with respect to an amendment that adds a claim to a pleading under two circumstances. First, an "amendment of a pleading relates back to the date of the original pleading when relation back is permitted by the law that provides the statute of limitations applicable to the action." FRCP 15(c)(1). Since the accident occurred in State Y, State Y law would provide the statute of limitations. Furthermore, since State Y has no rule allowing an amendment to relate back "under any circumstances," subsection (c)(1) would not permit relation back. Next, under subsection (c)(2), an amendment relates back if the claim asserted in the amended pleading "arose out of the conduct, transaction, or occurrence set forth or attempted to be set forth in the original pleading." This standard would appear to be satisfied since P's amended pleading raises a claim that arises out of the same accident that was the subject of his initial pleading. Hence, under the language of FRCP 15(c)(2), Paul ("P") would be entitled to have his amendment relate back to the date of the original filing.

Nonetheless, the U.S. district court's ruling denying relation back may have been correct. The essential question is whether application of FRCP 15(c)(2) to these facts would be proper in light of the standards of the Rules Enabling Act (REA). To resolve that question, three subsidiary questions must be answered: (1) Is the federal rule broad enough to control, and, if so, is there a direct collision between it and the state law? (2) Assuming a conflict, is the federal rule rationally classifiable as procedural? (3) Assuming affirmative answers to the first two questions, would application of the federal rule abridge, enlarge, or modify a substantive right?

On the first question, FRCP 15(c)(2) would appear to be broad enough to control since it addresses the specific circumstances under which relation back would be allowed. In addition, since the federal rule allows relation back (and, in fact, seems to require it) and state law does not, there would seem to be a conflict between the federal rule and state law. However, this conflict can be avoided. FRCP 15(a) permits a plaintiff to amend a pleading as of right if done within 20 days of the date on which the original pleading was filed. Otherwise, in the absence of consent by the adverse party, the pleading may be amended only by leave of court that "shall be freely given when justice so requires." The amendment here was filed one month after the initial pleading and it would not appear that D consented to it. Hence, the district court could avoid any conflict with state law by simply concluding that justice would not be served by allowing P to file this amendment. In essence, it would not be just to allow a plaintiff in federal court to enjoy the benefits of relation back when a plaintiff in state court would not reap those fruits. Since there is no conflict, the district court's ruling would be correct.

Assuming there is a conflict, the two elements of the REA must be satisfied if relation back is to be allowed, i.e., the procedural and substantive components of the statute must be applied. As to the first, FRCP 15 is rationally classifiable as procedural since it adopts a method through which to amend pleadings and provides standards for determining the effect of those pleadings. Hence, this low threshold test is easily satisfied here.

Next, assuming a conflict and assuming that the rule is rationally classifiable as procedural, we must determine whether application of the rule would abridge, enlarge, or modify a substantive right. D has a very strong argument that allowing relation back when the effect of doing so will be to revive a claim that otherwise would be barred by the state statute of limitations does abridge his right to be free from liability on claim that is no longer enforceable under state law. Similarly, D could argue effectively that the application of relation back enlarges P's right to assert that claim by essentially resurrecting the moribund state-created cause of action.

In short, D's motion to dismiss the personal injury claim was correctly decided, either because the district court avoided the conflict with state law by refusing leave to file the amended pleading or because application of FRCP 15(c)(2) under these circumstances would abridge, enlarge, or modify the underlying substantive rights asserted by P.

Did the court err in dismissing D's third-party complaint?

Insco ("I") has asserted three independent grounds for its contention that the district court should dismiss the third-party complaint against it.

(a) Lack of authorization under the FRCP: This assertion should not have prevailed since FRCP 14 specifically authorizes third-party claims.

(b) Lack of competency: Since D and I are both citizens of State Y, I's argument was probably that the U.S. district court was not competent to hear the impleader because diversity subject matter jurisdiction requires that no plaintiff and no defendant be citizens of the same state. However, impleader by a defendant falls within the court's supplemental jurisdiction. Thus, dismissing D's complaint on this basis would have been erroneous.

(c) Lack of substantive claim: I's argument appears to be that D, in fact, has no right of recovery against it since the policy in question was fraudulently obtained. However, FRCP 14(a) permits an impleader claim whenever the

impleaded party "may" be liable to the third-party plaintiff (i.e., the impleading party). Since whether the policy was wrongfully obtained appears to be a factual issue (to be decided at trial), dismissal of D's third-party complaint was therefore improper.

Admission of Wit's testimony:

Pretrial orders pursuant to FRCP 16(e) ordinarily describe matters that the parties have agreed on with respect to the conduct of the trial. Such matters can be modified at trial only to prevent "manifest injustice." Even though P might have been aware of Wit, he would have no reason to prepare to cross-examine him as a consequence of D's failure to list Wit in the pretrial order. Since (1) there is no indication that D had just discovered Wit, and (2) there was the possibility that Wit's testimony could tip the evidence in favor of D, the district court probably erred in permitting Wit to testify.

Answer to Question 7

Truco ("T")'s Motions to Dismiss

(a) Lack of subject matter jurisdiction: Where subject matter jurisdiction is based on diversity, the complaint must allege that no plaintiff and no defendant are citizens of the same state. T's contention that the complaint should be dismissed because of a lack of subject matter jurisdiction was probably based upon the fact that Pat ("P") has asserted only that she was a "resident" of State White. Thus, P could have resided in State White and yet have been a citizen of State Red. Yet, the word "resident" is often used synonymously with "domicile" or "citizenship." And under standards of notice pleading, P's allegations of residence probably would suffice as far as pleading goes. If there were any doubt as to whether P was, in fact, a citizen of State White, the district court would have a duty to require P to provide more specific proof as to her state of citizenship. Since the evidence later established that P was a citizen of State White at the time of filing, we can assume that the district court met its duty in this regard.

The fact that P was a citizen of State Red at the time the action arose is irrelevant because subject matter jurisdiction is determined at the time the complaint is filed. Since P had apparently made a bona fide relocation to State White before the action was commenced, diversity existed.

In summary, T's lack of subject matter jurisdiction defense was quite likely properly rejected.

(b) Failure to join Dan ("D"): Under FRCP 19(a), a person ought to be joined if (1) in his absence, complete relief cannot be accorded among those already parties; and (2) disposition of the action in his absence may (a) impede or impair his ability to protect his interest in the subject matter of the action, or (b) leave any of the parties subject to a substantial risk of incurring multiple liability. The Supreme Court has made it clear, however, that an absent party's status as a joint tortfeasor is not sufficient, standing alone, to satisfy the requirements of FRCP 19(a). In any event, P can clearly get complete relief from T in D's absence. Moreover, disposition of the action will not impair or impede any discernible interest of D; nor will it leave P or T subject to a substantial risk of incurring multiple liability. At most, if P prevails, T will be required to file a separate proceeding against D to enforce any joint liability between them and D will have ample opportunity to defend his rights against T in that proceeding.

T's motion for a judgment as a matter of law:

T would next contend that since (1) it and P had stipulated in a pretrial order that "T would be liable to P if D was an employee of T," and (2) it was proven that D was not employed by T, a judgment as a matter of law was appropriate. P could make two arguments in rebuttal. First, P and T agreed only that T would be liable if D were T's employee, not that there could be no other grounds on which T's liability to P could be established. Thus, liability could be predicated on the State Red statute, which enforces liability on the owner of the vehicle who gave the driver causing the accident permission to use his car.

Second, a pretrial order may be modified to "prevent manifest injustice." FRCP 16(e). It would arguably be unjust to permit T to avoid liability simply because P had inadvertently alleged an incorrect basis for recovery— especially since T was in a superior position to know that D was not its employee. However, T could respond that (1) a reasonable construction of the language in question would lead T to have assumed that liability could be premised only upon a finding that D was T's employee, and (2) there is no "manifest injustice" in holding P to a pretrial order into which she had voluntarily entered, especially when the stipulation in question probably induced T to refrain from contesting the admission of evidence that tended to show that D was driving the car with T's permission (since it would have been extraneous to T's potential liability). Under these circumstances, the stipulation, as interpreted by T, probably should be enforced.

P's motion to amend her complaint:

Assuming the stipulation was not deemed dispositive, P would argue (as mentioned above) that where an issue is actually "tried," the pleadings are deemed to conform to such evidence. FRCP 15(b). However, T could contend that the question of whether D drove the vehicle involved in the collision with T's permission was not "tried" since T had no reason to contest the introduction of this evidence because it was irrelevant to whether D was T's employee. Where evidence is objected to as being at variance with the pleadings, a court may nevertheless allow the pleadings to be amended at trial where "the merits of the action will be subserved thereby." FRCP 15(b). P alternatively could contend that justice is served by permitting the amendment since T knew (or should have known) from the commencement of the action that liability based on D driving with T's permission was a possible basis of recovery by P. However, T probably could successfully contend in rebuttal that an injustice would result by permitting such a post-trial amendment because, in light of the pretrial stipulation, it had no reason to rebut P's evidence bearing upon whether T permitted D to drive the vehicle that injured P.

Answer to Question 8

Does State White have personal jurisdiction over Albert ("A")?

A traditional basis for personal jurisdiction has been service of process upon the defendant when he was physically present in the forum. *Pennoyer v. Neff.* The Supreme Court reaffirmed that principle in *Burnham v. Superior Court,* where it held that the mere presence of a nonresident in the forum state is sufficient for the forum state to assert personal jurisdiction over him as long as service is made on the person while he is in the forum state. A's lack of other contacts with State White are irrelevant, so long as he was served in State White. Thus, State White may assert personal jurisdiction over A.

Does State White have personal jurisdiction over Par ("P")?

We'll assume that the State White legislature has enacted a long-arm statute that gives its courts all personal jurisdiction consistent with due process. Thus, there are no statutory interpretation issues.

To establish personal jurisdiction over P, Frances ("F") will have to satisfy the minimum contacts test by showing that P had purposeful contacts with State White and that F's claim arises out of those contacts. If F makes such a showing, then the burden will shift to P to demonstrate that the exercise of jurisdiction would nonetheless be unreasonable. As to purposeful avail-ment, F might rely on the stream of commerce (SOC) theory, arguing that P's clubs are distributed into the SOC, thereby subjecting P to jurisdiction in those states that may be included within that stream. Under this ap-proach, the reach of purposeful availment is extended from the state of manufacture to the state of retail sale. The difficulty in applying SOC here is that the club that caused the injury was purchased by a consumer in State Red. As a consequence, the SOC ended in State Red. Although Harold ("H") did bring the club into State White where the accident occurred, his actions are not attributable to P. Moreover, while F could argue that other clubs manufactured by P do wind up being sold at retail in State White, thus establishing purposeful availment of the State White market, those clubs were not the cause of her injuries. In short, F will not be able to show her claim arises out of any purposeful activity directed toward State White by P. The standards of minimum contacts not being satisfied, the court may not exercise jurisdiction over P.

Was P validly served?

First, it is unlikely that state law would permit service on A to constitute service on P. Although A is under contract to P, nothing in the facts indicates that he is authorized to accept service on behalf of P and that he could be reasonably presumed to have such authority. Cf. FRCP 4(h). Moreover, service of process, even if in conformity with the applicable state law, must comport with due process (i.e., give such notice as is reasonably calculated under the circumstances to apprise the defendant of the action). P might contend that service of process for it on A, a non-officer, is not constitutionally adequate. However, since P's president was also personally served, F should prevail on this issue.

Removal to the U.S. district court in State Red:

First, a case may be removed only to the federal district court embracing the geographic location of the state court. Hence, a case cannot be removed from a State White court to a federal court sitting in State Red. In theory, A and P could remove the case to a State White federal court and then seek to have it transferred to a State Red federal court pursuant to 28 U.S.C. §1404(a). The problem, however, is that there is no basis on which this case could be removed from state to federal court.

Removal is proper only if the case could have originally been filed in federal court. This means that the case would have to satisfy a federal court's subject matter jurisdiction. Since no federal question is presented by these facts, the only plausible basis for jurisdiction is diversity. Thus, F could initially contend that diversity does not exist since she and P are citizens of State Green. This assertion is premised on the argument that a corporation is a citizen of its state of incorporation and of the state in which it has its principal place of business. Since P's major manufacturing facility is in State Green, under a "place of activity" or "muscle" approach to determining "principal place of business," P would be a citizen of that state, thus destroying diversity.

The defendants would argue in rebuttal that a "nerve center" approach to determining P's principal place of business should be applied, and since the important decision making is done in State Red, P is a citizen of that jurisdiction only.

Typically, the nerve center test is applied only when the operations of the corporation are spread among several states. Here it appears that P's manufacturing is limited to State Green. Hence, a court likely would apply the "place of activity" test and conclude that P is a citizen of State Green. However, given that P distributes its products throughout the United States, it is possible that a court would apply the nerve center test and conclude that P's principal place of business is State Red.

Assuming that P is a citizen of State Red only, removal would be permitted so long as both defendants joined in the petition for removal and so long as neither defendant was a citizen of the forum state. The facts suggest that A and P joined in the petition for removal and neither of them is a citizen of State White. The next issue is whether the defendants' motion to transfer under §1404(a) should be granted.

Section 1404(a) allows a federal court to transfer a case in the interests of justice to another federal court where it could have been brought. Since both A and P are citizens of State Red, both would be subject to personal jurisdiction there. Moreover, under 28 U.S.C. §1391(a)(1), venue would have been proper in a State Red district court since both defendants are residents of that state. Thus, the case could have been filed in a State Red district court. The question, therefore, is whether the transfer from State White to State Red would be in the interests of justice. Given that the accident took place in State White and that much of the evidence would be in State White and given that State Red has no direct interest in this accident, it is quite unlikely that the State White federal court would grant the motion to transfer, especially considering the preference for plaintiff's choice of forum.

What use may Robert ("R"), P, and A make of the judgment?

(a) Assuming that F was successful, may R assert issue preclusion against P and A?

Under the issue preclusion aspect of *res judicata* doctrine, where an issue that was essential to the outcome of a case was actually litigated and decided in a prior lawsuit, and essential to the judgment in that case, relitigation of that issue by the defendant in a subsequent case between the same parties is precluded. Since F prevailed in the first lawsuit, it is fair to infer that the defectiveness of the golf club was litigated and decided in that proceeding. Moreover, in order for F to prevail, the resolution of that issue was essential. The question is whether R, a nonparty and nonprivy to the prior proceeding, can use the resolution of this issue to establish an element of his claims against A and P — so called offensive issue preclusion. The answer to this question depends on whether State White (assuming that the case remained in State White) has abandoned the doctrine of mutuality in the context of offensive uses of issue preclusion. (Note that under principles of intersystem preclusion, the State Green court would be compelled to follow the law that the State White court would apply to this issue.) That doctrine provides that only parties bound by a judgment can benefit from it. If State White has not abandoned this doctrine as to offensive uses of issue preclusion, then R, who is not bound by the State White proceeding, may not assert issue preclusion against A and P. Moreover, even if State White has abandoned mutuality in this context, the circumstances under which a person in R's position can use the doctrine are limited. If, for example, R could have joined in the prior litigation, a court is unlikely to allow him to assert issue preclusion in a subsequent proceeding because he has adopted an "inefficient" wait-and-see posture. In addition, if there is any unfairness to the defendants, issue preclusion will not be allowed. Thus, a determination of whether R may assert issue preclusion depends on the law of State White and on an examination of why R did not join in the earlier proceeding.

(b) Assuming that P and A were successful, could they assert collateral estoppel against R?

Robert was not a party to the previous proceeding, nor was he in privity with a party. Hence neither claim nor issue preclusion may be asserted against him in a subsequent proceeding.

Answer to Question 9

Did the U.S. district court in State X have personal jurisdiction over Devco ("D")?

In order for the U.S. district court to assert personal jurisdiction over D, both the standards of the state long-arm statute and the requirements of Fourteenth Amendment due process must be satisfied.

The state long-arm statute provides that jurisdiction may be asserted over a foreign corporation "only if" that corporation is "doing business" in the state. Hence, this statute provides the exclusive means provided by State X for asserting personal jurisdiction over a foreign corporation. The question, therefore, is whether D is "doing business" in State X within the meaning of this long-arm statute, as construed by the courts of State X. The facts state that D did "no business in State X." If this statement is dispositive, then Pete ("P") is out of luck. Indeed, D's only contacts with State X are the advertisement that was placed in a State Y newspaper and that also circulated in State X, and, arguably, the mailing of the stock certificate to Pete in State X. Unless the courts of State X would treat these contacts as "doing business," there would appear to be no statutory basis through which to assert jurisdiction over D in State X. The U.S. district court is, of course, bound by state law under these circumstances and cannot exercise personal jurisdiction over D in the absence of a state long-arm provision that would allow it to do so. This is true even if the standards of due process would be satisfied. Note, however, that some state courts construe their specific act statutes to extend jurisdiction to the full extent of due process. If State X is such a state, then the term "doing business" could be construed quite broadly to include the solicitation of business through a newspaper advertisement. If that is the case, then the statute might well be satisfied. Thus, whether the state long-arm statute is satisfied depends on how liberally the courts of State X have construed and applied that statute. Those constructions are binding on the U.S. district court.

Assuming that the state long-arm does allow for the assertion of personal jurisdiction over D, it must be determined whether the exercise of that jurisdiction would comport with the minimum contacts test embodied in the Fourteenth Amendment's Due Process Clause. To satisfy this test, P must show that D engaged in purposeful activities directed toward State X and that P's claim arises out of those contacts. If this standard is satisfied, the reasonableness of the exercise of personal jurisdiction will be presumed; however, D can then attempt to meet the heavy burden of rebutting that presumption by demonstrating that the exercise of jurisdiction would nonetheless be unreasonable.

Arguably, D has at least two purposeful contacts with State X: the newspaper advertisement circulated in State X and the delivery of the stock certificates to P in State X. As to the former, assuming D knew of the circulation in State X, this contact might well qualify as a purposeful contact, especially if the advertising had run over a lengthy period of time. In essence, D was soliciting business from potential clients in State X, a classic purposeful contact. On the other hand, the mailing of the stock certificate to P in State X, assuming that is what happened, might not qualify as a purposeful contact. If the certificate was mailed to P at his home address in State X, the contact might be seen as P's and not D's. As such, it represents a classic "unilateral" contact by the plaintiff that cannot be counted in the minimum contacts analysis. See *Hanson v. Denckla*. On the other hand, P could argue that the mailing was part of the overall solicitation of stock purchases within the state — i.e., D choose to promote its stock in the X market, and both the advertisement and the mailing were, in essence, part of the same purposeful transaction.

The next question is whether these purposeful contacts with State X — the newspaper advertisement and the mailing — are sufficiently related to Pete's claim to satisfy the standards of due process, i.e., does his claim arise out of D's purposeful contacts with State X? The resolution of that question depends on how strictly a court applies the "arises out of" principle. If that principle can be satisfied by a loose "but for" test — i.e., but for the advertisement P would not have purchased the stock, and but for that purchase he would not have been damaged — then the test would seem to be satisfied. If, as some courts do, the court requires that the D contacts with the forum be substantively relevant to P's claim — i.e., the contacts constitute an element of the claim — then the test would be satisfied only if the content of the advertisement were part of the fraud, which is certainly a possibility.

Assuming that the foregoing elements of the minimum contacts test have been satisfied, then D will have an opportunity to rebut the presumption that the exercise jurisdiction under these facts is reasonable. However, the burden here is a "heavy" one and is not likely to be met. D would have to demonstrate either that State X has no interest in this case — unlikely given that P is from State X — or that the burden on D of litigating in State X will be particularly onerous and prejudicial — the facts suggest no basis for such an argument.

In short, if the U.S. district court finds that both the state long-arm statute and the standards of due process are satisfied, it may exercise jurisdiction over D. As to the former, the resolution depends on how broadly the courts of State X have construed their long-arm statute. As to the latter, it depends on a combination of the sufficiency of the limited purposeful contacts and the relationship between those contacts and P's claim.

Did the U.S. district court in State X have subject matter jurisdiction over the action against Bull ("B")?

For a U.S. district court to be competent based upon diversity, (1) no plaintiff and no defendant may be a citizen of the same state; and (2) the amount in controversy must exceed $75,000, exclusive of interest and costs. It is assumed that the latter requirement is satisfied. The former criterion, however, would not be met if B is joined as a party-defendant. Individuals are considered citizens of the state in which they are domiciled (i.e., presently live and intend to remain). Although B works in State Y, for diversity purposes he is a citizen of State X. Thus, the U.S. district court would not have subject matter jurisdiction over the claim against B. Nor would the court have supplemental jurisdiction over this claim. Although any claim P would have against B would be part of the same constitutional case as P's claim against D, hence satisfying the standards of 28 U.S.C. §1367(a), since this is a diversity case, the limitations imposed by §1367(b) would apply. That section precludes the exercise of supplemental jurisdiction in diversity cases when doing so would violate the above principle of complete diversity and when the claim is one by a plaintiff, here P, against a party joined pursuant to FRCP 19, here B.

Assuming the U.S. district court had subject matter jurisdiction over P's claim against B, was it correct in ordering the latter to be joined as a party-defendant?

D's motion to bring B into the case would have been made pursuant to FRCP 19. Under FRCP 19(a), a person ought to be joined if (1) in his absence complete relief cannot be accorded among those already parties; and (2) disposition of the action in his absence may (a) impede or impair his ability to protect his interest in the subject matter of the action, or (b) leave any of the parties subject to a substantial risk of incurring multiple liability. It would not appear that B's joinder would satisfy any of these standards. Certainly, P can get complete relief without B's presence and there is nothing in the facts to suggest that D would be seeking any type of relief from B. Moreover, there is nothing in the facts to indicate that any interest of B would be impaired by the *P v. D* proceedings or that D would somehow be subjected to multiple liability. Hence, the standards of FRCP 19(a) having not been satisfied, joinder was improper. Moreover, as noted in the previous answer, the district court would not have subject matter jurisdiction over any claim by P against B; therefore, even if subsection (a) had been satisfied, under FRCP 19(b), B's joinder would not have been feasible. In that case, the district court could have proceeded without B since his absence would not prejudice him or the parties to the suit.

Did the district court err in striking P's demand for a jury trial?

Where a "common law" claim is brought in a federal district court, either party normally has a right to a jury trial, whether state law permits a jury trial or not. FRCP 38. A "common law" claim is one that courts of law recognized prior to the adoption of the Seventh Amendment in 1791. However, there appears to be a division of authority as to whether a case can be so exceedingly complex that the Fifth Amendment right to due process can be deemed to override the Seventh Amendment right to a jury trial. *In re Japanese Electronic Products Litigation* suggests that, in rare instances, a denial of a jury trial is appropriate. The Ninth Circuit, however, has refused to recognize a "complex case" exception to the Seventh Amendment. *In re U.S. Financial Securities Litigation.*

In any event, this case does not appear to constitute a situation where denying the normal right to a jury trial would be appropriate since laypersons should be able to determine if (1) the statements contained in the advertisement and promotional brochures were incorrect; and (2) D knew, or should have known, that those statements were (a) false, or (b) made without adequate knowledge as to their truth or falsity. Since P has asserted only common law fraud (rather than a federal securities violation) and such actions were recognized at "common law," the court erred in striking P's demand for a jury trial.

Answer to Question 10

Valvo ("V")'s objection to Peter ("P")'s failure to join Mity ("M") as a defendant:

The joinder of a party is necessary where (1) complete relief cannot be granted to those already parties in her absence; (2) disposition of the case in her absence will impede or impair an interest that she has in the matter; *or* (3) persons already parties to the action will, in her absence, be subject to substantial risk of multiple liability. If any of these factors is satisfied, the nonlitigant should be made a party if (a) she is subject to service of process; and (b) the court will not be deprived of subject matter jurisdiction if the party is joined.

In this instance, none of the elements is satisfied. P can obtain complete relief (i.e., a judgment for the full amount of his injuries) against V. M's interest in the subject matter of the action will not be impaired (i.e., any judgment against V will not have a collateral effect upon M since this doctrine cannot be used offensively against a party who is unrelated to the initial defendant).

V will not be exposed to double multiple liability since (1) it would retain the right to pursue an indemnity action against M if P were successful against it; and (2) in any event, a tortfeasor cannot complain about a plaintiff's decision to abstain from suing all possible joint tortfeasors. Thus, any objection by V that P must be joined would be incorrect.

May V bring M into the case as a defendant?

V could bring M into the case as a third-party defendant (assuming personal jurisdiction over the latter was satisfied) by means of a third-party complaint (sometimes called "impleader"). FRCP 14(a). This procedural device is appropriate where the third-party defendant (the impleaded party) may be liable to the third-party plaintiff (the impleading party) for all or part of the plaintiff's judgment against the latter. Subject matter jurisdiction would not be a problem (even though V and M are each citizens of State A) since impleader actions filed by defendants fall within the court's supplemental jurisdiction.

Joinder of parties (P and Q v. V and M):

Parties may be joined, as either plaintiffs or defendants, if (1) the claim asserted (or defended against) by them, jointly, severally or in the alternative, arises out of the same transaction or occurrence; and (2) there is a common question of law or fact. FRCP 20(a). These requisites appear to be satisfied in this instance since (1) both claims arise from the same occurrence (the explosion); and (2) there are common questions of fact (i.e., whether the valve "collar" was defectively or negligently made, whether the plaintiffs were advised of a possible malfunction). Thus, joinder of parties (subject to competency and personal jurisdiction questions discussed below) would be appropriate.

Joinder of causes of action (P and Q v. V and M):

A party asserting a claim to relief may ordinarily join all the causes of action she has against a particular defendant. FRCP 18(a). Since the plaintiffs probably would be asserting negligence, products liability, and breach of the implied warranty of merchantability against V and M, joinder of claims is appropriate.

Personal jurisdiction over the defendants:

Since this appears to be a diversity action, the U.S. district court would use (i.e., "borrow") the long-arm statute of State C, the forum in which it is located. It is assumed that the State C long-arm statute affords its courts all personal jurisdiction consistent with due process (and thereby avoids any possible statutory interpretation problems). It is also assumed that neither defendant was physically present within State C when service of process was effectuated. Service was not made upon an officer who was within the state, and neither corporation maintains a permanent office in State C from which business is solicited.

The assertion of personal jurisdiction over the defendants would still have to satisfy due process (i.e., the defendants must have such minimum contacts with the forum as not to offend traditional notions of fair play and substantial justice). In determining if this standard is satisfied, the courts ordinarily consider (1) the extent to which the defendant has purposefully availed itself of the benefits of the forum; (2) whether the claims by the plaintiff arise out of the defendant's forum contacts; and (3) assuming the first two elements have been satisfied, whether the defendant has rebutted the presumption of reasonableness.

The facts are not sufficient to determine whether the standards of due process have been satisfied. Certainly if V shipped the machinery into State C as part of a sale to P and Q, then the standards of due process would be satisfied. Such a direct sale would have been purposefully directed toward the forum state, and the plaintiffs' claims arising out of the explosion would also be deemed to arise out of the contacts. Moreover, under such circumstances, it would be highly unlikely that V could rebut the presumption of reasonableness. As to M, if M sold the collar to V as part of a regular course of business, under the stream of commerce test, the contacts of V with State C will be imputed to M. In essence, a court would conclude that M put the product into the stream of commerce with the reasonable expectation that it would be placed on a product and sold in another state. M would have purposeful contacts, therefore, with the state of sale, here, at least hypothetically, State C. On the other hand, if the arrival of the machinery in State C was completely fortuitous — e.g., P and Q purchased it from a third party in State X — then neither V nor M would be subject to personal jurisdiction in this State C proceeding. This is particularly true if the purchaser buys the product in one state and then brings it into another.

Subject matter jurisdiction over the parties:

For diversity subject matter jurisdiction to exist, (1) no defendant and no plaintiff may be citizens of the same state, and (2) the amount in controversy must exceed $75,000.

Since V and Q are citizens of State B (a corporation is a citizen of the states in which it is incorporated and has its principal place of business, and an individual is a citizen of his state of domicile at the time the action is commenced), a U.S. district court would *not* be competent to hear this matter.

Must P plead a lack of contributory negligence ("CN")?

U.S. district courts adhere to the FRCP whenever a valid federal rule is broad enough to cover the circumstances. *Hanna v. Plumer.* Under FRCP 8(c), CN must be set forth as an affirmative defense. Thus, P would not be required to plead that he was not contributorily negligent. Rather, the defense, if relevant, would have to be pled by the defendant.

Does P have the burden of persuasion on the issue of CN?

In a diversity case, where a matter is not dealt with directly in the FRCP and pertains to a substantive aspect of the case (the burden of proof on an issue would arguably constitute a substantive issue since it goes to establishing a claim or defense), state law will ordinarily be followed. Whether the federal judge will apply the law of State A (where the action has been commenced) or State C (where the cause of action allegedly arose) depends upon State A law. If State A applies its own law, it should be adhered to by the federal judge. However, if a State A court would (under its conflict of law rules) apply the law of State C, the federal judge should also apply the law of State C.

Answer to Question 11

Bigbucks ("BB") v. Palladium Corporation ("PC"):

(a) Subject matter jurisdiction: PC (or any party or the court itself) could successfully contend on appeal that diversity subject matter jurisdiction was lacking on either of two grounds: (1) PC and BB are citizens of New York, and (2) the amount in controversy is not "in excess" of $75,000. While BB could contend that PC waived these defects by filing an answer that failed to question the district court's subject matter jurisdiction, a lack of subject matter jurisdiction cannot be waived and can be raised at any time, FRCP 12(h)(3), including while on appeal. Thus, the court of appeals should dismiss the appeal and remand with instructions to the district court to dismiss the case for want of subject matter jurisdiction.

(b) Personal jurisdiction, service, and venue: Whatever objections PC may have to personal jurisdiction, service of process or venue were waived when PC filed an answer without raising these defects. Thus, although PC may have had a tenable personal jurisdiction argument, that argument is no longer available on appeal. As to service of process, even if the claim had not been waived, there is a plausible argument that the secretary to the president of a corporation falls within the meaning of FRCP 4(h)(1)'s requirement that service on a corporation be made by delivering a copy of the summons and complaint to an "officer, managing or general agent, or to any other agent authorized by appointment or by law to receive service of process." As to venue, again assuming no waiver, it is unlikely that venue was proper in Massachusetts since all the defendants do not reside there (28 U.S.C. §1391(a)(1)) and since no events giving rise to the claim occurred there (§1391(a)(2)). Additionally, the fallback provision of §1391(a)(3) is not available since there are other states in which substantial events giving rise to the controversy occurred, including Illinois (the discussions between Don and Merv), New York (where the telegram was sent and the contracted breached), and possibly California (where the Pallidium concert was to take place and where negotiations between Merv and PC may have taken place). Importantly, subsection (a)(2) is designed to establish proper venue in a range of locations; in other words, the underlying assumption of that subsection is that there may be more than one place where substantial events giving rise to the claim occur.

(c) Motion to transfer venue: Any party may make a motion to transfer an action in U.S. district court to a different U.S. district court, provided the case could have been commenced in the latter court. In other words, both venue and personal jurisdiction must have been available in the potential transferee forum at the time the original suit was filed. As to venue, venue

is proper in a diversity action in a judicial district in which (1) any defendant resides, if all defendants reside in the same state; (2) a substantial part of the events or omissions on which the claim is based occurred or a substantial part of the property is located; or (3) if there is no jurisdiction where the suit may otherwise be brought, any defendant is subject to personal jurisdiction at the time the action commenced. 28 U.S.C. §1391(a). California would provide a proper venue if substantial events giving rise to the plaintiff's claim occurred in a judicial district in that state. It is possible that the negotiations between Merv and PC took place partly in California, where the Palladium is located. If that's the case, then the district in which the Palladium is located would have been a proper venue. Venue would not be proper in California under subsection (a)(3) since there are other districts where venue may have been proper, namely, Illinois and New York under subsection (a)(2). See discussion in the preceding subsection of this answer. However, in addition to establishing venue, the party seeking a transfer must also establish that personal jurisdiction over all defendants would have been available in the transferee state at the time the action was commenced. It is not clear that Don would have been subject to personal jurisdiction in California at that time since the facts do not indicate any contacts he may have had with California other than his plans to perform there on a future date. If personal jurisdiction would have been lacking, transfer would be inappropriate. Assuming that California would be a proper transferee state — i.e., both venue and personal jurisdiction would have been satisfied — it remains within the discretion of the district court to transfer or not in the interests of justice. In this case, the district court may have abused its discretion since Massachusetts has no connections with this case while California at least has some. The ultimate conclusion on this issue, however, would depend on a balancing of the interests of the parties, the witnesses, and the judicial system. Additional facts would be required to make that judgment.

BB v. Don Pickles ("D"):

(a) *Personal jurisdiction:* BB could contend that she obtained personal jurisdiction over D since the latter was served within Massachusetts. *Pennoyer v. Neff.* However, there is dicta in *Shaffer v. Heitner* that all assertions of personal jurisdiction must meet the minimum contacts standard articulated in *International Shoe* (i.e., the defendant must have sufficient minimum contacts with the forum so as not to offend traditional notions of fair play and substantial justice). Nevertheless, the U.S. Supreme Court has held that service in the forum state establishes personal jurisdiction over the defendant no matter how brief the defendant's presence in the state. *Burnham v. Superior Court.*

(b) Venue and waiver: Even if D prevailed on the issue of personal jurisdiction discussed immediately above and could have successfully objected to venue (see discussion of venue under *BB v. PC*), these objections were waived by his failure to raise them in his initial response to BB's complaint. FRCP 12(h)(1).

D v. Merv ("M"):

(a) The Federal Rules: Since BB was not seeking monetary damages from D, D's action against M was presumably for the lost income that D would have earned from appearing at the Palladium. This is not a proper claim for impleader since D does not allege that M may or will be liable to him for any liability D has to BB, the plaintiff. Hence, FRCP 14 is not available. Moreover, since D has not filed a counterclaim against BB, FRCP 13(h) (joinder of additional party to a counterclaim) is also not available. In fact, there are no federal rules that would allow D to file this claim, although he plausibly could have filed a motion to dismiss for failure to join a necessary party under FRCP 19. But the facts do not indicate the filing of any such motion. The claim against M, therefore, should be dismissed.

(b) Subject matter jurisdiction: Assuming there was a federal rule that allowed D to file his claim against M, the court would have supplemental jurisdiction over the claims since they arise from the same transaction as the plaintiff's primary claim. 28 U.S.C. §1367(a). Moreover, although this is a diversity suit, nothing in §1367(b) would preclude this claim. The fact that D and M are citizens of the same state would be irrelevant.

(c) Service of process: Next, M could have argued that service of process should be quashed because he was "lured" into the jurisdiction (i.e., he entered Massachusetts in response to D's telephone call and D had a process server waiting at the airport). While D could argue that the thought of serving D at the airport occurred *after* the telephone conversation and there was nothing dishonest about his statements (i.e., D intended to seek another agent if BB's action against him was not dismissed), the court probably should have ruled in favor of M on this issue.

(d) Personal jurisdiction: M could argue that his temporary physical presence did not establish sufficient minimum contacts with the forum state for it to assert personal jurisdiction over him. D could counter that since M was served in Massachusetts, the district court in that state could constitutionally assert personal jurisdiction over M (see discussion of jurisdiction under *BB v. D*). However, in *Burnham v. Superior Court*, at least five members of the Court suggested that principles of fairness might limit the scope of territorial jurisdiction, and given the possibility that M was lured into the jurisdiction, that principle may apply here.

PC v. M

(a) Subject matter jurisdiction: Since PC is a citizen of New York and possibly California (if Massachusetts follows the "muscle approach" to determine the principal place of business of a corporation) and M is a resident of Illinois, diversity subject matter jurisdiction exists over this claim. However, since PC is asserting an indemnification-type claim against M (M is arguably more culpable than PC because the latter entity would have had no reason to believe that D was already under contract with another person), the third-party action would fall under the court's supplemental jurisdiction.

(b) Service of process: Service of process was properly effected. A copy of the summons and complaint was delivered to M's office and received and acknowledged by M's secretary, who is presumably an authorized agent to receive service of process. FRCP 4(e)(2). Since this apparently did not occur, service by another means was required (unless Massachusetts law permits service by mail; FRCP 4(e)(1)). If Massachusetts does permit service of process in this manner, however, M could raise a due process objection (i.e., permitting service by mail without any initial attempt at personal delivery of the summons and complaint is arguably *not* reasonably calculated to inform the defendant of the lawsuit). However, given that M received actual notice, this argument is not likely to succeed. Moreover, since the summons and complaint were sent by certified mail, requiring a signature by a responsible party, it seems that the service was reasonably calculated to apprise M of the pending litigation.

(c) Personal jurisdiction and venue: Once a court gains jurisdiction over a party in a litigation, it continues during the entire litigation. Assuming M's receipt of service in Massachusetts gave the district court there personal jurisdiction over M, it retains jurisdiction over M for the remainder of the litigation. Assuming venue was proper between the original parties, venue is proper for the third-party claim.

(d) Determination of BB's right to an injunction: Under FRCP 38(a) and the Seventh Amendment, there is an absolute right to a jury trial with respect to legal claims in federal courts. In *Beacon Theaters, Inc. v. Westover*, the Supreme Court held that in a federal court, legal claims *must* be tried

prior to equitable ones in order to preserve a party's right to a jury trial. Since BB's right to injunctive relief would be premised upon the "legal" question of whether D was in breach of his contract with BB, the judge incorrectly determined the equitable issue first. Under the Supremacy Clause of the U.S. Constitution, any state rule that is inconsistent with the Supreme Court's interpretation of the Seventh Amendment as applied to federal court cases will be superseded. Thus, the fact that Massachusetts law permits resolution of equitable issues first is irrelevant.

D's defense of minority:

Amendments to pleadings are permissible at trial if the court determines that (1) "the merits of the action will be subserved" thereby, and (2) the objecting party fails to satisfy the court that the admission of such evidence will prejudice her defense on the merits. FRCP 15(b). Although D could have contended that this standard is satisfied because BB could not have defended against this assertion in any event (i.e., either D is under the age of majority or he is not), the court could have decided that D's making this assertion near the end of the litigation was prejudicial to BB. If the prejudice could not be avoided, then the district court's decision was correct. However, if any prejudice to BB could have been mitigated (e.g., by imposing costs on D), the district should have allowed the amendment.

Answer to Question 12

Ped ("P")'s motion to remand:

Removal to a U.S. district court when no federal question is involved is proper where (1) no defendant is a citizen of the state(s) in which the action has been commenced, and (2) "diversity" subject matter jurisdiction requirements are satisfied.

P could have contended that removal to the U.S. district court was improper on two grounds: (1) Health ("H") is a citizen of State A (a corporation is a citizen of the states in which it is incorporated and has its principal place of business) since that is where H's business is conducted (and therefore one of the defendants is a citizen of the state in which the action was commenced); and (2) "diversity" is lacking because P and H are both citizens of State A (diversity requires that no plaintiff and no defendant be citizens of the same state). Thus, federal court subject matter jurisdiction does not exist. If, however, the board of directors of H ordinarily met in State H *and* State A follows a "nerve center" approach in determining a corporation's principal place of business (i.e., a corporation's principal place of business is deemed to be located where the central decision making takes place), H would be a citizen of State H only, and removal would have been proper.

However, since (1) the day-to-day corporate decisions are presumably made at the hospital in State A, and (2) State A is where H's entire business operations are conducted, State A would probably be deemed to be H's place of business for citizenship purposes. Thus, remand back to the state court was proper.

H's demurrer:

In some states, defendants can be joined only if their liability to the plaintiff arises out of the same "transaction or occurrence." Thus, H would contend that joinder of D and H was not proper since two distinct occurrences were involved: (1) the traffic accident involving P and D, and (2) the treatment that P subsequently received at H's hospital.

In determining if claims arise from the same "transaction or occurrences," state courts typically apply one of two standards: (1) whether the events that serve as the basis for each claim are "logically related," *or* (2) whether "common evidence" would be introduced in trials regarding each claim. Either test appears to be met in this instance.

The claims are "logically related" in that H's liability should be diminished to the extent it can be shown P's injuries in the traffic accident are distinguishable from those that he allegedly sustained at the hospital. Also, an initial tortfeasor is ordinarily liable for additional injuries caused to the plaintiff by medical personnel acting in a negligent manner, unless the latter's conduct can be characterized as "reckless" (in which case, the initial tortfeasor is *not* responsible for the subsequent enhancement of the plaintiff's injuries). Since a determination of each defendant's conduct is pertinent to deciding the extent of liability properly allocated between them, the claims are probably "logically related." The "common evidence" test would also be satisfied for the reasons described above (i.e., evidence as to P's initial injuries and the conduct of H's medical personnel would be pertinent in an action against either D or H for purposes of determining each party's precise liability to P).

Finally, it should be mentioned that a few jurisdictions follow the FRCP. Under the applicable rule, claims against multiple defendants can be joined as long as (1) they arose out of the same transaction or occurrence, and (2) there is at least one common issue of law or fact. FRCP 20(a). Since this provision has been liberally construed, it probably would be concluded that (1) P's claims against both D and H "arose" from the same occurrence (i.e., the traffic accident), and (2) there are common questions of fact (i.e., the extent to which each defendant's conduct caused injury to P and whether H's personnel performed their duties in a reckless or merely negligent manner).

Thus, joinder of claims was proper, and H's demurrer was properly denied.

P's request for admissions:

In many states, requests for an admission of a legal conclusion are *not* permissible. However, requests for admissions relating to facts or the application of law to facts (e.g., leaving a rake on a sidewalk is negligent) are ordinarily proper. In states that follow the FRCP, a party may request admissions pertaining to (1) statements or opinions of fact, or (2) the application of law to facts. FRCP 36(a). P's request is probably improper because it basically asks H and D to admit all of the elements of P's cause of action (which apparently is negligence). As such, it is requesting admission of a purely legal conclusion. Thus, the court properly sustained the objections to P's request for admissions.

P's motion for a new trial:

Misconduct by jurors is an established ground for granting a mistrial. Quotient verdicts (i.e., where the verdict is determined by dividing a particular sum by the number of jurors) are usually viewed as improper since the figure does not represent the collective decision of the jury as to the actual damages sustained by a plaintiff. The verdict is arguably subject to this defect because the amount of P's damages was determined by adding the differing opinions as to liability and dividing by the total number of jurors.

In rebuttal, however, P could have made two arguments. First, some jurisdictions (including the federal courts) do not permit evidence of jury deliberations (except to show the possible influence of external factors upon the jurors). If this were such a jurisdiction, the affidavits could not be considered in the determination of whether a new trial should be granted. Second, the use of a quotient verdict as a **starting point** for discussing the amount of a judgment that should be rendered is not improper. Since the jury agreed on the $43,652.89 amount after that figure was derived from the quotient method, P probably could successfully argue that the verdict was proper (despite the occurrences described in the affidavits).

Assuming evidence of jury deliberations is admissible, D might also have contended that the total lack of discussion on the substantive issues was improper because **immediately** after entering the jury room, a vote of liability was taken and returned against the defendants. However, P could have argued that since the jury members presumably understood the legal issues under consideration, their verdict of liability evidenced a determination by each juror that P had successfully satisfied the burden of proof on the *prima facie* elements of his action.

In summary, the court's refusal to order a new trial (on any aspect of the case) was probably correct.

Answer to Question 13

Was Dod ("D") an indispensable party?

A person should be joined if, in her absence, (1) complete relief cannot be accorded to the existing parties, (2) disposition of the case will impair her ability to protect an interest that she has in the action, or (3) disposition of the action without her could result in an existing party's being exposed to multiple liability.

Cozy Nook ("CN") could contend that D is person who should be joined because (1) he has an interest in the action (the apartment D now occupies could be jeopardized) since Abel ("A") seeks to lease the dwelling now rented by D; and (2) CN would be exposed to multiple liability since a verdict in favor of A would oblige CN to dispossess D, thereby exposing CN to an action by the latter for breach of the lease agreement.

However, A could argue in rebuttal that D's interest would not necessarily be affected by A's action because (1) A has alternatively sought a similar apartment in the building; and (2) even if no similar apartment were available, A probably could be adequately compensated by monetary damages (the rental differential between the initial apartment and the one in which A is now living, as well as any moving expenses attendant upon the relocation).

Additionally, CN is not exposed to the risk of multiple liability for the same obligation since it knew (or should have known) that its conduct toward A could result in liability by a subsequent tenant if A subsequently asserted his legal rights. Therefore, it appears that D is not a person who should be joined in the proceedings. Even if D were a person who should be joined, that joinder would not likely be possible since D does not appear to have any contacts with State White. Given that D's joinder is not feasible and assuming that D ought to be joined, D could not be characterized as an indispensable party since the court could avoid any potential prejudice to CN or D by shaping the relief. Thus, should P prevail, CN could be ordered to give P an alternate apartment. Accordingly, the court should overrule CN's motion to dismiss on this basis.

Did the court lack personal jurisdiction over CN?

A traditional basis of obtaining personal jurisdiction over an out-of-state defendant is service of process within the forum. Thus, A would contend that since CN's president was personally served within State White, personal jurisdiction over that entity was obtained.

CN, however, could make two arguments in rebuttal. First, there is language in *Shaffer v. Heitner* that indicates all assertions of personal jurisdiction over an out-of-state defendant must be tested by the "minimum contacts" standard set forth in *International Shoe*. The defendant must have such minimum contacts with the forum as to not offend traditional notions of fair play and substantial justice. This approach, however, was rejected by the Supreme Court in *Burnham v. Superior Court*. There the Court reaffirmed the constitutionality of the territoriality principle, holding that service within the forum was sufficient to establish personal jurisdiction. This principle likely would be controlling here. On the other hand, if service on the CN president was not deemed sufficient (see next paragraph), CN could contend that attachment of a single account within a jurisdiction that is unrelated to the plaintiff's action does not constitute an adequate basis for making it stand trial within State White. Although A could argue that by maintaining the account, CN is availing itself of the protection of State White's banking laws, CN is likely to prevail on this question given the ruling in *Shaffer*, cited above, that exercises of *quasi in rem* jurisdiction over personal property must comport with the minimum contacts test. At a minimum, Abel would have to establish some relationship between his claim and the attached property. The facts here indicate no such connection.

Was service of process on CN's president proper?

CN alternatively could contend that, even if physical presence within the jurisdiction is still a valid means of obtaining personal jurisdiction over an out-of-state defendant, the service of process upon CN's president should be quashed. CN's argument would be that since its president was responding to a legal proceeding (the attachment hearing) when he was served with process, the court should exercise its discretion to grant immunity from service of process in this instance.

A, however, could argue that this theory has ordinarily been applied where the defendant had voluntarily chosen to assist in a forum-related proceeding (i.e., been a witness to a legislative hearing or at *another's* trial). It has *not* traditionally been extended to situations where the defendant was in the jurisdiction to protect his personal interests (i.e., to release CN's bank account from A's attachment). Nevertheless, an enlightened court probably would rule in favor of CN. To hold otherwise would almost always result in a defendant's being required to stand trial in any state in which he had an asset. This outcome would frustrate the Supreme Court's effort in *Shaffer v. Heitner* to make the assertion of *quasi in rem* jurisdiction roughly equivalent to *in personam* jurisdiction.

Is State White an inconvenient forum?

In its discretion, a court may decline to exercise jurisdiction. Factors considered in making this determination are access to proof, ability to secure attendance of key witnesses, the forum's relationship to the matter, and the potential necessity of viewing the premises.

CN could contend that since (1) the action arose in State Red, (2) D is domiciled in State Red, and (3) CN is a State Red corporation, dismissal is proper. A could then reinstitute the action in State Red.

However, A could argue in rebuttal that (1) the presentation of evidence would not be significantly impaired by conducting the trial in State White (i.e., the matter will primarily involve the oral testimony of A and CN's representatives; the mere fact that D subsequently rented the apartment desired by A does not make D's testimony essential), and (2) State White has an interest in affording its citizens a convenient forum. Thus, dismissal is unlikely.

Is CN entitled to a jury trial?

In *Dice v. Akron, Canton & Youngstown Railroad Co.*, the Supreme Court held that a state procedural rule (which did not permit a jury trial with respect to the particular issue under scrutiny) is overridden where it conflicts with a federal statute that allowed a jury trial on the claim in question. The court reasoned that where a procedural aspect is embodied in a U.S. statute that creates a federal cause of action and is important to the successful assertion of that claim, it must be observed by a state court. The only difference between the *Dice* case and the present situation is that in the latter the right to a jury trial has been judicially (as opposed to legislatively) created. However, since an interpretation of federal law by the U.S. Supreme Court is binding upon a state court, CN's demand for a jury trial should be granted (regardless of any contrary local procedure).

Answer to Question 14

Was dismissal because of lack of subject matter jurisdiction correct?

Federal district courts are competent to hear diversity actions where no plaintiff and no defendant are citizens of the same state and the amount in controversy exceeds $75,000, exclusive of interest and costs. Since there is no question that Don ("D") and Tinselware ("T") are citizens of different states, whether the court's dismissal was proper will turn on whether D's damages were in excess of $75,000.

T could contend that since D expended exactly $75,000 to purchase the widgets, the "in excess of" $75,000 requirement was not satisfied. However, since D intended to resell the widgets, he is entitled to recover consequential damages, including lost profits; his damages therefore meet the monetary requirement for diversity. Thus, assuming there was no "legal certainty" that D's claim would not exceed $75,000, dismissal for failure to satisfy the amount in controversy would not have been correct.

Did the court lack personal jurisdiction over T?

U.S. district courts "borrow" the long-arm statute of the state in which they are located. Since the facts do not describe the California long-arm statute, it is assumed that the courts of that state have been legislatively authorized to assert all personal jurisdiction is consistent with due process.

Nevertheless, personal jurisdiction could not be exercised over T unless due process is also satisfied (i.e., T had such minimum contacts with California as not to offend traditional notions of fair play and substantial justice). To satisfy this test, D must demonstrate that T had purposeful contacts with California and that D's cause of action arose out of those contacts. T could contend that since (1) it does no business in California, (2) the contract was made in Arizona, and (3) the items in question were delivered to D in Arizona, it would not be constitutionally permissible to require it to defend the action in California. In essence, T would argue that it has no purposeful contacts with California.

In response, D will argue that Maureen ("M"), an employee of T, initiated this business transaction by placing a call on behalf of T to D in the state of California. Moreover, M's purpose was to promote resale of T's products in California and, as such, represents an effort by T to purposefully avail itself of the California market. A single contact with the forum state can be sufficient to establish personal jurisdiction over an out-of-state defendant so long as the claim arises out of that contact such that it is reasonably foreseeable for the defendant to expect to be haled into a court of the forum state. Here there is certainly a "but for" relationship between Maureen's phone call and the breach of contract action filed by D. However, given the paucity of contacts with the forum, a court might require a tighter substantive connection between the contacts and the claim. Hence, unless M made certain representations concerning the widgets that form a part of the breach of contract claim, a court might find the necessary relationship between the contacts and the claim inadequate for due process purposes.

In short, D has an argument that due process would be satisfied under these facts, but it is not a strong argument. Hence, in the absence of some additional facts showing a tighter connection between the contacts and the actual breach, the court's ruling was probably correct.

Was the court correct in dismissing the action because of lack of proper service?

Under the FRCP, service may be made upon a corporation by delivering a copy of the summons and complaint to an officer, a managing or general agent, or to any other agent authorized by appointment or law to receive service of process. The burden is on the plaintiff to establish a proper inference of agency. M, as an employee of T, might well be authorized by T to accept service of process, and courts tend to be quite liberal in applying this principle. The fact that she is an employee with the authority to promote out-of-state business might support an inference of agency for service of process purposes. However, the facts here are insufficient to arrive at a definitive conclusion.

However, under FRCP 4(h)(1), a summons and complaint may be served in accordance with the law of the state in which the U.S. district court is located.

Since California has a statute that permits service of process upon a corporation by mailing, the issue is whether the application of this statute is constitutionally valid. Due process requires that a defendant be given such notice as is reasonably calculated under the circumstances to apprise him of the lawsuit.

While D might argue that service by mailing to the president of a corporation is proper, this assertion probably would fail. This is the correct result because pieces of mail sent to a corporation are rarely received directly by the individual addressee. Thus, there would be a significant possibility that the document could be received by an employee who is unhappy with management or might not understand the importance of legal papers. As a consequence, the summons and complaint could intentionally or inadvertently be discarded (without ever reaching the hands of the proper person). Thus, dismissal for improper service was probably correct.

Could the court have transferred the action to the U.S. district court in Nevada?

Under 28 U.S.C. §§1404(a) and 1406(a), a U.S. district court may transfer a case to any federal district court where the case could have filed originally. This requires that both personal jurisdiction and venue would have been satisfied in the transferee district at the time the action was commenced. As to personal jurisdiction, there are no facts indicating that T has any contacts with Nevada. Hence, under the given facts, there is no reason to believe that D could have commenced this action in Nevada against T. The fact that T might waive any objection to the exercise of personal jurisdiction is irrelevant. Venue is similarly problematical. Where subject matter jurisdiction is based on diversity, venue is proper in a judicial district in which (1) any defendant resides, if all defendants reside in the same State; (2) a substantial part of the events or omissions on which the claim is based occurred or a substantial part of the property is located; or (3) if there is no jurisdiction where the suit may otherwise be brought, any defendant is subject to personal jurisdiction at the time action commenced. 28 U.S.C. §1391(a). Since Nevada meets none of these criteria, the court could *not* have transferred the action to the U.S. district court in that state.

Was the dismissal of D's action against M correct?

D's action against M is not an amendment to an existing lawsuit (the initial case having already been dismissed). Hence, there is no basis on which to discuss relation back under FRCP 15(c). Moreover, in a diversity case, the federal court must apply the substantive law that a state court of the forum state would apply. Given that under the applicable law the state statute of limitations has run, a federal court would be required to enforce the statute of limitations and dismiss the case. To do otherwise would plainly violate the *Erie* doctrine and the refined outcome determinative test as defined by the Supreme Court in *Hanna v. Plumer*. Thus, dismissal of D's complaint against M was proper if the applicable statute of limitations had expired.

Answer to Question 15

Is the U.S. district court competent?

For diversity purposes, a corporation is deemed to be a citizen of the states in which it is incorporated or has its principal place of business. Although Defendant ("D") is incorporated in Massachusetts, the facts are unclear as to its principal place of business. If the district court in California adheres to a "muscle approach" in determining this question, D could contend that there is a lack of diversity since its main booking terminal (which presumably is the place at which orders for Defendant's services are accepted and therefore at which Defendant's revenues produced) is in Arizona — the same state of which Pete ("P") is a citizen. (The domicile of the class representative of a class is controlling for diversity purposes.)

P, however, could make two arguments in rebuttal. First, if the California district court adheres to a "nerve center" approach, D's principal place of business would be where its corporate decision making takes place. Second, the booking terminal should be viewed merely as a place where tickets for D's flights are recorded. The "business" is actually done where orders are given to a travel agency or where D's ticket personnel are stationed. Although more information is needed, it will be assumed that most reservations for D's flights are initiated outside of Arizona. Given this scenario that D's business activities are spread out among several states, it is most likely that the district court will apply the nerve center test. Thus, Arizona is probably not D's principal place of business, and the diversity requirement is satisfied.

Additionally, in a class action based on diversity, the claim of **each member** of the class must exceed $75,000. Thus, any passenger who did not suffer injuries and losses in excess of $75,000 would have to be dropped from the class (the facts indicate that only "minor" injuries were suffered by the persons on the plane). However, since mental distress could have been suffered (in addition to physical injuries), an allegation that the jurisdictional amount is satisfied for each member of the class probably would be accepted by the court (i.e., it could **not** be determined to a "legal certainty" that a verdict exceeding $75,000 would not be rendered for each member of the class).

Is a class action maintainable?

For a class action to be maintainable, four requisites must be met: (1) the class is so numerous that joinder of all members is impracticable, (2) there are questions of law or fact common to the class, (3) the claims of the representative are typical of the class she seeks to represent, and (4) the representative is capable of fairly and adequately protecting the interests of the class. Assuming these conditions are satisfied, P is apparently asserting an FRCP 23(b)(3) class action (i.e., common questions of law or fact predominate and a class action is superior to any other method of adjudication).

D could contend that (1) the class is not sufficiently numerous (only 40 persons, even assuming that each member of the class has a claim in excess of $75,000); and (2) since each passenger's injuries are different, common questions of fact do not predominate.

While 40 is not a large number, joinder of claims is probably impracticable since the plaintiffs are from various states, and therefore many members of the class could assert venue objections. Additionally, the objective of judicial economy is realized by combining 40 potential lawsuits into one action. Finally, any plaintiffs who did not desire to be a part of the class would have a right to opt out of the group. FRCP 23(c)(2). Thus, a "numerosity" objection by D should be overcome.

Finally, while each plaintiff's injuries are different in type and extent, common questions of law or fact probably still predominate since the initial question of D's liability to the group for the accident is common to the entire class. Thus, a class action is probably appropriate.

Is venue proper?

A diversity action may be brought in a judicial district in which (1) any defendant resides, if all defendants reside in the same State; (2) a substantial part of the events or omissions on which the claim is based occurred or a substantial part of the property is located; or (3) if there is no jurisdiction where the suit may otherwise be brought, any defendant is subject to personal jurisdiction at the time the action is commenced. 28 U.S.C. §1391(a). This suit clearly could have been brought in Massachusetts under either subsection (a)(1) or (a)(2). D resides there and the accident took place there. Therefore, subsection (a)(3) — the fallback provision — cannot be relied on to establish venue in the Central District of California. Nor will (a)(2) work since substantial events giving rise to the claim did not occur in the Central District of California. The only possibility is that D might be treated as a resident of California for purposes of subsection (a)(1). In this regard, §1391(c) provides that a corporation will be deemed a resident of any judicial district in which it would be subject to personal jurisdiction at the time the suit commenced. Hence, D will be treated as a resident of the

Central District of California if its contacts with that district are sufficient to satisfy the minimum contacts test. The facts state that a majority of D's flights originate and land on the West Coast. The contacts are purposeful, but there are two problems here. First, the contacts are not necessarily with the Central District of California, and second and more important, there is no showing that the claim asserted by P arises out of the California contacts. Thus, unless D's contacts with California are so systematic and continuous so as to satisfy the standards of general jurisdiction, venue will not be proper under the residency prong of §1391(a). This seems unlikely since the standards of general jurisdiction require a presence in the state that is the practical equivalent of citizenship. The facts here would not support such a claim. In short, it is unlikely that venue is proper in the Central District of California.

Should the action be transferred to Massachusetts?

On motion of any party, an action pending in a U.S. district court may be transferred to any other U.S. district court where the case could have originally been commenced, if the "convenience of the parties and witnesses" and "the interest of justice" so require. Since the accident occurred in Massachusetts (when the aircraft was taking off from Boston), the action could have been commenced in that state. While a plaintiff's choice of forum is not easily disturbed, it is likely that all nonparty witnesses reside in Massachusetts and medical records pertaining to the victims are located in that jurisdiction (presumably, the victims were treated at the airport or taken to hospitals in the Boston area). Thus, D's motion to transfer probably will be granted.

Can the Doeing Company ("DC") be impleaded by D?

A third-party claim (sometimes referred to as "impleader") is appropriate where the complainant has a indemnity-type claim against the third-party defendant (the party being impleaded). FRCP 14. DC could contend that impleader is improper because (1) the evidence of engine malfunction is "nonconclusive," (2) D and DC are citizens of the same state (and thus, subject matter jurisdiction is lacking), (3) personal jurisdiction is lacking, and (4) venue is improper.

D could respond that (1) it is necessary only that the third-party claimant "may" have an indemnity-type claim against the third-party defendant (there need not be a strong likelihood that liability will actually be established at trial); (2) impleader actions satisfying the standards of FRCP 14(a) fall squarely within the court's supplemental jurisdiction under 28 U.S.C. §1367; (3) since DC presumably knew that (a) its engines were ordinarily integrated in D's aircraft, and (b) D's airplanes often flew into and out of Massachusetts, DC should have reasonably foreseen being haled into court in that state, and thus, the "minimum contacts" necessary to satisfy due process are met (this of course assumes that the case has been transferred to Massachusetts); and (4) venue is established by the original parties to the case; hence if venue was proper as to the original parties, as it would be if transferred to Massachusetts, then the court will have supplemental venue over the impleader action against DC.

There is, however, one additional problem with D's impleader against DC. If D is alleging that the accident was not its fault but the fault of DC, then this is not a proper impleader. The only basis on which D may implead DC is on allegations that if D is liable to P, DC may or will be required to indemnify D, in whole or in part. Thus, the impleader is appropriate only if D is alleging that DC, as a joint tortfeasor, is or may be liable for contribution and indemnity (or, less plausibly under these facts, as an insurer).

Answer to Question 16

Paul ("P")'s motion for leave to file his first amended complaint:

(a) Would an amendment to P's complaint be permitted under the FRCP?
Under FRCP 15(a), a party may amend his pleading any time before
a responsive pleading is served. If a responsive pleading has been served,
a pleading may be amended with leave of court (which "shall be freely given
when justice so requires"). FRCP 15(a). The facts are unclear as to whether
Doe ("D") answered P's initial complaint prior to July 1. If no answer had
been served, then P would have had an absolute right to file his first
amended complaint.

Even if D had filed an answer, no prejudice (i.e., inability to locate an important witness) appears to result to D by permitting P to amend his complaint
for the purpose of attempting to recover for the fracture of his other leg.
Thus, P's first amended complaint would be proper under the FRCP.

(b) Is the amendment barred by the Rules Enabling Act (REA)? Under
FRCP 15(c), an amendment to a complaint relates back to the original filing
for purposes of tolling the statute of limitations, if doing so would be permitted by the law that provides the statute of limitations or if the claim
asserted in the amendment arose out of the same transaction as the originally
asserted claim. Thus, if State X would allow relation back under these circumstances, then FRCP 15(c) would do so as well. If State X law does not
allow relation back, however, there is a conflict between State X law and
FRCP 15(c) since under the federal rule, relation back would be allowed as
this amendment asserts a claim (or an aspect of a claim) that arises out of the
same transaction as the original claim. Given the conflict, we must determine
whether the standards of the REA would allow the federal court to ignore the
state law. The problem here is that application of the federal rule may run
afoul of the second sentence of the REA in that it may abridge, enlarge, or
modify a substantive right by allowing P to proceed with a state law claim
under circumstances where State X law would not. As a consequence,
application of the REA under these circumstances would be inappropriate.
While P could have contended that the statute of limitations is not applicable
to the initial amendment, since recovery for the fracture of his other leg does
not constitute a new cause of action, this argument also depends on state law.
If state law would treat the amendment as not presenting a new cause of
action, then under FRCP 15(c), the federal court must do so as well. Hence,
relation back will be allowed. Conversely, if state law would treat the amendment as presenting a new claim and, as a consequence of that, would not
permit relation back, then the federal court must do the same.

P's motion for leave to file his second amended complaint:

As noted above, leave to amend a pleading may be granted prior to trial whenever "justice so requires." Since the alleged rescission occurred on February 20, 1990, P's request for leave to file a second amended complaint (presumably made within 30 days of D's answer, which was filed on July 25, 1990) would still be within the one-year statute of limitations.

It should be noted that D's claim that P had executed a release of all claims held by the latter against D probably would constitute an affirmative defense. Since P is asserting that the purported release was invalid, it was probably unnecessary for him to amend his complaint a second time. This is because statements in a pleading to which no response is required (such as an affirmative defense) are taken to be denied. FRCP 8(c), (d).

D's application for an order for a medical examination and copies of medical reports:

(a) The medical examination: When the physical condition of a party is in controversy, the court may order the individual to submit to an examination by a physician for good cause shown. FRCP 35. The notice of examination should specify the scope of the examination and the person or persons by whom it is to be made.

Since P is seeking to recover for personal injuries suffered as a consequence of D's allegedly negligent driving, D probably would be entitled to conduct a physical examination of P. Without such an examination, it would be virtually impossible to contradict evidence introduced by D to prove the extent of the injuries he suffered. Thus, the court's order for the medical examination was proper.

(b) Copies of all medical and hospital records: A party may ordinarily discover any nonprivileged matter relevant to the pending action. FRCP 26(b)(1). The fact that the information sought to be obtained would be inadmissible at trial is **not** a basis for a successful objection, if such data appears to be reasonably calculated to lead to the discovery of admissible evidence.

P could contend, however, that (1) pursuant to FRCP 34(a), he could be required to produce the documents in question only for the purpose of permitting D to copy them (P would not be obliged to make the copies); (2) P's hospital records are within the physician-client privilege; and (3) while medical and hospital records since the date of the accident might be pertinent, P's medical history one year prior to the accident is not relevant.

With respect to P's second argument, D could contend that the physician-patient privilege is ordinarily not extended to situations where the party involved has placed his own physical condition in issue (which P has done in this instance by claiming damages for injuries sustained as a consequence of the accident).

P's third objection probably also could be overcome because P's pre-accident physical condition is pertinent for purposes of verifying that the injuries for which P is demanding damages were not extant at the time the accident occurred. However, there does not appear to be a satisfactory rebuttal to P's initial contention (i.e., that he is obliged to permit D only to copy the medical and hospital reports). However, even if the court did rule improperly in requiring P to furnish copies of his medical records to D, this determination probably would constitute "harmless error." The question of who should bear the expense and inconvenience of copying particular items is probably not so "inconsistent with substantial justice" as to constitute a basis for granting a new trial. FRCP 61.

D's motion for a separate trial without a jury with respect to the issues raised by the second amended complaint:

The Seventh Amendment assures litigants in a federal court the right to have all "legal" claims determined by a jury. FRCP 38(a). In *Beacon Theatres, Inc. v. Westover*, the U.S. Supreme Court held that where an issue of fact is common to both a legal and equitable claim, trial of the legal issues by a jury should precede determination of the equitable claims by the judge (except, possibly, where the party asserting an equitable claim would be irreparably harmed by the delay necessarily inherent in a full hearing on the legal issues).

D's action for rescission (while traditionally viewed as an "equitable" claim) embodies the "legal" issue of whether the release was fraudulently obtained. (In *Dairy Queen v. Wood*, the U.S. Supreme Court held that the nature of a claim is not determined by the label attached to it in the pleadings.) Thus, even if it were proper to try the rescission issue before the question of D's possible liability for the accident (i.e., if P's release was valid, it would be unnecessary to determine D's alleged liability and P's damages), P probably would still be entitled to have the jury determine the fraud issue. If the fraud allegation is resolved in favor of P, the court would then decide the strictly equitable question of whether it should exercise its discretionary power to negate the release.

Thus, D's motion should *not* have been granted.

Answer to Question 17

Zonco ("Z")'s motion to dismiss for failure to join Smith:

A person who is subject to service of process and whose joinder will not deprive the court of subject matter jurisdiction must ordinarily be joined as a party to the action if (1) in her absence complete relief cannot be accorded to the existing parties, (2) disposition of the case in her absence may impede her ability to protect an interest relating to the subject matter of the action, or (3) her absence may subject a party to a substantial risk of incurring multiple liability for a single obligation. FRCP 19(a).

First, complete relief can be afforded to Patricia ("P") since she could obtain a judgment against Z for the full amount of his injuries. Second, Smith ("S")'s interest in the action will not be impaired by his absence (in fact, his presence in the litigation could result in liability only to him). If, for example, a judgment is entered for P against Z, S will not be bound by that judgment since he was not a party to that proceeding and since, as an employee, he will not be treated as being in privity with his employer when a judgment is entered against the employer on a theory of respondeat superior.

Finally, Z is not exposed to multiple liability because (1) it probably can assert an indemnity action against S for any judgment obtained by P, and (2) the risk of a judgment being recovered entirely from one of the tortfeasors is always a possibility when two or more parties are jointly and **severally** liable for the plaintiff's injuries.

Thus, the court correctly denied Z's motion to dismiss for failure to join S.

P's notice to produce:

A party may obtain discovery of documents prepared for litigation or trial (1) for another party, or (2) by or for that party's representative (including her insurer) only upon a showing that substantial need for such materials exists and they are otherwise unobtainable without undue hardship. FRCP 26(b)(3).

Since the co-worker's statement was made to Z's insurer, Z could contend that it is within the work product privilege. However, P could argue that there is a "substantial need" for the co-worker's statement since it presumably was given relatively soon after the accident and would therefore be the most reliable version of the incident. While Z could depose the co-worker and arguably obtain the same information, since the co-worker probably would be a hostile witness (i.e., the co-worker is employed by Z and might therefore be reluctant to make any comments that could adversely affect her employer in the litigation), the co-worker's statements to Z's insurance adjuster (which were not made to an adversarial party) are arguably not otherwise discoverable. Nevertheless, the trial court was probably correct in sustaining Z's refusal to produce the statement without at least an initial attempt by P to take the co-worker's deposition.

P's summary judgment motion:

A summary judgment should be granted when there is no genuine issue as to any material fact and the moving party is entitled to prevail as a matter of law. FRCP 56(c).

At trial, the burden of proof on the question of liability would be P's. Therefore, on summary judgment, P had the burden of producing sufficient evidence on which a rational trier of fact could find for P as to each element of the claimed liability. Thus, P would be required to introduce evidence (1) that S was driving the truck within the course of his employment by Z; and (2) that the cause of the accident was attributable to Z, either vicariously or directly. The deposition of S satisfies the second element by providing evidence that the cause of the accident was the brakes on the truck driven by S and owned by Z. If, in addition, the deposition provided evidence that the accident occurred while S was driving on behalf of Z, P would have met her burden production on summary judgment (i.e., a rational finder of fact could have found for P). Under these circumstances, the burden would have shifted to Z to contest one or both of the elements of P's claim. On the other hand, if P did not produce evidence on the latter point, the burden would have shifted to Z only with respect to the question of causation (i.e., the failure of the brakes).

Assuming the burden of production shifted, to meet its burden of production (i.e., to demonstrate the existence of a genuine issue of material fact), Z would be required to provide evidence that refuted those facts on which P met her burden of production. As to the failure of the brakes, Z could meet its burden of production by providing proof that there was another cause for the accident (e.g., eyewitness testimony that P jumped in front of the truck). As to Z's vicarious liability, and assuming P provided evidence that the accident occurred while S was driving on Z's behalf, Z could meet its burden of production by providing proof that S was not driving on Z's behalf or under circumstances for which Z would be vicariously liable. Similarly, if the substantive law provided a defense premised on the recent inspection of the brakes, Z could introduce proof of that fact. It, however, would not be sufficient for Z to speculate or argue about these possibilities. The burden on Z is to produce evidence.

At the very least, P was entitled to a partial summary judgment on the question of causation since it does not appear that Z provided any evidence that would create a genuine issue of material fact on that point. As to liability, the information is not sufficient to establish whether P met her burden of production on that issue and, if so, whether Z responded through the introduction of evidence.

Z's motion for a judgment notwithstanding the verdict ("JNOV") (now called "judgment as a matter of law"):

A JNOV (which results in the entry of judgment for the party who lost the trial) is proper where there is no legally sufficient basis for the determination reached by the jury. Z could have contended that while there was uncontradicted testimony that S was employed by Z and that P had suffered personal injury as a consequence of Smith's conduct, there apparently was no proof that S was acting within the course and scope of his employment (or at least with Z's knowledge). Thus, even if S was responsible for the accident, P failed to introduce any proof that Z was vicariously liable for S's conduct. However, if the accident occurred during regular business hours, it is possible that the jury could have inferred that S was employed by Z and was acting within the scope of his employment at the time of the accident. Thus, the court properly denied Z's motion for a JNOV.

P's motion for a new trial:

A federal court may grant a new trial if the verdict (1) is against the clear weight of the evidence;, or (2) will result in a miscarriage of justice, even though there may be substantial evidence that would prevent a judgment as a matter of law from being granted. The trial judge's determination that $85,000 does not adequately represent the pain and suffering probably would not be reversible. This is because the judge had the opportunity to personally observe the witness's testimony and evidence. However, granting a new trial unless the defendant agreed to raise the damage award was improper since *additur* (a judicial order for a new trial unless the defendant consents to higher damages) has been found to be a violation of the Seventh Amendment for federal trial purposes. *Dimick v. Schiedt.* Thus, the trial court probably could grant a new trial solely on the issue of damages, but could not condition it upon Z's agreement to pay P an enhanced verdict.

Answer to Question 18

Dumbo ("D")'s motion to dismiss:

(a) Personal jurisdiction: To establish personal jurisdiction over D, Paul ("P") would have to satisfy the elements of the minimum contacts test. Although the presence of D's warehouse in Ohio is not irrelevant, standing alone, its presence in the state is not sufficient to establish personal jurisdiction. Rather, P must show that D has engaged in purposeful activity directed toward the state of Ohio and that his claim arises out of that activity. If P meets this burden, D will have the opportunity to rebut the strong presumption that the exercise of jurisdiction over D would be reasonable, i.e., that it would comport with due process.

D does have purposeful contacts with Ohio. The presence of the warehouse is one such contact. In addition, D's sales of Enemy Attack, even sales outside of Ohio, may constitute a purposeful contact with Ohio under the effects test. In essence, by selling this product in violation of Paul's common law copyright, D is engaging in an intentional act with foreseeable effects in Ohio, namely, the damages suffered by Paul. If, as the facts suggest, D is aware that Paul was from Ohio (they had entered into a contract), then the locus of the effect or the "brunt of harm" in Ohio was also foreseeable to D.

The next question is whether P's claim arises out of those purposeful contacts. As to the sales through the warehouse, unless the sales are of Enemy Attack, then it is unlikely that the relationship between this contact and P's claim are sufficient for purposes of due process. On the other hand, if the "effects" felt in Ohio are sufficient to satisfy the first element of the minimum contacts test, then almost by definition, P's claim arises out of those contacts.

If both purposeful availment and "arising out of" are satisfied, D will have a difficult time rebutting the presumption of reasonableness, especially given the presence of D's warehouse in the state.

(b) Service of process: Pursuant to FRCP 4(h)(1), service of process may be accomplished in accordance with the law of the state in which the U.S. district court is located. Thus, service of process was, in effect, accomplished in compliance with the FRCP. Also, since process was personally served upon each member of D's board of directors, it probably would be deemed constitutional (i.e., reasonably calculated to inform the defendant of the lawsuit against it). Thus, the court correctly denied D's motion to dismiss upon this ground.

(c) Failure to state a claim upon which relief could be granted: A motion to dismiss under FRCP 12(b)(6) challenges the legal sufficiency of the claim asserted by the plaintiff. In other words, in the context of this case, D would argue that the common law copyright claim asserted by P does not provide a basis for relief when the purported copyright involves the creation of a video game. This presents a question of law for the district court, the resolution of which depends on whether the asserted claim by P is tenable as a matter of substantive federal law. The fact that D attached a Points and Authorities to the motion is a red herring. While the attachment of factual matter to a motion under FRCP 12(b)(6) can convert the motion into a motion for summary judgment, the filing of a Points and Authorities or a brief would have no such effect and, indeed, would be expected.

Was the entry of default valid?

A party who has filed a counterclaim may move for a default judgment on that counterclaim after the expiration of 20 days from service of the counterclaim. Under FRCP 5, service of the answer and counterclaim on P's attorney would trigger the running of the 20 days. Since 2001 was not a leap year, P would be required to file his answer to the counterclaim no later than March 15. As a consequence, the entry of the default on March 14 was one day early.

D could argue in rebuttal that even if the entry of default was one day early, this fact is inconsequential since (1) P did not file an answer by March 15 (the 20th day), and (2) the default judgment was not entered until March 16. However, given the usual judicial reluctance to grant default judgments, it is likely that P would prevail on this question.

Was the entry of a default judgment valid?

A default judgment may be entered by the clerk only if the damages sought are for a sum certain and only if the defaulting party has made no appearance. Here neither requirement is satisfied since the $10,000 in damages relating to the materials delivered to P is not a sum certain and, most importantly, since P has made an appearance in the case as the plaintiff. As a consequence, a default judgment in this case could be entered only by the court. FRCP 55(b)(1) & (2).

D's motion for judgment on the pleadings:

D's assertion that P admitted the allegations of its affirmative defense by not responding to them is incorrect. Under the FRCP, averments in an affirmative defense are deemed to be denied if no responsive pleading is made. FRCP 8(d). D's assertion that *res judicata* principles preclude a successful action by P probably would be successful. In a majority of jurisdictions, P would be precluded from relitigating the breach of contract action inherent in D's judgment. However, if, as discussed above, the purported default judgment is probably invalid, D's motion for judgment on the pleadings should not be granted.

Should P's motion to set aside the default judgment be granted?

The court may set aside the entry of default for good cause shown. Since the default was entered prematurely, P could easily satisfy this standard. Moreover, pursuant to FRCP 60(b), a default judgment may be set aside where it is the result of a mistake, inadvertence, or excusable neglect. Here, at the very least, the clerk mistakenly entered a default judgment under circumstances in which it was impermissible to do so, i.e., against a person who had made an appearance in the case.

Additionally, P's attorney could assert that the summer clerk's accidental misplacement of D's responsive pleading comes within this standard. D probably would prevail on this issue. P's attorney should have entered the date to respond on her calendar prior to giving the document to the summer clerk. However, since (as discussed above) both the entry of default and the entry of the default judgment are invalid, no valid judgment against P exists.

Answer to Question 19

The FRCP 12(b) motion to dismiss the case:

Since U.S. district courts "borrow" the long-arm statute of the state in which they are located, it is assumed that the State B legislature has enacted a law that gives its courts all personal jurisdiction consistent with due process.

Salco ("S")'s FRCP 12(b) motion probably asserted that it does not have the minimum contacts with State B necessary to satisfy due process (i.e., S does not have sufficient minimum contacts with the forum as to avoid offending traditional notions of fair play and substantial justice). S would contend that it has not availed itself of the benefits of the forum because (1) it employs no agents or salespersons within State B, (2) its advertising is purchased in magazines published outside State B, and (3) the amount of business done with citizens of State B ($75,000) is relatively small.

Poe ("P") could argue in rebuttal, however, that S should have reasonably foreseen being haled into the forum because it was aware (via its employees who received the orders and sent the items) that numerous persons from State B were purchasing its clocks. If the facts are as P alleges — i.e., that S's employees accepted orders from State B residents and sent the products to those purchasers in State B — then, given that the claims arise out of those transactions, there would be a strong presumption that the assertion of jurisdiction was reasonable. On the other hand, the facts do not indicate where the purchases were made. If the purchases were made by citizens of State B while they were in State A, for example, the key element of purposeful contacts by S with State B would be lacking.

Hence, whether S's motion to dismiss for want of personal jurisdiction should have been granted depends on a consideration of additional facts.

S could have also asserted that the notice that it received was constitutionally defective (i.e., not reasonably calculated under the circumstances to give it notice of the action against it). (The fact that service of process was made in accordance with State B law presents no problem since the service took place while the case was still pending in a State B court.) S probably contended that service by mail (even a registered mailing) in the first instance is impermissible where the summons and complaint could probably have been personally served upon the defendant (i.e., presumably, the names and addresses of S's officers or directors could have easily been obtained from the State A corporate records). Registered mailing is always fraught with the possibility that someone could sign for the item and yet (not appreciating the legal significance of the document contained inside) fail to read it or deliver it to the appropriate person.

However, P could argue that the president of a corporation is likely to appreciate the potential importance of registered mail. Moreover, if the president of S actually received the notice, as it appears from the question, any potential defect in the method will be ignored since actual notice satisfies due process. Since courts generally have accepted registered mail as consistent with due process and since it seems that the president of S received actual notice, the motion to dismiss on this grounds was properly denied.

The motion to remand the case back to the state court:

An action cannot be removed to a U.S. district court unless the case could have been filed in a federal court originally. S's motion to remand was probably based upon the assertion that the case could not have been filed in a federal court because subject matter jurisdiction was lacking. S is correct. Since the claims do not arise under federal law, the only potential basis for subject matter jurisdiction would be diversity. While the standards of diversity are satisfied — the named class representative, P, and the sole defendant are from different states — the amount in controversy requirement is not. In *Zahn v. International Paper Co.*, the U.S. Supreme Court held that the claims of the class may *not* be aggregated for the purpose of satisfying the amount in controversy requirement. Hence, both P and each member of the class must assert an individual claim that exceeds the $75,000 minimum. Yet, as to actual damages, P and each class member have suffered only $250 in damages.

P could contend in rebuttal that if the $25 million in punitive damages were distributed amongst each of the members of the plaintiff class, the claims of each person would exceed $75,000. P would also point out that the "amount in controversy" requisite should be considered satisfied, unless the court determines "to a legal certainty" that the damages sought by the plaintiff could not be recovered. It is, however, legally certain that neither P nor any individual class member will be entitled to sufficient punitive damages to satisfy the amount in controversy. Under the Due Process Clause, any award of punitive damages must bear a reasonable relationship with the actual damages, usually something below a 4-1 ratio. To satisfy the amount in controversy here, the ratio would have to be 300-1, an outcome that would clearly violate due process. Thus, the motion to remand was improperly denied.

The motion for a more definite statement:

If a complaint is so vague or ambiguous that the defendant cannot reasonably be required to frame a responsive pleading, he may move for a more definite statement. FRCP 12(e). S could have contended that since allegations of fraud must be stated with particularity (FRCP 9(b)), its motion for a more definite statement is appropriate. P's complaint apparently alleged only that the clocks were purchased as a consequence of S's misrepresentations, without any description of the allegedly fraudulent statements. While P could contend in rebuttal that the exact wording upon which the complaint is predicated could be developed during discovery, the court's denial of S's motion for a more definite statement was probably improper.

Was Jones ("J") barred from suing S?

If, as discussed above, subject matter jurisdiction was lacking because each class member's claim did not exceed $75,000, the district court judgment could be subject to rescission on the ground that it is void. FRCP 60(b)(4). To accomplish this, J would have to file a Rule 60 motion for relief from judgment in the original U.S. district court. Alternatively, J could collaterally attack that judgment, but under the modern approach to collateral attack, the general rule is that such attacks are not allowed, the presumption being that the prior court correctly decided the question of its subject matter jurisdiction. This is particularly so where, as here, the prior court actually decided the question.

Assuming J could not prevail on the subject matter jurisdiction issue and that the U.S. district court in *P v. S* certified the action as a class action, more facts would have to be ascertained to determine whether J's claim was barred. Under FRCP 23(b)(3) actions, each member of the class must be given notice and an opportunity to "opt out" of the action if she desires to do so. FRCP 23(c)(2). Assuming J received adequate notice of the action, his claim would be barred. If adequate notice had not been received by J, his present action against S could be maintained.

Answer to Question 20

A default judgment is valid when it is statutorily and constitutionally sound. We'll assume that the Calvada state court is competent to hear the matter upon which Paula ("P") sued Glassco ("G") for $100,000.

Did P comply with the statutory requirements of the Calvada long-arm statute?

G could contend that the Calvada long-arm statute does not apply to it because (1) it is not a "person"; and (2) since the defective manufacture of the glasses occurred in State White, the cause of action did not arise out of "a tortious act" in Calvada. P would argue in rebuttal that (1) a corporation should be deemed a "person" since it is an independent legal entity and the word "natural" would have been inserted before the word "person" by the legislators if they had intended the statute to pertain only to individuals; and (2) the action arose when P was injured, and that "act" occurred in Calvada. On the first point, P is likely to prevail since the word "person" is typically used to encompass artificial entities such as corporations. On the second point, the resolution depends on how the state court interprets the phrase "tortious act." Some courts have construed this phrase to focus on the location of the act itself, and others have it interpreted it broadly to include any element of the tort. If the former definition is adopted, G will prevail since the "act" took place in the location of manufacture. If the latter definition is adopted, P will prevail.

Can the Calvada court constitutionally exercise personal jurisdiction over G?

To establish personal jurisdiction over G, P must establish that G engaged in purposeful activity directed toward the state of Calvada and that her claim arises out of those purposeful contacts. If P satisfies this burden, there will be a strong presumption that the exercise of jurisdiction would be reasonable and would comport with due process. G, however, will have an opportunity to rebut that presumption.

As to purposeful contacts, P will cite the fact that G, through the agency of the Krispy promotional campaign, solicited the sale of its glassware within the state of Calvada. In addition, G intentionally sent the allegedly defective product into the state as part of a commercial exchange with P. P will further assert that her claim arises directly out of the latter contact since she is claiming that the shipped product was the cause of her injuries. As such, P would have established the presumptive reasonableness of the exercise of personal jurisdiction over G. G might attempt to rebut that presumption by asserting that the contract for sale was completed in State Black and that the amount of the sale was marginal. However, given a state's strong interest in protecting its consumers from dangerous products, G's arguments would be insufficient to rebut the presumption of reasonableness. P will prevail.

Was there statutory compliance with the notice (i.e., service of process) statute of Calvada?

A default judgment is not valid if service was not accomplished in conformity with the applicable statute and in a constitutionally valid manner. G would argue that the statutory words "its place of business" should be construed to mean its "principal place of business" since the word "its" suggests a single place, and therefore only the primary place of business would suffice. While P would contend in rebuttal that "its place of business" means the place where the plaintiff conducted her business with the corporation, it is unclear who should prevail on this issue since the question is one of statutory construction. A state court would be free to adopt either interpretation; however, service of process statutes are usually construed liberally to validate process, and substantial compliance with the terms of the statute is typically considered adequate. Given that G used the State Black address as a business address for purposes of engaging in business in the state of Calvada, it is possible that a Calvada court would find substantial compliance here. On the other hand, there is a presumption in favor of allowing a party to defend on the merits, and the court may construe the statute narrowly to void the default.

Assuming, however, there was compliance with the Calvada notice statute, is the statute constitutionally valid?

Notice must be "reasonably calculated" under the circumstances to apprise the defendant of the action. G would contend that mailing a registered or certified letter to a corporation should not suffice since relatively low-level personnel in a mailroom could either (1) lose a certified letter; or (2) if unhappy with management, deliberately misplace such an item.

P could argue in rebuttal that a registered or certified mailing should suffice since people ordinarily recognize that important documents come by such means. Therefore, there is little likelihood that documents mailed in this manner would ***not*** come to the attention of the proper persons.

Whether service by registered mail satisfies due process is an open question. Most courts addressing the issue have affirmed the use of registered mail under most circumstances, including the type of circumstances presented here. If the mail is returned "not accepted," some courts treat the nonacceptance as proof of service, while others require the plaintiff to engage in additional efforts to serve. Thus, whether service would be considered adequate here, where the defendant refused the mail, is an open question.

If the judgment is valid, should it be overturned?

G may seek to set aside the default judgment under the appropriate provisions of state law. Typically a default judgment may be set aside for good cause shown, including mistake, inadvertence, surprise, or excusable neglect. Using these principles, G might argue that its failure to respond was due to the excusable neglect of its employees in State Black who were not accustomed to receiving service of process. Whether to grant this motion would be within the discretion of the trial court and would depend largely on the evidence produced by G regarding the nature of its State Black operations.

Is P likely to prevail on the same evidence?

G could also contend that there was insufficient evidence for the court finding it liable since P failed to show that G was negligent in the manufacture of the glasses. However, P could argue that under the theories of products liability—breach of the implied warranty of merchantability or negligence (via use of the *res ipsa loquitor* doctrine)—there was adequate evidence to prove the default judgment. It is unclear, however, as to how the court determined that P's damages were $25,000. Without proof of medical bills or lost income, there was arguably insufficient proof for this aspect of the judgment. While P could contend that the trier of fact could infer that she suffered pain and suffering in the amount of $25,000, more evidence probably would have to be introduced to sustain this aspect of the judgment.

Answer to Question 21

The FRCP 12(b) motion to quash:

It is assumed that Peter ("P") claimed damages in excess of $75,000, for if he did not, subject matter jurisdiction would be lacking.

Although service within a jurisdiction has been a traditional basis for obtaining personal jurisdiction over an out-of-state citizen, Stanford James ("SJ") could have contended that service here was ineffective since he was "lured" into the jurisdiction. If a defendant is "lured" into a jurisdiction by means of trickery or fraud, a court, in its discretion, may quash the service of process. FRCP 12(b)(5).

In response, P would assert that there was no evidence of trickery or fraud. He "invited" SJ into State White to discuss his claim and made no representation that service of process would not be made. If SJ was concerned about being served in State White, he could have (1) refused P's offer, or (2) required P to stipulate in advance that no attempt to serve him would be made. In the absence of some showing of trickery or fraud by P, a court would not quash service under these circumstances.

Given the foregoing, as to personal jurisdiction, P could also assert that the Supreme Court has held service of process within a forum is still a valid means of obtaining personal jurisdiction over an individual. *Burnham v. Superior Court.* Thus, since SJ was properly served while within the territory of the forum, the court's ruling on SJ's Rule 12(b) motion was probably proper.

SJ's motion to transfer:

An action commenced in a U.S. district court may be transferred to another federal court in a different judicial district if (1) the action could have been commenced in the latter district court, and (2) the "convenience of the parties and witnesses" would be accommodated by the transfer. Since P's action is based upon diversity, it could have been initiated in State White (the jurisdiction in which the defendant resides and in which substantial events giving rise to the claim occurred; 28 U.S.C. §1391(a)(1) & (2)). Since venue was not proper in State Red (the defendant does not reside there, no events giving rise to the claim occurred there, and there is a district — State White — where venue would be proper), the motion to transfer would be pursuant to 28 U.S.C. §1406(a). Under this section, the U.S. district court would have discretion to either dismiss the case or transfer it to a federal district court in State White. While the court could dismiss the case for lack of proper venue, in the absence of a showing of injustice to either party, the court is more likely to transfer the case to a State White district court. In no event, however, may the court retain jurisdiction over the case since venue is clearly improper in State Red.

P's motion to amend his complaint:

Under the FRCP, a party may amend her pleading at any time before a "responsive" pleading has been served. FRCP 15(a). Since FRCP 12(b) and venue transfer motions are not pleadings to which a response must be filed, P was entitled to amend his complaint as of right.

SJ's motion for a judgment on the pleadings:

SJ apparently contended that since the amendment (which correctly stated SJ's name) was not made until the applicable statute of limitations had expired, he was entitled to a judgment on the pleadings. P could point out that the FRCP provides that an amendment *changing the party* relates back to the date of the original pleading if within the 120-day period for service of the summons and complaint the party named in the amended pleading (1) has received such notice of the action that it will not be prejudiced in defending itself; and (2) knew (or should have known) that, but for the mistaken identity, the action would have been brought against him. FRCP 15(c).

While the two conditions appear to be satisfied, it is unclear whether P amended his complaint within 120 days of filing the original complaint. If not, P could argue that he is not attempting to *change* or *add* a party. Rather, he simply desires to correctly state the name of the person he is already suing. P is more likely to prevail on this issue since SJ (1) has apparently not suffered prejudice by the delay in effectuating the name change; and (2) in effect, has waived any objection by responding to P's action (via the FRCP 12(b) and venue transfer motions, as well as his answer).

Since there is no FRCP provision precluding the correction of a party's name, the amendment probably would relate back to P's original complaint (and therefore be within the statute of limitations).

The facts are silent as to whether there is a State Red rule of law that specifically precludes relation back for statute of limitations purposes in a situation such as that posed by the present case. If there were such rule, SJ would argue that application of the FRCP under these circumstances would violate the second requirement of the Rules Enabling Act, which provides that the federal rules may not abridge, enlarge, or modify a substantive right. The argument in favor of this position is that application of the federal rule appears to extend the statute of limitations and, hence, to permit the vindication of a state substantive right that is otherwise barred as a matter of state law. The contrary argument is that state substantive policy is fully served since the case was filed within the state statute of limitations and SJ received timely notice of that proceeding. (This presumes that the state statute of limitations would have been tolled by the filing of the suit had SJ been properly identified in the complaint.) The resolution of this conflict is not obvious, though the strong presumption of the validity of the federal rules may tip the balance in favor of the federal rule given that the case was filed within the statute of limitations, the only error being that SJ's first and last names had been inverted. Certainly, in the absence of any State Red rule of law specifically stating that a name change may not relate back to the original pleading, as indicated above, P should prevail.

Answer to Question 22

Question 1:

The defendants could appear in the U.S. district court in Oklahoma and make an FRCP 12(b)(2) motion to dismiss the action for want of personal jurisdiction. In determining whether the minimum contacts standard (i.e., an out-of-state citizen has minimum contacts with the forum as not to offend traditional notions of fair play and substantial justice) is satisfied, a court will ordinarily weigh (1) the extent to which the defendant has availed him of the benefits of the forum, and (2) the relationship between the wrong allegedly committed by the defendant. As to Bobb ("B"), Paul ("P") would contend that the limited partnership activities in Oklahoma constitute purposeful availment; however, even if these activities are sufficient to establish purposeful availment, they have no relationship with P's claim against B. Similarly, although Silley's ("S") does have some business contacts with Oklahoma, none of those contacts are related to P's claim against S. As a consequence, P would be unable to satisfy the standards of the minimum contacts test. Nor would P be able to assert *quasi in rem* jurisdiction over B by attaching B's limited partnership assets. There being no relationship between those assets and P's claim against B, due process could not be satisfied under these circumstances.

In the unlikely case that their 12(b)(2) motion were to fail, B and S could also make (simultaneously with their 12(b)(2) motion) a 12(b)(3) motion to dismiss for lack of proper venue. In a diversity case such as this, venue is proper in the judicial district where one of the defendants resides if all defendants reside in the same state; where substantial events giving rise to the claim occurred; or, if there is no other district available under the first two standards, where personal jurisdiction could be established over one of the defendants. 28 U.S.C. §1391(a)(1)-(3). None of these alternatives establishes proper venue in Oklahoma. Neither defendant resides there, no events giving rise to the claim occurred there, and since venue would be proper in the district embracing Austin, Texas, the third alternative is not available. The district court would grant this motion.

Alternatively and in conjunction with the 12(b)(3) motion to dismiss for lack of proper venue, B and S could file a motion to transfer to the U.S. district court that encompasses Austin, Texas. 28 U.S.C. §1406(a) (motion to transfer where venue improper in the originating court). Venue for a diversity action would be satisfied in the district embracing Austin because substantial events giving rise to the claim occurred in that judicial district. In support of this motion, the defendants could argue that all witnesses to the incident probably live in that area. In lieu of dismissing, the court in Oklahoma could transfer the case to Texas. Given the lack of personal jurisdiction in Oklahoma and the fact that venue was improper in Oklahoma, the court could not retain the case. Its only options are to dismiss or transfer.

Question 2:

Joinder of claims against multiple defendants is permissible where (1) the claims asserted against them arise out of the same transaction or occurrence, and (2) there is common question of law or fact. FRCP 20(a). Most federal courts adhere to the view that claims arise from the same occurrence if they are "logically related." Since all of P's claims arise from the incident that occurred outside S's store, the initial condition is probably satisfied. As to the second condition, a factual issue that must be resolved in both actions would be whether P had actually taken something from S. If he had, then B's conduct may have been privileged (assuming he had not used excessive force) and the arrest would not have been "false." Thus, the claims probably could be joined.

Question 3:

The court would have subject matter jurisdiction over P's claims. First, the claim against B is predicated upon a federal statute (i.e., a federal claim). The U.S. district court would have jurisdiction over this claim as a case arising under federal law pursuant to 28 U.S.C. §1331 (federal question jurisdiction). Next, the court would have supplemental jurisdiction (28 U.S.C. §1367) over P's factually related assault and battery claim since it arises out of the same common nucleus of operative facts as his federal claim. Finally, the claims against Mary ("M") and S also arise out of the same transaction or common nucleus of operative facts as the federal claim against B. Hence, the U.S. district court would have supplemental jurisdiction over these claims as well. 28 U.S.C. §1367. Note that §1367 specifically permits the exercise of supplement jurisdiction over parties in federal question cases. The claims against M and S may also come within the court's diversity jurisdiction if the amount in controversy is satisfied as to each.

Question 4:

The ATPD could make an FRCP 12(b)(6) motion (i.e., that P failed to state a claim upon which relief could be granted). If this motion failed, the ATPD could file an answer alleging that it did not authorize the particular conduct in question (i.e., B's applying the chokehold upon P), and then move for a judgment on the pleadings. FRCP 12(c).

Question 5:

B could assert a cross-claim against the ATPD if his action against that entity is deemed to arise out of the occurrence that is the subject of P's claim. The ATPD could contend that no logical relationship between the two claims exists because (1) P's injury arose out of a physical act (the chokehold), and (2) B's action arises from a written agreement.

However, B could argue in rebuttal that (1) the ATPD's liability to him, if any, arises from his conduct vis-à-vis P; and (2) FRCP 13(g) specifically states that a cross-claim may include an action for indemnification. Thus, B's claim against the ATPD probably would be allowed by the district court.

The facts that (1) B and the ATPD are citizens of the same jurisdiction, and (2) the amount involved is unstated, are not relevant since supplemental jurisdiction exists with respect to cross-claims that satisfy the standards of FRCP 13(g).

Question 6:

A person may intervene as of right into a federal case where (1) she has an interest in the subject matter of the action, (2) the action may impair her ability to protect that interest, *and* (3) her interest is not adequately represented by an existing party. FRCP 24(a). P probably could contend that there is no right to intervene because (1) a decision by a U.S. district court in Texas would not be binding upon federal courts outside of that district, and (2) there is (presumably) no reason to believe that the ATPD's counsel would not adequately assert its contention that no federal claim exists. The potential intervenors could argue in rebuttal that if B prevailed, and the decision was affirmed on appeal, (1) a precedent would be set in that circuit, and (2) the ruling could have a persuasive effect on other district courts in the nation.

Additionally, since P is claiming only $85,000, the ATPD may not have retained the best counsel available to defend this matter. Nevertheless, a court probably would hold that the other police departments could **not** intervene as of right.

Intervention is permissible where the applicants wish to assert a claim or defense similar to that alleged by an existing party. FRCP 24(b). While permissive intervention will not be granted where the applicant's presence would serve no useful purpose (i.e., the ATPD could effectively argue against B's conduct being interpreted as a federal claim), the court, in its discretion, could allow intervention in these circumstances. Since the intervenors would merely be submitting a brief in opposition to the legal aspects of P's claim (i.e., that the conduct in question constituted a federal claim), intervention would not have a disruptive impact upon the case.

Answer to Question 23

1. Was the court correct in denying P's motion for summary judgment?

When a summary judgment motion is supported by an affidavit based upon personal knowledge that describes facts that are admissible into evidence at trial, the adverse party may ***not*** rest upon the allegations contained in his pleadings. The latter must respond with affidavits or statements made under oath during discovery. FRCP 56(e). Thus, Pam ("P") probably contended that, because D's attorney failed to respond with a statement made under oath, summary judgment upon the question of liability was appropriate.

However, while the failure to install a smoke detector in a patient's room constitutes ***negligence per se***, it does ***not*** establish liability. It establishes only that one element of negligence (i.e., the defendant failed to have acted reasonably) is present. In this case, D might still be able to successfully contend that causation is absent (i.e., even with a functioning smoke detector, P would have suffered exactly the same injuries).

Thus, the court was correct in denying P's summary judgment motion, although the court could have, and perhaps should have, entered a partial summary judgment with respect to D's breach of its duty of due care (i.e., its failure to act reasonably).

2. Was the court correct in ordering D to produce the fire investigator's report?

A party may ordinarily obtain discovery of documents prepared by another party in anticipation of litigation or trial only upon a showing that the former (1) has a substantial need for the item; and (2) is unable, without undue hardship, to obtain the equivalent by other means. FRCP 26(b)(3). P probably argued that (1) there is a substantial need for the report since it greatly assists in establishing an important fact (i.e., P's room did not have a smoke detector in it), which D has denied; and (2) this fact can no longer be verified by P since the home has been demolished.

D might have contended in rebuttal that the appropriate corporate officer had already admitted in an interrogatory that there was no smoke detector in P's room. Therefore, there was no substantial need for the report. However, the court was probably correct in ordering D to produce this item since a statement made in an interrogatory may be contradicted by that party at trial (as occurred in this case).

3. Was the court correct in holding D in contempt for refusing P's discovery request?

When a party does not furnish information sought to be discovered, the party seeking discovery must ordinarily seek an FRCP 37(a) order compelling discovery. If such an order is obtained *and* the discoveree *persists* in his refusal, the court may order a variety of sanctions (including holding the disobedient party in contempt). FRCP 37(b). However, since the court in this instance held D in contempt *at the same time* that it issued the Rule 37(a) order compelling production of the inspection, the contempt ruling was probably improper.

4. Was the court correct in denying P's motion to disallow Mac ("M")'s testimony?

There is no rule that precludes testimony simply because it is inconsistent with an answer to an interrogatory. The statement made in the interrogatory may be used (1) to impeach M, and (2) as substantive evidence against D (under the Federal Rules of Evidence, the corporate official's response is *not* hearsay; FRE 801(d)(2)). The court, therefore, was correct in denying P's motion.

Answer to Question 24

1. Borrow's ("B") motion to remand:

When the plaintiff's complaint is premised upon a federal claim, the defendant (regardless of citizenship) can have the action removed to the federal district court that encompasses the place where the action is pending. Since B's claim is based upon a federal statute (the TLA), Finco ("F") was entitled to have the action removed to the applicable U.S. district court.

If a federal judge subsequently concludes that removal does not satisfy the applicable statutory requirements, the case must be remanded back to the state court. Additionally, the judge may, in his discretion, remand the case back to state court if there is also a pendent state claim and it is likely that the federal claim will be dismissed before trial. Since neither of these circumstances is present, the court correctly denied B's motion to remand.

2. B's motion to amend her complaint:

Dealer ("D") probably contended that, since (1) it is a citizen of State A (where it is incorporated and conducts all of its business), and (2) B is a resident of State A, diversity subject matter jurisdiction is *not* satisfied for the state law claim that B is asserting against Dealer. Additionally, only $20,000 in damages is being asserted (far short of the necessary jurisdictional amount of "in excess of" $75,000). Thus, the federal court had to deny the motion.

However, under **supplemental party jurisdiction** principles, where a valid federal claim has been asserted, a federal court may hear a claim against a party over whom it otherwise would *not* have subject matter jurisdiction, if that claim is **transactionally related** to the underlying federal claim. D could contend that the claims are **not transactionally related** since B is contending that D provided B with erroneous information while the claim against F asserts complete failure to disclose required data. However, since both of B's claims pertain to the circumstances surrounding her signing of the papers with regard to her vehicle purchase, it is likely that the "transactionally related" requirement is satisfied.

Thus, the court incorrectly ruled that it lacked subject matter jurisdiction over B's action against D.

3. B's motion for partial summary judgment:

Summary judgment is proper when there is no "genuine issue of material fact" with respect to one or more aspects of the lawsuit.

B is apparently contending that F should be precluded from relitigating the issue of its violation of the disclosure provisions of TLA. Under the doctrine of issue preclusion (collateral estoppel), where the identical issue was actually litigated in a prior lawsuit by the party, a court may preclude relitigation of that issue in a subsequent proceeding. The question is whether B may rely on issue preclusion in the present proceeding.

B's argument must overcome several obstacles. First, there is a question as to whether the courts rendering the previous judgments were in jurisdictions that recognize the "mutuality rule." If they were, then issue preclusion is not available to B since the federal court in the immediate proceeding is required to apply the rules of preclusion that would be applied by the courts previously rendering a judgment against F. If those courts adhered to "mutuality," the federal court must do so as well, and since B is not mutually bound by those previous judgments, she may not benefit from them.

If the prior courts had abandoned mutuality in the context of offensive issue preclusion (i.e., issue preclusion asserted by a plaintiff attempting to satisfy one of the elements of her claim), then the federal court must determine if B should be allowed to benefit from the prior judgment in accord with the law of those jurisdictions. Assuming that scenario, the critical question is whether the precise issue decided against F in those prior proceedings is the same as the issue B now wishes to preclude. Thus, if the contracts in both proceedings are essentially identical and the question is whether the contractual language provides an adequate disclosure under TLA, then the issue is likely to be treated as the same. On the other hand, if the contracts or disclosures differ in any significant fashion, the issue is not the same and preclusion will not be available.

Assuming that mutuality has been abandoned in the context of offensive issue preclusion and that the issue now presented is the same as the issue previously litigated and decided in the prior proceeding, the court then must be determine if it would be fair to allow B to benefit from the prior proceeding. Two factors will be considered: whether B could have intervened in the prior proceedings and whether there would be any unfairness to F in permitting B to benefit from the prior judgments. As to the first point, there are no facts that suggest that B was even aware of any of these earlier proceedings; hence, it is unlikely that B would have been expected to intervene in them. Second, as to fairness to F, the use of the issue in the present case cannot be a surprise and one can assume that F had a complete incentive to litigate this issue in the prior proceeding.

Moreover, the facts at least suggest that F has had several opportunities to litigate this issue.

If any of the prior judgments were rendered in courts that have abandoned mutuality and if the issue presented here is not significantly different from the issue decided in those case, then B's summary judgment on the question of TLA liability should have been granted.

Answer to Question 25

1. *Motions for judgment on the pleadings:*

A motion for judgment on the pleadings challenges only the sufficiency of the adversary's pleadings (i.e., it does not assert defects that do not appear on the face of the pleadings). In federal court, a complaint need only adequately inform the defendant of the nature of the action against her and state the relief requested.

Dave ("D") might have argued that the complaint (1) failed to describe the basis of his negligent conduct (i.e., it merely stated he was "negligent" as a legal conclusion), and (2) prayed for an amount ($250,000) far in excess of Paul ("P")'s alleged injuries (i.e., $25,000). However, P probably successfully asserted in rebuttal that (1) it should have been obvious to D that P was contending that the former had not operated his vehicle in a reasonable manner, and (2) the mere fact that the prayer did not coincide with the injuries set forth in the body of the document does not cause a complaint to fail (damages must always be proven).

An answer must effectively deny the plaintiff's allegations for those assertions to be put into issue. Failure to adequately deny allegations contained in a complaint constitutes an admission of those assertions. However, damages are always deemed to be in issue (even if not adequately denied). FRCP 9(d). Since D's answer does not unequivocally "deny" the assertions contained in P's complaint, P probably argued that D, in effect, admitted them (except for damages). D could have argued that, since his answer stated that he did not "admit" the assertions contained in P's complaint, he impliedly denied them. This argument probably would fail, however, since D's answer stated that the allegations in P's complaint were not denied. Thus, the district court should have granted P's motion for a judgment on the pleadings (exclusive of his prayer for damages).

2. *Al ("A")'s motion to dismiss:*

Under the FRCP, an amendment of a pleading relates back to the date of the original pleading when (1) relation back is permitted by the law that provides the statute of limitations applicable to the action; (2) the claim or defense asserted in the amended pleading arose out of the conduct, transaction, or occurrence set forth or attempted to be set forth in the original pleading; or (3) in the case of an added party, that party knew (or should have known) that, but for a mistake pertaining to the identity of the proper party, the action would have been brought against him, and the claim is asserted within the applicable statute of limitation period. FRCP 15(c). These provisions are disjunctive; hence, satisfaction of any one will permit relation back. The second provision, relating only to added claims or defenses, does not apply since this amendment applies to an added party. The third provision arguably applies but, since A had no notice of P's action prior to the expiration of the statute of limitations, it would not permit relation back under these facts. The first provision, however, does apply and mandates the application of relation back. Since the accident occurred in State Y, State Y law provides the relevant statute of limitations. Accordingly, since the law that provides the relevant statute of limitations mandates relation back, under FRCP 15(c), the district court was correct in denying A's motion (i.e., in allowing the amendment to relate back to the date of the original filing). Importantly, FRCP 15(c)(1) was designed to avoid conflicts with state law under precisely this type of situation.

3. A's motion to compel an answer to his interrogatory and the production of documents:

A party may obtain relevant papers that were prepared in anticipation of litigation by (or for) another party, or her representative, only upon a showing that the party seeking discovery (1) has a substantial need for them, and (2) is otherwise unable to obtain those materials without undue hardship. FRCP 26(b)(3). The work product privilege, however, prevents discovery of opinions, legal theories, or mental impressions of another party's attorney.

P might have asserted that A's demand does not meet the requirements of FRCP 26(b)(3) because (1) Wilma ("W") was acting pursuant to his direction when she obtained the statements from the two witnesses, and (2) A could obtain this information by directly questioning those persons. If that is true, then the information was obtained in anticipation of litigation, and A can easily obtain that information. The statements, therefore, are not discoverable. However, there was no indication that W was acting pursuant to P's instructions or under his direction. Second, there is a substantial need for this information because, even if A's attorney questioned those witnesses directly, there is no other means of determining if their answers were consistent. Moreover, given that the statements were made contemporaneously with the accident, there is no way that A can now recreate the circumstances surrounding those initial impressions. Thus, P should be required to answer A's interrogatory and provide

the statements. (Interestingly, P could have possibly answered D's interrogatory in the negative, since W, rather than P, took the statements in
question.)

If, however, the notes that P's attorney made on these statements contain
legal theories, impressions, or conclusions, they are protected by the work
product privilege. A can obtain these statements, but Len's notes must be
somehow deleted.

Answer to Question 26

1. Was the denial of Danielle ("D")'s motion to make Trucko ("T") a party proper?

A person should be joined as a party when the failure to do so (1) will result in the inability of the court to grant complete relief to persons who are already parties, (2) may impair that person's ability to protect an interest relating to the subject matter of the action, or (3) leaves any party to the action subject to a substantial risk of incurring liability or inconsistent obligations. FRCP 19(a). If such a person is not subject to service of process, or if his joinder will deprive the court of subject matter jurisdiction, the court must determine whether in "equity and good conscience" it can proceed with him. FRCP 19(b).

Price ("P") can contend that T is not a necessary party. Complete relief can be given to P (i.e., he can obtain a judgment for the full amount of his injuries against D).

Additionally, D's interests are not prejudiced by the absence of T. Even assuming D could show P's truck headlights were off, T's absence as a defendant would *not* preclude D from offering evidence of this fact in her defense (i.e., to show there was no causal relationship between D's conduct and P's injuries). As to any prejudice to T, if D offered such evidence and prevailed, the determination of this issue would not preclude T from re-litigating this question if P subsequently sued T. Hence, the failure to join T will not prejudice T in any manner, and the court was correct in denying D's motion to join T.

However, the court's statement that it had no personal jurisdiction over T is probably incorrect. Assuming State Z has a long-arm statute that applies to T, the minimum contacts test is likely to be satisfied by the fact that P's injury arose from T's conduct within the jurisdiction. Finally, it's difficult to know what the court intended by its statement that "service of process would be difficult." If personal jurisdiction can be exercised over T, effectuating service is usually a relatively facile matter.

Thus, the court probably ruled correctly, but for the wrong reasons.

2. Was the order approving an examination of D's physical capabilities proper?

Under FRCP 35, upon a showing of good cause, the court may order a physical examination of a party when his condition is in controversy. D can argue that, since P has alleged that the accident was caused by the former's failure to use carburetor heat, D's physical condition is **not** in controversy. P can respond that, while the lack of carburetor heat may have caused D to land the plane, a pilot possessing ordinary physical attributes would have nevertheless been able to avoid the accident.

The court's decision was probably incorrect. It should have awaited discovery by P of evidence that tended to show that D's physical impairment contributed, in some manner, to the accident. Once this was established, P's FRCP 35 motion would be proper.

3. Was the court's instruction to the jury that it could consider evidence of P's contributory negligence proper?

Affirmative defenses ordinarily must be specifically pleaded by a defendant. FRCP 8(c). However, when issues not raised by the pleadings are litigated at trial, those issues are treated as if alleged in the pleadings. FRCP 15(b). Since D introduced evidence at the trial showing that P's truck lacked lights without objection by the latter party, the pleadings are deemed to be amended to contain an assertion of P's contributory negligence.

Thus, the court's instruction permitting the jury to consider P's possible contributory negligence was proper.

Answer to Question 27

To satisfy the standards of federal question jurisdiction, the plaintiff's claim must satisfy either the creation test or the essential federal ingredient test. 28 U.S.C. §1331. Since the cause of action here is breach of contract, a state-created claim, the creation test is not satisfied (i.e., the claim is not one created by federal law). As to the essential federal ingredient test, two preliminary aspects of that doctrine are satisfied. This is a state-created cause of action (element one) that includes an essential federal ingredient (element two). As to the latter, the question of whether there is a breach of contract depends on whether Daz is in compliance with the CWA, a federal statute. However, there must be some showing that there is a strong interest in providing federal jurisdiction over the claim, as would be the case with issues of constitutional law or with respect to such quintessentially federal matters as the collection of federal taxes. Moreover, the court must be convinced that the exercise of jurisdiction over this particular claim will not open the floodgates of litigation in federal court. The federal element here does not pertain to constitutional law; nor is there anything about it that implicates federal policy in the same manner or to the same degree as the collection of federal taxes. Moreover, given that Congress has provided no private right of action, which suggests the absence of an interest sufficient to invoke federal jurisdiction, the court is unlikely to exercise jurisdiction over this claim. The district court is likely to grant the motion to dismiss.

Answer to Question 28

May Bob ("B") implead Carl ("C")?

Yes. This represents a classic example of impleader. FRCP 14(a). C, as a surety, is a person who is or may be liable to B if B is found liable to Abe ("A") under the primary claim. The U.S. district court would have jurisdiction over the impleader since it is part of the same constitutional case or controversy as A's claim against B—by definition, the impleader (i.e., the claim for indemnity) is factually and legally related to A's claim. 28 U.S.C. §1367(a). In addition, nothing in §1367(b) precludes a defendant (B) from bringing in an additional party pursuant to FRCP 14. The fact that C is not diverse from A is irrelevant. One could also assert an independent basis of jurisdiction over the impleader since B and C are diverse from one another and the amount in controversy exceeds $75,000.

May C file a claim against A related to the construction project?

Yes. FRCP 14(a) specifically allows the third-party defendant (C) to file a transactionally related claim against the original plaintiff. Section 1367(a) creates the jurisdictional premise for doing so (same constitutional case or controversy), and §1367(b) imposes no limits on claims filed by third-party defendants such as C. The fact that C is not diverse from A is irrelevant.

May C file a claim against A unrelated to the construction project?

Perhaps, but unlikely. If C files a transactionally related claim against A under FRCP 14(a) as in the question answer directly above, he may attach other unrelated claims against A pursuant to FRCP 18(a). However, those unrelated claims must have an independent basis of jurisdiction—by definition, they are not transactionally related to the 14(a) claim and therefore would not satisfy §1367(a). Since A and C are from the same state, diversity cannot be satisfied. If, however, the unrelated claim arises under federal law within the meaning of §1331, C may file it along with the FRCP 14(a) claim.

May A file a claim against C related to the construction project?

Yes, but only if the claim presents a transactionally related federal question. FRCP 14(a) allows a plaintiff to file a transactionally related claim against the third-party defendant, and this standard would seem to be satisfied here. However, in a diversity case such as this one, there is no supplemental jurisdiction over such a claim since the text of §1367(b) excludes from the coverage of §1367(a) any claim by a plaintiff against a person joined pursuant to FRCP 14—precisely the problem presented here. Thus, even though §1367(a) would be satisfied, §1367(b) would bar the exercise of supplemental jurisdiction in this diversity case. Hence, A can file this claim only if there is an independent basis of jurisdiction over it. Since A and C are not diverse from one another, the only potentially independent basis of jurisdiction would be §1331.

If B does not attempt to implead C, may C intervene?

C could attempt to intervene as a defendant relying on FRCP 24. Assuming his application has been timely (no facts indicate otherwise), under FRCP 24(a)—intervention as of right—he would have to claim (1) an interest in the transaction that is the subject matter of the suit (the breach of contract claim as it relates to his obligations as a surety); (2) that the disposition of the case may, as a practical matter, impair his ability to protect that interest (if a breach were found, he would have to indemnify B); and (3) and that his interest is inadequately represented by B (B has little incentive to fully defend the suit given that C will pay the judgment). Under subsection (b), C could also seek permissive intervention by showing a common question of law or fact between the primary action and any claim or defense he might have. If FRCP 24 is satisfied, jurisdiction would be established pursuant to §1367(a)'s same case or controversy test, with no limitations imposed by §1367(b) since C most likely would be aligned as a defendant. Alternatively, as to the previous point, one could argue that although C is a defendant joined pursuant to FRCP 24, the plaintiff is now filing a claim against him in violation of §1367(b)—no claims by plaintiffs against persons joined under FRCP 24. Under this approach, there would be no jurisdiction.

May B file a counterclaim against A, joining Donna ("D") as a defendant on that counterclaim?

The claim against A would be a compulsory counterclaim within the meaning of FRCP 13(a). If the amount in controversy were satisfied, it would have an independent basis of jurisdiction since A and B are diverse from one another. It would also satisfy the supplemental jurisdiction standards of §1367(a), given the close factual relationship between this claim and A's claim against B. Section 1367(b) would impose no limits on the exercise of supplemental jurisdiction since B is not a plaintiff. Next, the claim against D could be brought pursuant to FRCP 13(h) since doing so would satisfy the requirements of that rule, including the permissive joinder standards of FRCP 20. As to jurisdiction, although B and D are not diverse from one another, supplemental jurisdiction could be exercised over this factually related claim under §1367(a); moreover, subsection (b) imposes no limitations on defendant B's use of this joinder device.

May D intervene?

First, the standards of FRCP 24 would have to be satisfied, and it is not entirely clear how D's tortuous interference claim would be impaired by this suit. Permissive intervention is a possibility, though a court might conclude that D's intervention would change the basic contours of the lawsuit (a breach of contract suit). But even if the rule allowed intervention, the bottom line is that D would be intervening as a plaintiff and that doing so would destroy complete diversity. As a consequence, there would be neither an independent basis for jurisdiction — absent a federal question — nor supplemental jurisdiction over her claim. As to the latter, §1367(b) precludes the filing of a claim by a party made a plaintiff pursuant to FRCP 24 when doing so would violate the jurisdictional principles of §1332. That appears to be the case here.

May A file a claim against D related to the underlying dispute between A and B?

FRCP 13(g) might allow A to do this depending on how one interprets the scope of that rule. Assuming, as it appears to be the case, that the claim is transactionally related to the primary claim (i.e., to the breach of contract claim), some courts would treat the co-plaintiffs as co-parties and allow the filing of the claim. Other courts, however, would not treat co-plaintiffs as co-parties unless both co-plaintiffs were made defendants on a counterclaim, which is not the situation here. Assuming the rule is satisfied, subject matter jurisdiction must be satisfied as well. Since A and D are diverse, §1332 would be satisfied if the amount in controversy were met. If the amount is not met, the claim would appear to satisfy the standards of §1367(a), but then runs afoul of §1367(b) since it would be a claim by a plaintiff (A) against a party (D) joined under FRCP 24 under circumstances that would undermine the jurisdictional requirements of §1332.

Answer to Question 29

Surety ("S")'s 12(b)(7) motion requires an application of FRCP 19(a) and (b). That inquiry is divided into three parts. First, is Delmore ("D") a party who should be joined if feasible? Second, assuming an affirmative answer to that question, is D's joinder feasible? And third, assuming that his joinder is not feasible, may the action, in equity and good conscience, proceed without him? As to the first inquiry—the 19(a) inquiry—D is a person who ought to be joined. He has an interest in the performance bond, and that interest may be impaired by an adverse judgment against S. For example, a finding that S is liable to Patricia ("P") might require D to indemnify S, or it might reduce the amount of protection available to D with respect to other subcontractors. In addition, S may be subjected to inconsistent obligations if P prevails against D (triggering S's payment obligation) but loses against S (nullifying S's payment obligation). There is also an "inefficiency" prejudice to the judicial system. Next, as to feasibility of joinder, if D is joined as a defendant, complete diversity would be destroyed, and although the claim against D would be part of the same constitutional case within the meaning of §1367(a), the principles of §1367(b) would be violated since P, the plaintiff, would now be asserting a claim against a party joined pursuant to FRCP 19 where complete diversity is lacking. The same situation would occur were D to intervene under FRCP 24. On the other hand, S could file a counterclaim for declaratory relief and join D as a 13(h) defendant on that counterclaim. With this approach, there would be no violation of §1367(b). Alternatively, S might file a counterclaim in interpleader against P and D or an impleader against De, which would also avoid the §1367(b) problems. (Note that these alternative approaches could also be discussed under the "shaping the relief" principle.) Finally, assuming joinder is not feasible, one must reconsider the prejudice to P (minimal since she chose to split her claims), S (potential inconsistent obligations), D (diminution of his security bond), and the courts (inefficiency), and then determine whether this prejudice can be avoided or lessened by shaping the relief. Among other things, the court simply could withhold any judgment in this proceeding pending the outcome of the state court lawsuit between P and D. Alternatively, the court could stay this proceeding until such time as S had an opportunity to intervene in the state court proceeding. In general, since there are alternative ways of bringing D into the suit and ways of shaping the relief that would avoid any prejudice to S, the motion should be denied.

Answer to Question 30

Is A bound by the finding in the first proceeding that the contract allowed B to make the delivery within four months of July 1?

No. The decision on that issue was not necessary to the previous judgment. Excise that decision from the judgment, and the judgment would still stand.

If B raises a defense of claim preclusion, how should the court rule? Does it matter whether the breach at issue in the first proceeding was considered material?

The claim preclusion defense should be denied since the temporal scope of the claim in the first proceeding was limited to 1999-2000. If the breach had been "material," then, in some jurisdictions, A would have been required to sue for both past and future damages. Under this scenario, the claim preclusion defense would prevail. Under these facts, however, there is no basis on which to conclude that the breach was material.

Since the court in the first proceeding made several findings, is B bound by the finding of no fraud?

Yes, B is bound. That issue was actually litigated, decided, and necessary to the previous judgment. As to the latter point, the court could not have found in A's favor in the absence of this finding.

If in the first case the court found for B, would A be precluded from bringing the second suit?

It depends. Under the Restatement (Second) of Judgments, neither issue would be binding unless A appealed and both were affirmed on appeal. Under the original Restatement, however, both would have been binding even in the absence of an appeal. Finally, under an approach adopted by some states, the issue would be binding so long as it was "squarely addressed and specifically decided." (Note this presents a problem of issue preclusion, not claim preclusion. It is the "issue" of fraud that will potentially bar the subsequent suit.)

If A attempts to sue B for damages to the loading dock, may B rely on the prior judgment in favor of D as bar to that suit?

Yes. Under the substantive standards of vicarious liability, B (employer) and D (employee) would be deemed to have been in privity with one another for purposes of claim preclusion. B, therefore, may assert claim preclusion as a defense in the second suit.

If the judgment in the A v. D *proceeding was against D and in favor of A, would B be bound by that judgment?*

No. Under these circumstances, the substantive policies of vicarious liability would not be advanced by creating a privity relationship between B and D. B, therefore, would be treated as a nonparty. As a nonparty, and consistent with the Due Process Clause, B is not bound by the prior judgment.

Multiple-Choice Questions

1. Paul, a state district attorney, files a complaint in the proper U.S. district court seeking to enjoin a pro-communist rally. He alleges the rally is being held without a license, in violation of a state statute. Paul asserts federal question jurisdiction by alleging that the defendants have publicly claimed immunity for such rallies on First Amendment grounds.

   Denton, the group leader, files an FRCP 12(b)(1) motion to dismiss for lack of subject matter jurisdiction. He alternatively claims immunity from prosecution under the First Amendment as an affirmative defense.

   Denton's motion should be

   A. granted, because there is no subject matter jurisdiction.

   B. granted, because Denton has asserted a First Amendment defense.

   C. denied, because there is "federal question" subject matter juris-diction.

   D. denied, because Paul's claim involves the U.S. Constitution.

2. Paula and Pete were hit by a truck driven by an employee of the D Corporation. The accident occurred in California, where Paula and Pete were living at that time. D's headquarters are in Florida, but its principal place of business is in Michigan. It is incorporated in Delaware. After the accident, Paula and Pete moved to Miami, Florida, where they planned to retire.

   After moving, they contacted a lawyer who filed suit against D in the appropriate U.S. district court where Paula and Pete lived, alleging diversity jurisdiction. The suit alleged that each plaintiff had suffered personal injuries in excess of $75,000. D moved to dismiss the case for lack of subject matter jurisdiction.

   D's motion should be

   A. granted, because the plaintiffs were citizens of California when they were injured.

   B. granted, because D's headquarters are in Florida.

   C. denied, because diversity subject matter jurisdiction exists.

   D. denied, because D is a citizen of Delaware only.

3. P files suit in the U.S. district court in Nevada alleging a federal claim (i.e., racial discrimination against him occurring in Texas). The defendant is a citizen of California, and all of the witnesses live in Texas. P lives in Nevada. The defendant moves to change the venue to

California or, alternatively, to Texas. Which of the following is correct?

A. The action may be transferred only to California.

B. The action may be transferred to California or Texas.

C. The action must be dismissed since it was commenced in an improper forum.

D. It is discretionary with the court whether to retain the action or transfer it to California or Texas.

4. Priscilla filed suit against Derek for recovery of a shipment of cargo lost at sea. The suit was filed in a court of general jurisdiction in State A. Derek was personally served at his home in State B. He has no contacts with State A. Derek made a general appearance in the State A court and filed a demurrer to the complaint. The demurrer was overruled and the case proceeded to trial, where Priscilla prevailed.

You may assume that Priscilla's claim is in admiralty, which is within the exclusive jurisdiction of the federal courts. On appeal, Derek asserted (1) lack of personal jurisdiction, and (2) lack of subject matter jurisdiction. Derek should

A. prevail on both (1) and (2).

B. prevail on (1) only.

C. prevail on (2) only.

D. lose on both (1) and (2).

5. Plaintiff, a citizen of State A, filed suit against Defendant in a State A court, alleging a claim based upon a federal statute. Defendant, also a citizen of State A, filed a petition for removal to the federal court that encompasses the judicial district in which the state court is located.

Should the action be removed?

A. No, because the action could not have originally been brought in the U.S. district court to which removal has been requested.

B. Yes, because Plaintiff's action arises under a U.S. statute.

C. Yes, because state courts, even those of general jurisdiction, do not have subject matter jurisdiction over federal claims.

D. No, because Defendant is a citizen of State A.

6. Acme became involved in a labor dispute with the Steamroller's Union (the entity that ordinarily supplied workers for Acme's plant).

Acme brought an action against Steamroller's Union ("Union") in the appropriate U.S. district court, claiming $75,000 in damages as a consequence of Union's conduct in harassing and intimidating nonunion workers in violation of the National Labor Relations Act and applicable state law.

Acme is an Indiana corporation, and Union (an unincorporated association) has members who are domiciled in every state, except New York and New Jersey. Union answered by denying Acme's allegations and filing a $15,000 counterclaim (which asserted that Acme had deliberately made false accusations about Union to the local papers for the purpose of obtaining favorable press coverage).

If Union moves to dismiss for lack of subject matter jurisdiction, it should

A. prevail, because there is no diversity.

B. prevail, because Acme has not claimed monetary damages in excess of $75,000.

C. lose, because subject matter jurisdiction is satisfied.

D. lose, because a state claim has been asserted in a federal court.

7. Bank is a Missouri corporation. Bank has a savings account in the name of one of its customers, Harvey Hunt, who was domiciled in California. Harvey recently died. In his will, Harvey left the entire account (in the specific amount of $7,000) to his nephew Sam, a citizen of Texas. On the same day that Sam showed up to claim the money, Jay appeared at Bank and presented a notarized agreement signed by Harvey assigning the entire bank account to Jay. Jay is a citizen of New York.

Bank filed a statutory interpleader action in the U.S. district court for the judicial district of California in which it is located. Which of the following statements is correct?

A. The case should be dismissed because the citizenship of Sam will be imputed to Harvey. Thus, diversity of citizenship will be lacking.

B. Although there is complete diversity between adverse parties, the case lacks the necessary amount in controversy. Thus, it should be dismissed for lack of subject matter jurisdiction.

C. The case would be subject to a motion to dismiss under Rule 12(b)(3) because venue in a statutory interpleader action would be proper only in a district where one of the claimants resides.

D. Both A and B.

8. In a state court of general jurisdiction, Pete sued the Big Time Corporation for personal injuries he received in an auto collision with a truck driven by a Big Time truck driver. Doris was the president of Big Time when the accident occurred. Pete personally served Big Time Corporation by handing the summons and complaint to Doris the day before she retired. In the excitement of her retirement, Doris neglected to deliver the papers to anyone else at Big Time. A default was entered against Big Time.

Other than service upon Doris, Big Time never received notice of the pending lawsuit prior to the entry of a default judgment. Big Time now moves to quash service of process. You may assume that applicable state law pertaining to service of process is identical to the Federal Rules of Civil Procedure. Which of the following statements is probably correct?

   A. Service should be quashed because Big Time Corporation did not receive actual notice of the pending lawsuit.

   B. Service should be quashed because Doris was not an officer of Big Time at the time an answer was due.

   C. Service should be quashed because the summons and complaint was served by Pete.

   D. Big Time's motion should be denied.

9. Plaintiff, a citizen of California, sues the Bank of Nevada ("Bank") in the U.S. District Court for the District of Nevada. Bank has its only place of business in Nevada. Plaintiff seeks an order directing Bank to deliver the proceeds of a savings account in the amount of $80,000 to her. She alleges an agreement between her and Krooke, also a California citizen, whereby they each deposited an equal amount of money in the account, to be held solely in the name of Krooke.

The Bank answers by alleging that it refused to make the transfer because Krooke claims that Plaintiff assigned her interest in the account to him as repayment for a loan. Bank makes a motion to dismiss for failure to join Krooke as a party. At a hearing on this issue, the court dismisses the case for P's failure to join an indispensable party. Which of the following statements is correct?

   I. Plaintiff will not be barred from refiling the action in a state court since the dismissal on the grounds provided in FRCP 12(b)(7) does not constitute an adjudication on the merits.

   II. The court should have ordered Bank to interplead P and Krooke.

   III. The court correctly dismissed the action because there was no way to shape the relief in a manner that would avoid prejudice to Bank.

IV. The court should not have dismissed the action because there was diversity between Plaintiff and Bank.

A. I and II

B. I and III

C. I and IV

D. II only

10. P, a citizen of Idaho, brings a multimillion dollar diversity action for wrongful death in the proper U.S. district court against his wife's employer, D Construction Company, a Washington corporation. He alleges that D negligently allowed scaffolding to collapse while his wife was walking beneath it. D impleads T, the manufacturer of the scaffolding, alleging that it would have a right to indemnity from T as a consequence of the latter's negligent manufacture of the equipment. T is an Idaho corporation.

P was granted leave to file an amended complaint alleging negligent manufacture against T. Thereafter, T moved to dismiss P's action against it for lack of subject matter jurisdiction. Which of the following statements is correct?

A. The motion should be denied because of the pendent jurisdiction doctrine.

B. The motion should be denied because of the ancillary jurisdiction doctrine.

C. The motion should be granted because diversity is lacking.

D. The motion should be granted because there is diversity between P and D.

11. P, a citizen of California, filed an action in the U.S. district court in Los Angeles against D, a Texas corporation, and Z, a New York corporation, alleging that (1) they were engaged in a conspiracy to fix prices in violation of the Sherman Act, 15 U.S.C. §1, and (2) that his actual damages from the conduct of the defendants was $73,000.

P further alleged in a second cause of action that D is wrongfully withholding $1,000 that P paid to D as a deposit for a computer that was not delivered. Which of the following statements is correct?

A. The action should be dismissed by the district court since the value of the aggregated claims does not meet the amount in controversy requirement.

B. The district court may exercise pendent jurisdiction over the second cause of action only if it arises from a common nucleus of operative facts with the first cause of action.

C. The federal court has subject matter jurisdiction because there is complete diversity of citizenship between all plaintiffs and defendants.

D. None of the above.

12. P brings an action against D in a state court of general jurisdiction in California. P is a citizen of California. D is a citizen of New York. P alleges that D has infringed upon a patent recently granted to P by the U.S. Patent and Trademark Office. P seeks $75,000 in damages and an injunction barring D from further acts of infringement. Patent infringement matters are within the exclusive jurisdiction of the federal courts.

D is personally served with a copy of the summons and complaint when his airplane lands in Los Angeles International Airport on a brief stopover. The flight was bound for Hawaii. D fails to answer the complaint, and P obtains a default judgment. P then seeks to enforce the judgment in a New York state court.

Which of the following statements is correct?

A. The court in California did not have subject matter jurisdiction over the action. Thus, P's judgment is not entitled to full faith and credit from a New York court.

B. Even if *Shaffer v. Heitner* does not alter the traditional rule that service of process within a state is a valid means of obtaining personal jurisdiction over a defendant, the California state court never obtained personal jurisdiction over D since he does not reside in California. Thus, the judgment is not entitled to full faith and credit from a New York court.

C. By failing to appear, D waived his right to object to subject matter and personal jurisdiction.

D. None of the above.

13. P, a citizen of Arizona, was injured in an automobile accident in New Mexico. The driver of the other vehicle was D, a citizen of Texas. New Mexico is a comparative negligence state whose law would apply to this action. P knows that D's damages are $46,000. P brings her action in the only U.S. district court in Arizona, alleging in good

faith that she has incurred damages in the total amount of $75,000. Which of the following statements is correct?

I. Venue is not proper.

II. The federal court lacks subject mater jurisdiction because the claim does not meet the amount in controversy requirement.

III. The federal court has subject matter jurisdiction because the parties are diverse, and P's claim satisfies the amount in controversy requirement.

A. I only

B. II only

C. III only

D. I and II

14. Packer, a New York citizen, purchased a mountainside home in Lake Tahoe, Nevada, from Denton. Packer asked Denton if Denton was sure that the land on which the home is situated was geologically sound. Denton (aware that there was a major fault under the home) nevertheless responded to Packer's question in a positive manner. Two months after Packer occupied the house, it collapsed. Packer brings an action for fraud against Denton in the appropriate U.S. district court. The complaint alleges that "Denton fraudulently induced Plaintiff to enter into the purchase agreement for the house and land." Denton moved for a more definite statement under FRCP 12(e). Which of the following statements is correct?

   A. The motion should be granted since the FRCP requires that circumstances constituting fraud must be stated with particularity.

   B. The motion should be denied since the FRCP requires only that the pleader give a short, plain statement of the claim for relief.

   C. The motion should be denied if the complaint is adequate under Nevada law.

   D. None of the above.

15. D, a Michigan corporation, sells its automobiles through independent dealers. D's principal place of business is Detroit. All dealers have dealership agreements that they executed with D at the time they were appointed to be dealers. Their agreements entitle them to sell in their areas cars manufactured by D. This year, D has produced a new sports car that is a radical departure from its

previous automobiles. D decides that it will not sell this car to its existing dealers, but instead will enter into agreements with new dealers to handle the new sports car line. Twelve dealers in California jointly file actions for breach of contract and an injunction against D in the appropriate U.S. district court. D moves to sever the actions. Which of the following statements is correct?

A. The motion should be granted since the plaintiffs are all citizens of the same state.

B. The motion should be denied because plaintiffs are compelled to join their actions if their claims arise out of the same transaction or series of transactions.

C. The motion should be granted if (a) the court finds that the claims arise out of the same transaction or series of transactions, and (b) there are common issues of law and fact to all of the claims.

D. None of the above.

16. North America Insurance Company ("NAIC"), an Illinois corporation with its principal place of business in New York, is sued by two of its policyholders in a class action filed in a U.S. district court in Illinois. The complaint alleges that NAIC overcharged them and 5,000 other similarly situated policyholders for automobile insurance. The class seeks a refund of the overcharges, which equal slightly over $5 million in the aggregate.

The plaintiffs in the action are Adams ("A"), a citizen of Illinois, and Baron ("B"), a student domiciled in New York, but attending law school in California. The amounts of the overcharges claimed by the named plaintiffs are A, $5,000, and B, $8,000. The members of the class are domiciled in roughly equal proportions in ten states, including New York and Illinois. Which of the following statements is correct?

A. The federal court lacks subject matter jurisdiction over the action since the complete diversity requirement is not met.

B. The federal court lacks subject matter jurisdiction over the action because the claims of the named representatives do not satisfy the amount in controversy requirement.

C. The federal court has subject matter jurisdiction since the aggregate claims of the class meet the amount in controversy requirement and since minimal diversity is satisfied.

D. Both A and B.

17. P, a citizen of New York, brings an action against D, in the U.S. district court in New York (the judicial district in which P lives). D is a citizen of Michigan. P alleges $90,000 in damages based on an alleged breach of contract by D to manufacture equipment for P's restaurants.

Subsequently, D brings an action against P for $80,000 in a New York court of general jurisdiction for personal injuries suffered by D when he slipped on a banana peel while at P's restaurant in New York three weeks before the parties were initially introduced. P seeks to remove the state court action to the New York U.S. district court. Which of the following statements is correct?

I.   D's action may not be removed.

II. Assuming the state court action meets applicable subject matter jurisdiction requirements, it could be removed to the appropriate U.S. district court in New York.

III. D was not required to assert his action in the original federal court litigation initiated by P since it did not arise out of the same transaction or occurrence as P's action.

A. I only

B. II only

C. II and III

D. III only

18. Abel, a Colorado citizen, is injured when her car is hit by Chance, also a Colorado citizen. Chance is a minor who was served drinks illegally at a bar located in Wyoming owned by Baker, a Wyoming citizen. Abel brings an action in the only U.S. district court in Colorado against Baker, alleging negligence and breach of a statutory duty.

Thirty days after answering, Baker files a motion seeking leave to file a third-party claim (i.e., an impleader action) against Chance, based entirely upon Chance's unpaid bar bill, and failure to pay for a used car that Baker had sold to Chance. Which of the following statements is correct?

I.   The motion will be denied because Baker's claim does not assert that Chance may be liable to Baker on all or part of Abel's claim.

II. If the court finds that Baker may properly implead Chance, the federal rules will permit Chance to assert any claims he has against

Baker so long as doing so is consistent with principles of subject matter jurisdiction.

III. Chance cannot be made a party to the action by Baker because that would destroy diversity subject matter jurisdiction.

A. I only

B. II only

C. I and III

D. I and II

19. Paul, a citizen of Ohio, was involved in a three-car auto collision with Peter and Mary. Paul sued Peter and Mary in the only U.S. district court in Maine. The defendants were citizens of Maine. Paul's action against each defendant was for personal injuries in the amount of $70,000 and property damage in the amount of $9,000. Which of the following statements is correct?

I.   Paul might be permitted to assert a $1,000 breach of contract action against Mary.

II. Peter might be permitted to assert a $12,000 breach of contract action against Mary.

III. Paul's action should be dismissed because no single claim satisfies the "amount in controversy" requirement.

A. I only

B. II only

C. I and II

D. I and III

20. Railroad Corporation brings a class action in the U.S. District Court for the Eastern District of Ohio against the members of the United Railroad Fireman's Union ("Union"). The class action complaint names four officers of Union as class representatives. The action asserts that members of Union destroyed railroad property in Pennsylvania during a strike. The railroad seeks seeks an aggregate of over $5 million in damages against the class.

Railroad is a Pennsylvania corporation, which has its principal place of business in New York. Union is an unincorporated association that has its headquarters in Ohio, where the major portion of its administrative work is performed. All of the officers of Union are citizens of Pennsylvania. The membership of Union includes railroad employees who are domiciled in equal numbers in Michigan, New York, Pennsylvania, and Ohio.

Which of the following statements is true?

A. Venue is proper only in Ohio, assuming Union has sufficient contacts there to satisfy personal jurisdiction.

B. The action cannot be brought in a U.S. district court unless it is based on a federal claim.

C. Since this is an action involving an unincorporated labor organization, it is outside the subject matter jurisdiction of federal courts.

D. The federal court would have subject matter jurisdiction over the controversy.

21. Joan owns Riverdale, a palatial residence. Bill owns the adjoining residence. One day Matt, Bill's butler, started a fire on Bill's estate to burn some excess rubbish. Unfortunately, the fire got out of control and burned down Joan's residence. It also caused considerable damage to the rest of Riverdale. Joan sustained some injuries and was hospitalized for ten days. Joan files an action against Bill, in which she seeks damages in excess of $300,000 for property loss caused by the fire.

If Joan obtains a judgment against Bill, which of the following statements is correct?

A. Bill cannot sue Matt.

B. Any action by Joan against Matt is barred.

C. The judgment against Bill would not be binding upon Matt in a subsequent lawsuit by Joan against Matt.

D. Joan's claim against Bill for personal injuries is not barred by *res judicata* principles followed by a majority of jurisdictions because that claim was not litigated in the *Joan v. Bill* lawsuit.

22. Acme became involved in a labor dispute with the Steamroller's Union ("Union"), the entity that ordinarily supplied workers for Acme's plant. Acme commenced an action against Union in the appropriate U.S. district court, claiming $90,000 in damages as a consequence of Union's conduct in harassing and intimidating nonunion workers in violation of the National Labor Relations Act and applicable state law.

Acme is an Indiana corporation, and Union (an unincorporated association) has members domiciled in every state, except New York and New Jersey. Union answered by denying Acme's allegations and filing an $80,000 counterclaim that asserted that Acme deliberately made false accusations about Union to the local papers for the purpose of obtaining favorable press coverage. If Acme moves to dismiss Union's counterclaim for lack of subject matter jurisdiction, it should

A. lose, if Union's counterclaim is mandatory in nature.

B. prevail, if Union's counterclaim is permissive in nature.

C. prevail, since Acme has asserted a state cause of action.

D. lose, because diversity does not exist.

Questions 23–25 are based upon the following facts:

Paul was injured while operating a drill press manufactured by Manco. Paul properly commenced an action against Manco in the appropriate U.S. district court. Prior to trial, Paul sought discovery of a report that had been made to Manco by Brown, a claims investigator for Manco. Brown had inspected the machine and investigated the circumstances of the accident immediately thereafter. The machine was subsequently destroyed in a fire, and Brown has retired and moved, leaving no forwarding address.

In selecting the jury, the judge conducted the *voir dire*, but refused Manco's request that the judge ask the members of the jury panel whether any of them were prejudiced against corporations. A verdict was returned in favor of Paul for $75,000. Manco moved for a new trial.

The trial judge agreed to grant a new trial, unless Paul accepted a reduction in the verdict from $75,000 to $25,000. Paul agreed to the reduction under protest. Paul then appealed. He asserted as error the trial court's order granting a new trial unless he accepted a reduction in the verdict from $75,000 to $25,000.

23. Paul's request for Brown's report should be

    A. granted, because tangible items prepared in anticipation of litigation or trial are not discoverable.

    B. granted, even if prepared in anticipation of litigation or trial, provided Paul can show that there is a substantial need for the information and he is otherwise unable to obtain it without undue hardship.

    C. denied, because it was apparently prepared at Manco's request (rather than at the instigation of Manco's attorney).

    D. denied, if Manco procured the report at the suggestion of its legal counsel.

24. The trial judge's refusal to comply with Manco's request at the *voir dire* was

A. correct, because the question was irrelevant to the issues of the case.

B. correct, because Manco could have exercised a peremptory challenge against the potential juror.

C. erroneous, because prejudice against a party is a proper subject for inquiry at *voir dire.*

D. erroneous, because when the trial judge conducts the *voir dire*, he must ask any questions requested by counsel.

25. Paul's appeal from the order of remittitur should be

A. successful, since the court's order violated Paul's Seventh Amendment right to a trial by jury upon the issue of damages.

B. successful, unless the trial court abused its discretion in ordering a new trial if Paul had not agreed to the lessened sum.

C. unsuccessful, because Paul elected to accept the remittitur.

D. unsuccessful, because the Seventh Amendment does not apply to damage issues.

Questions 26–28 are based upon the following facts:

Ten college students in State X filed a class action in U.S. district court. The complaint requested that five specifically named state officials, the defendants, be enjoined from enforcing the state's flag desecration statute, which was alleged to be unconstitutional. The class that the plaintiffs sought to represent was all college students in State X. The defendants filed motions requesting that

(1) the complaint be dismissed on the grounds that the court lacked subject matter jurisdiction; and

(2) the court deny certification of the class.

26. The defendants' motion to dismiss for lack of subject matter jurisdiction should be

A. denied, because a First Amendment claim is involved.

B. denied, only if there is diversity of citizenship between the plaintiffs (representatives) and the defendants, and the amount claimed by each member of the plaintiff class satisfies the "amount in controversy" requirement.

C. granted, because no specific assertion has been made that each plaintiff has suffered damages in excess of $75,000.

    D. granted, if any member of the plaintiff class and any defendant are citizens of the same state.

27. The defendants' strongest argument to deny certification of the plaintiff class would probably be that

    A. the "numerosity" element is absent.

    B. the plaintiffs have failed to allege that each member of the prospective class will suffer damages in excess of $75,000.

    C. the representatives do not adequately represent the interests of the entire class.

    D. it would be impossible to individually notify each member of the proposed class by mail.

28. If the court refused to certify the class, which of the following would be true?

    A. The plaintiffs could immediately appeal the court's decision.

    B. The plaintiffs could not appeal immediately, but would be obliged to try the action on the merits as a nonclass action.

    C. The plaintiffs would waive any right to appeal if they elected to first try the case on its merits.

    D. The court would be obliged to dismiss the case.

Questions 29–31 are based upon the following facts:

Arnold and Bates, citizens of State Z, are plaintiffs in an action brought in the U.S. district court in State X against Manco, a State Y corporation, and Storeco, a State X corporation. Manco's office and plant are located in State Y. At no time has Manco had an office or sales staff in State X. Storeco's sole place of business is in State X.

The complaint alleges that each of the plaintiffs sustained serious personal injuries when a blade broke on an electric lawn mower while the equipment was being demonstrated by a clerk in Storeco's store in State X. Each plaintiff requested damages in the sum of $80,000. The mower had been manufactured by Manco and shipped to Roe in State Z. Roe had a contract with Manco to act as exclusive distributor of Manco products in 11 states, including X and Z.

Process was served personally on the president of Manco at Manco's office in State Y and on the president of Storeco at its office in State X. Thereafter, the following occurred:

    (1) Manco moved to dismiss the action on the ground that the court had no jurisdiction over it.

(2) Storeco filed a counterclaim against Arnold for $72,000 alleged to be due for merchandise previously sold to Arnold.

(3) Manco filed a cross-claim against Storeco for $12,000 alleged to be due for merchandise previously sold by Manco to Storeco.

29. The U.S. district court can assert *personal* jurisdiction over Manco:

   A. if State X has an appropriate long-arm statute, and the assertion of personal jurisdiction would comport with due process.

   B. if the assertion of personal jurisdiction would comport with due process. There is nationwide service of process in actions commenced in federal court.

   C. if the amount in controversy exceeds $75,000, exclusive of interest and costs.

   D. if process was served upon Manco in accordance with both federal and State X law.

30. A motion to strike Storeco's counterclaim should be

   A. dismissed, because there is supplemental jurisdiction.

   B. dismissed, because Arnold has implicitly consented to personal jurisdiction by commencing an action in State X.

   C. granted, because the amount owed to Storeco is only $72,000.

   D. granted, because Storeco's counterclaim is compulsory.

31. A motion to strike Manco's cross-claim against Storeco should be

   A. granted, because the cross-claim is unrelated to the plaintiff's action.

   B. granted, because Manco and Storeco are not adverse to one another.

   C. denied, if the court believes that Manco's action will not confuse or divert the jury with respect to the original claim.

   D. denied, because there is diversity subject matter jurisdiction with respect to Manco's cross-claim against Storeco.

32. You may assume that this jurisdiction has abandoned the "mutuality rule" pertaining to collateral estoppel.

   Paul is the executor of the estate of Carol. Paul files an action on behalf of the estate in an appropriate State X court against Doris (Carol's nurse) alleging that Doris converted Carol's money.

Although Doris was authorized to deposit funds into Carol's account at the local bank ("Bank"), Paul claims that Doris also withdrew funds for her own use. At trial, the jury found that Carol had made an *inter vivos* gift to Doris of the money in question.

Thereafter, Paul commenced an action against Bank in the applicable U.S. district court sitting in State X, alleging that the withdrawals by Doris were not authorized by Carol, and therefore Bank had breached its contractual relationship with Carol. Which of the following statements is correct?

A. There will be no collateral estoppel from the first case because that action was not commenced in a federal court.

B. Bank should be able to use the factual determination in favor of Doris in the first case as a shield to the claims of Paul in the second action.

C. Since Carol and Bank are in privity, Paul will be bound by the issues determined in the first case.

D. None of the above.

33. On behalf of herself and the 92 specific students in her class, P brought an FRCP 23(b)(2) class action against D, claiming that D had arbitrarily assigned final grades in a law school course by drawing names and numbers from two different hats.

P sought declaratory relief and an injunction, forcing the teacher to withdraw the original grades and submit a new set based upon actually having read the students' papers. While P was a citizen of State Z, all of her classmates and D were citizens of State Y. The suit was filed in a U.S. district court in State Y, which entered judgment for D after the jury found that P had failed to prove that D did not read the exams. The judgment was affirmed on appeal.

Thereafter, X, one of the students in the class who had received a grade of 65, brought an action against D in a State Z court, seeking $76,000 in damages for D's alleged failure to actually read X's exam, as a result of which X received his lowest grade in law school. Which of the following statements is correct?

A. The judgment rendered in the first action is not entitled to full faith and credit in the present suit, if the U.S. district court lacked subject matter jurisdiction.

B. The U.S. district court lacked subject matter jurisdiction because members of the plaintiff class and D were citizens of the same state (State Y).

C. Assuming the federal court had subject matter jurisdiction, D can preclude X from seeking to prove that D failed to read the exams, even though X's action seeks to recover monetary damages (rather than injunctive relief).

D. None of the above.

34. P and D had an automobile accident in State X. P, a citizen of State Y, sued D, a citizen of State X, in a State Y court of general jurisdiction. D had recently inherited some vacant land in State Y. D was also personally served with process at his home in State X. Assuming *Hess v. Pawloski* is no longer "good law," which of the following statements is correct?

I.   If State Y has a typical nonresident motorist statute, there is an adequate basis for obtaining personal jurisdiction over D.

II.   Even in the absence of a long-arm statute, most courts probably would hold that D's inheritance of property in State Y, coupled with notice of the suit by personal service, is sufficient for the exercise of personal jurisdiction over D in State Y.

A. I only

B. II only

C. I and II

D. Neither I nor II

35. P, who had been employed by D, was fired when D learned that P, who was unmarried, was living with Q. P and Q sued D in the appropriate U.S. district court. P sought $58,000 for breach of their employment contract, $10,000 for violation of a federal civil rights statute, and $9,000 for damages that D had caused to P's car after P loaned it to D earlier that year. Q claimed $12,000 in damages as a result of P's wrongful termination since she is now obliged to pay their entire apartment rental by herself. Prior to his discharge, P contributed one-half of the rental amount.

P and Q are both citizens of State X. D is a citizen of State Y. Which of the following statements is correct?

A. The FRCP do not allow all the claims of P and Q to be joined together in a single action.

B. A U.S. district court would have subject matter jurisdiction over Q's claim.

C. If P failed to assert the claim for damages to his car in this action, it would be barred.

D. None of the above.

36. In a three-car collision, P's car was rear-ended by D, who in turn was rear-ended by E. P brought an action against D in the U.S. district court in the state in which P was domiciled. P sought to recover $80,000 for damages to his Mercedes. D filed a counterclaim against P, seeking $1,152 for damages to his Volkswagen.

   D also filed two claims against E, the driver behind him, one seeking $80,000 in the event that D was liable to P, and the other seeking $1,152 for the damages caused to D's Volkswagen. P and D are both citizens of State X; E is a citizen of State Y. Judgment was entered for P against D, but all the other claims were found to be without merit.

   E has now filed a lawsuit against P and D in the U.S. district court in X, seeking $1 million for personal injuries suffered in the earlier auto accident. P and D have each counterclaimed, seeking $1 million for their own personal injuries, and have filed similar cross-claims against each other. Which of the following statements is correct?

   A. The court in the initial action lacked subject matter jurisdiction.

   B. Apart from any possible subject matter jurisdiction problems in the prior suit, E could have filed any claim arising out of the prior accident that he had against P.

   C. Apart from any possible subject matter jurisdiction problems in the prior suit, P and D may not assert their claims against each other in the present action.

   D. All of the above.

37. P brings an action against D, E, and F, asserting (1) infringement of copyright, and (2) breach of contract. Copyright actions are exclusively within the subject matter jurisdiction of federal courts.

   All of the claims arose from the defendants' having produced a television show based upon a script that P had written for them. P seeks to recover $80,000 from each of the defendants. All of the parties are citizens of California. Which of the following statements is correct?

   A. If this action is filed in a California state court, the defendants could have it removed to federal court.

   B. If this action is filed in federal court, dismissal for lack of subject matter jurisdiction would be required.

C. If this case goes to trial in a state court, and judgment is entered against P, P will have waived any lack of subject matter jurisdiction by failing to assert it before or during trial.

D. None of the above.

38. P, the publisher of a magazine, announced that D was the winner of a $5,000 prize for the best poem of the month. However, before P awarded the prize to D, P received a letter from E. E claimed he had written the poem and D's entry was stolen from him or F, E's agent.

P, a citizen of State X, brought a statutory interpleader action in the appropriate U.S. district court against D and E, seeking a declaratory judgment as to which of them was entitled to the prize money. D is a citizen of State Y, and E is a citizen of State X. Which of the following statements is correct?

A. The federal court lacks subject matter jurisdiction over this action.

B. E may file a third-party claim based upon negligence against his agent, F, a citizen of State X, seeking $5,000 from F in the event the prize money is awarded to D.

C. Venue is proper in either State X or Y.

D. None of the above.

39. Plaintiff, a citizen of Arizona, sued Defendant, a citizen of Washington State, in the U.S. district court in Arizona for breach of contract seeking $78,000 in damages. Defendant answered by denying that a contract was formed.

Plaintiff and Defendant stipulated that the jury would consist of eight persons. Trial was held, and seven jurors voted in favor of Plaintiff. One juror voted for Defendant. The jurors then deliberated on the amount of damages and rendered a verdict in favor of Plaintiff for $18,500. Defendant appealed the ruling. On which of the following grounds would Defendant be most likely to prevail on appeal?

A. The ruling was defective because it was rendered by less than twelve jurors.

B. The ruling was defective because it was based on a nonunanimous vote.

C. The court did not have subject matter jurisdiction because the verdict did not exceed $75,000.

D. The court lacked personal jurisdiction.

40. An automobile accident occurred in State Y involving P, Q, and a vehicle driven by an employee of D. The car in which P and Q were riding was a Ferrari, which they had purchased together for $79,000 (P contributing $40,000 towards the purchase price, and Q the remaining $39,000). The car was destroyed in the collision.

P and Q are citizens of State X, and D is a corporation organized under the laws of State Z, with its principal place of business in Y. It does business in all 50 states. One year after the accident, P and Q sued D to recover a total of $79,000 in damages for the loss of their car. Which of the following statements is correct?

A. If this suit was properly commenced in a state court in State Y, D could have the action removed to a federal court.

B. If this action was filed in the U.S. district court in State W, D probably could have the action transferred to a U.S. district court in State Y, and the federal court in State Y would then apply the statute of limitations that a state court in State Y would apply.

C. Subject matter jurisdiction does not exist because neither P nor Q had invested a sum in excess of $75,000 in the car.

D. None of the above.

Questions 41–42 are based upon the following facts:

Phil was driving his car in San Diego, California, when he was involved in an accident with Dowd. Phil is domiciled in San Diego. Dowd is a citizen of Alabama. The registered owner of the car Dowd was driving is Ellwood (a citizen of Kentucky). Phil filed a timely action against Dowd in the appropriate U.S. district court in California. The complaint contained a proper subject matter jurisdiction allegation.

41. The complaint alleged only that there was a collision between the cars driven by Phil and Dowd, and that Phil suffered personal injuries and property damage in the amount of $85,000. If Dowd filed a motion to dismiss for failure to state a claim upon which relief could be granted, the court would probably

A. grant the motion, without leave to amend.

B. overrule the motion, since the allegations of Phil's complaint are sufficient to state a claim on which relief can be granted.

C. overrule the motion, since Phil's complaint fails to identify the legal theory upon which his claim is predicated.

D. grant the motion, but only if the applicable statute of limitations under California law had expired subsequent to the filing.

42. The complaint contained a proper subject matter jurisdiction allegation and asserted that (1) the collision was caused by Dowd's negligence in driving into the rear of Phil's car while Phil was lawfully stopped at a red light; or (2) alternatively, the collision was caused by Dowd's negligence in driving through a red light and into Phil while the latter was lawfully driving through an intersection. If Dowd filed a motion to dismiss for failure to state a cause of action upon which relief can be granted, the court would probably

A. grant the motion, on grounds of inconsistency.

B. grant the motion, since Phil has pleaded a legal conclusion (i.e., that Dowd was negligent in his conduct).

C. overrule the motion, since alternative grounds for relief are permissible under the FRCP.

D. overrule the motion, but require Phil to strike one of the inconsistent claims.

43. P is a citizen of New York who works in New Jersey. D and E are citizens of New Jersey who work in that state. One day, D borrowed E's car, advising E that he intended to use it to pick up his sister in Trenton (the capital of New Jersey).

However, D drove to New York to take a new girlfriend to Coney Island (which is in Brooklyn, New York). Unfortunately, D became involved in a traffic accident with P while driving in New York City.

P brought an action against E in the proper U.S. district court in New York for personal injuries and property damages in the amount of $80,000. A New York statute permits an action against the owner of a motor vehicle when he loaned the car to the person who was driving it when the incident occurred. If E makes an FRCP 12(b)(2) motion to dismiss the action for lack of personal jurisdiction, he should:

A. prevail, since the assertion of personal jurisdiction over him probably would violate due process.

B. lose the motion, but the court may possibly require Phil to amend the complaint to make it more definite.

C. lose, because federal courts have nationwide service of process.

D. prevail, if the applicable statute of limitations under New York state law had expired subsequent to commencement of the suit.

44. P is incorporated in State X, but has its principal place of business in State Z. P does substantial business in every state except W. P filed an action against D Insurance Company and E. D is a corporation existing under the laws of State Y, where it has its principal place of business. D also does business in States X and Z. E, a natural person, is a citizen of Ontario, Canada.

P's claim against E arises out of a fire occurring at P's plant in State X. P's claim against D is for breach of contract, based upon D's refusal to pay P the proceeds under a fire insurance policy that P had purchased from D. Both claims are for $100,000. Which of the following statements is correct?

I.   If this action were filed in the U.S. district court for State Y, subject matter jurisdiction would exist and venue would be proper.

II.   If this action was properly commenced in a State W court, the defendants could remove the action to the appropriate U.S. district court, even though the action could not have been commenced in a U.S. district court in State W.

III. P's joinder of D and E in one action is not proper since P is asserting two distinct causes of action.

A. I alone

B. III alone

C. I and II

D. None of the above

45. P suffered permanent personal injuries in an auto accident with D and E. D and E were each driving separate cars. X, P's insurance company, paid P the maximum limit of $100,000 under the policy.

Having collected from her insurance company, P then brought an action against D in the proper U.S. district court, seeking $500,000 for her personal injuries. Assume the "collateral source" rule is in effect in this jurisdiction (i.e., a plaintiff's recovery in tort from a defendant is **not** diminished by any insurance or other collateral sources that reimbursed the former for all or any portion of her damages). P is a citizen of State X, and D and E are citizens of State Y. Which of the following statements is correct?

I.   D may object to P's bringing this action on the ground that the insurance company, rather than P, is the real party in interest (under the insurance agreement, X is subrogated to P's rights to the extent that P's claim against D is paid by X).

II. If D contends that the accident was caused exclusively by the negligence of E, D may implead E seeking to recover $77,000 from the latter for the damages that E caused to D's car.

III. Whether or not D files a claim against E, E may intervene as of right as a defendant and file actions for her damages against both P and D.

A. I and II only

B. II and III only

C. III only

D. None of the above

46. Delbert liked to cut across Pat's land on his way to law school. Pat, however, disliked Delbert because Delbert had become somewhat arrogant since he made Law Review. When Pat asked Delbert to cease using the shortcut, he responded that his time was "extremely valuable" and therefore it was a "private necessity."

Pat instituted an action against Delbert in the appropriate U.S. district court, demanding that Delbert be enjoined from using her land. You may assume that competency and jurisdictional requisites are satisfied. Although her real property had not been damaged by Delbert's constant encroachments, she also requested nominal monetary damages. Which of the following statements is correct?

A. Delbert is entitled to a jury trial with respect to the trespass issue.

B. Delbert is not entitled to a jury trial on the trespass claim since the primary relief Pat is seeking is an injunction.

C. As a consequence of the "clean-up doctrine," the court, in its discretion, may decide both the legal and equitable issues.

D. There is no right to a jury trial because trespass was not a "suit at common law" under the Seventh Amendment.

47. P, a citizen of State X, and Q, a citizen of State Y, sued D, a citizen of State Z for breach of contract occurring in State Z. The action was filed in the U.S. district court in State Y, and D was *improperly* served. Upon learning of the suit, D made a successful motion to transfer the case to the U.S. district court in State Z. Which of the following statements is correct?

A. The federal court properly transferred the action to State Z.

B. The federal court in State Y should have dismissed the action because venue in the U.S. district court in State Y was improper.

C. The federal court in State Y should have denied D's motion to transfer the case since he was improperly served.

D. None of the above.

Questions 48–50 are based upon the following facts:

E, a State X corporation, designed a building for Smith, a citizen of State Y, six years ago. Part of that building collapsed last year, causing damage in excess of $80,000.

Smith filed an action against E in the U.S. district court in State X, alleging that his damages resulted from the negligent design of the building. E filed an answer denying negligence and asserting as an affirmative defense that the statute of limitations for negligence is two years.

At the time the building was being constructed, Jones, an attorney and member of E's board of directors who occasionally handled legal matters for E, prepared and sent the following memorandum to the president of E:

> I have been informed by Tom Withers, an architect who used to work for E, that the materials being used by the contractor, Builder Corp., in constructing the building are substandard.

Smith filed a timely motion for pretrial production of the Jones memorandum. The motion was denied.

Smith filed a timely motion for summary judgment, relying on an affidavit made by Withers that set forth facts consistent with Jones's memorandum. E also filed a motion for summary judgment, accompanied by an affidavit that the building had been constructed six years ago. Both motions were denied.

48. If E asserted the work product privilege in response to Smith's motion for production of Jones' memorandum:

A. E should prevail, because Jones was an attorney.

B. E should prevail, because it reflects Jones's impressions about E's potential liability.

C. Smith should prevail, because it is relevant to his action.

D. Smith should prevail, if Jones is not representing E in the present action.

49. Smith's motion for summary judgment was properly denied

A. because, based upon Withers's affidavit, genuine issues of fact remain as to causation.

B. because Withers's affidavit did not address E's affirmative defense.

C. for the reasons set forth in (A) and (B).

D. for neither of the reasons set forth in (A) or (B).

50. E's motion for a summary judgment was

A. improperly denied, because the building was constructed six years ago.

B. improperly denied, because Smith failed to file a responsive affidavit.

C. properly denied, because the accident occurred only recently.

D. properly denied if E has the burden of proof with respect to its statute of limitations defense.

51. P and D were involved in a car accident in Texas. P is a citizen of State X, and D is a citizen of New York. The State X service of process statute is similar to FRCP 4. P sued D in a State X court of general jurisdiction. P served D by sending, via first-class mail, the summons and complaint to D in New York. D received these documents, but failed to respond to them. P then obtained a default judgment. If P sought to enforce the judgment in New York:

A. the judgment should be given full faith and credit by a New York court since D had actually received the summons and complaint.

B. D may collaterally attack the judgment for insufficient service of process.

C. the judgment should be given full faith and credit because a default judgment is usually deemed to be "on the merits."

D. choices (A) and (C) are correct, but (B) is not.

52. P commenced an action against D in a State X court of general jurisdiction. D is a citizen of State Z, and P is a citizen of State X. D owned a boat that he kept at a pier in State X.

Pursuant to State X law, P obtained an attachment against D's boat. When properly served with notice of the attachment, D moved to quash it. The boat is probably worth $20,000. P's action is for breach of contract and alleges damages in the amount of $15,000. Which of the following statements is correct?

A. The attachment should be quashed if a State X court could not constitutionally assume personal jurisdiction over D.

B. Prejudgment attachments are *per se* unconstitutional.

C. If D's motion was denied, P could apply all of the proceeds from the sale of the boat to his obligation.

D. Choices (A) and (B) are correct, but (C) is not.

53. P, a citizen of Utah, was involved in an auto accident with D, a citizen of Minnesota. The accident occurred in Utah.

Pursuant to the applicable Utah long-arm statute, P sued D in a Utah state court of general jurisdiction for $80,000. P also named C as a defendant. C was D's insurer. Pursuant to Utah law, this type of action was permissible. C is incorporated in Delaware and has its principal place of business in Utah.

D's petition to remove the case to the applicable U.S. district court should be

A. granted, because D is not a citizen of Utah.

B. denied, because C's principal place of business is Utah.

C. denied, unless C joins in the petition.

D. granted, because the amount in controversy requirement is satisfied.

54. Dr. Dumb, a citizen of State A, performed emergency surgery upon Pam, a citizen of State B, for which he charged $5,000. Pam was injured during the surgery. She filed a negligence lawsuit against Dr. Dumb in the appropriate U.S. district court in State A for $90,000. Dr. Dumb impleads Insurance Company, a corporation incorporated in State B and doing business in States A and B, for payment on his malpractice insurance policy if Pam should win her lawsuit. Which of the following causes of action may be joined?

    I.   A $3,000 counterclaim by Dr. Dumb against Pam for damage done when Pam, angry at the results of the operation, broke three of Dr. Dumb's office windows, if the counterclaim is deemed "permissive."

    II.   A claim by Pam against Insurance Company for the nonpayment of a $76,000 claim on an insurance policy she maintained with Insurance Company when her car was stolen, if Insurance Company's principal place of business is in State A.

A. I only

B. II only

C. I and II

D. Neither I nor II

55. A (plaintiff) properly commenced a diversity action in the applicable U.S. district court against B. A claimed that he and B had entered a valid contract, that B had repudiated the agreement, and that as a consequence A had sustained economic losses in the amount of $90,000. B denied the existence of a contractual agreement.

At trial, B attempted to introduce evidence that A had made an anticipatory repudiation of the alleged agreement prior to the time that B's performance was due. If this assertion is correct, B would have an affirmative defense to A's action (even if a valid contract had been formed).

If A made a timely objection to the introduction of B's evidence pertaining to anticipatory repudiation:

A. his objection must be sustained, because the evidence is outside the pleadings.

B. the evidence may be admitted, in the discretion of the court.

C. the objection must be sustained, because amendments to pleadings cannot be made after trial has been commenced.

D. the evidence must be admitted, since it is relevant to B's defense. However, if it is admitted, A is entitled to a continuance to meet such evidence.

56. The State X Rules of Civil Procedure are equivalent to the FRCP. Paul sued Donna in a State X court, alleging that, at Donna's home, Donna hit Paul on the head with a hammer and that Paul suffered injuries in the amount of $15,000. Donna moved to dismiss the case, but her motion was denied.

Paul then amended his complaint to add as damages the lost wages resulting from having to miss work. Donna answered by denying that she hit Paul and, as an affirmative defense, claimed that she hit Paul because he was attacking her.

Paul then moved for summary judgment based on an affidavit signed by his cousin, Bill, stating that Paul told him Donna struck Paul out of jealousy (rather than because Paul was attacking her). Which of the following statements is correct?

A. Donna's motion to dismiss should have been granted since Paul did not state his legal theory.

B. Donna's pleadings are defective because they are inconsistent, answering that she did not hit Paul and also stating as a defense the reason why she had hit Paul.

C. Paul's amendment is permissible, even without leave of court.

D. Paul's summary judgment motion should be granted because it was supported by an affidavit.

57. X, a citizen of Oregon, sued Y, a large Colorado corporation doing business only in Colorado. The action asserted that Y failed to provide training, support, and service for a $85,000 computer system that Y had sold to X.

X sued Y in the U.S. district court in Oregon. Although the contract was accepted and signed in Colorado, there was a provision that stipulated that in the event of litigation, Y could be sued by X in Oregon. Y moved for transfer of the action to the U.S. district court in Colorado, claiming that its training, support, and service personnel, who would be witnesses, are domiciled in Colorado. The Colorado damage remedies are more favorable to Y than the corresponding rules in Oregon.

Which of the following statements is correct?

A. Transfer of the action probably will be granted.

B. If Y's motion is granted, the law of Oregon regarding damages will be applied.

C. The provision stipulating that Y would stand trial in Oregon is unconstitutional if Y did not have "minimum contacts" with Oregon.

D. None of the above.

58. Daleon Motors, a Delaware corporation that has its principal place of business in Michigan, created the Daleon automobile. Approximately 3,000 of these vehicles were sold before it was discovered that the brake lining was defective. As a consequence, the car became virtually undrivable after about 500 miles. Paul, a citizen of Rhode Island, purchased a new Daleon automobile in that state.

Paul commenced an FRCP 23(b)(3) class action in the U.S. district court for Rhode Island against Daleon on behalf of all of the purchasers of automobile, contending that the plaintiff class is entitled to return of the purchase price for fraud. Daleon Motors had advertised its car as being the "safest" in the world. Each Daleon car cost $77,000.

After Paul commenced the action, Daleon claimed that its offices had been broken into and its records of Daleon purchasers destroyed. Paul personally knows of two other purchasers of Daleon cars. One is a citizen of New Mexico and the other is a citizen of Delaware.

Which of the following statements is correct?

A. Daleon could successfully make a motion to dismiss the class action, since at least one of the purchasers is a citizen of Delaware.

B. Notice to the prospective class by publication in the major newspapers throughout the country probably will be permissible (except that mailing to the two known buyers will be required).

C. Notice to the class may be dispensed with in light of the suspicious destruction of the names and addresses of prospective class members while such data was within Daleon's possession.

D. None of the above.

59. P sued Amusement Company for injuries sustained when she fell while getting off a ferris wheel at the Amusement Company's park. The lock holding the seat had prematurely broken open. At P's suggestion, her boyfriend immediately took pictures of the broken lock. Since the park was still open, Amusement Company hired a locksmith to replace the lock that same afternoon. The locksmith had to completely disassemble the broken lock. P's attorney hired an expert locksmith to prepare a report and testify at trial regarding the defective nature of the lock.

Amusement Company moved to discover the report prepared by P's expert and the pictures taken by P's boyfriend of the broken lock. P claims both the pictures and the report are covered by the work product privilege.

Which of the following statements is correct?

A. Amusement Company may not view the pictures or the report.

B. Amusement Company may view the pictures and obtain the report.

C. Amusement Company may view the pictures, but not obtain the report.

D. Amusement Company may not view the pictures, but may obtain the report.

60. Acme is a Georgia corporation that has its principal place of business in Alabama. Polly used to live in Alabama and work at Acme's Arkansas plant. However, she was recently terminated from her employment with Acme. She consulted an attorney, who advised her that her termination was wrongful under a law recently enacted by Congress. The lawyer also informed Polly that Georgia had the most liberal procedures for prosecuting this type of action.

Polly moved to Georgia, where she is now working as a waitress, and commenced an action in the appropriate state court against Acme for wrongful termination under the applicable U.S. law and a similar Georgia statute. Polly seeks $80,000 in damages. Acme filed a petition to remove the case to the U.S. district court in Georgia.

The petition should be

A. denied, because Polly moved to Georgia only for the purpose of acquiring a more advantageous forum for litigation.

B. denied, because there is a lack of diversity.

C. granted, because one of her actions is a federal claim.

D. granted, because there is no diversity of citizenship because citizenship is determined at the time the cause of action arose.

61. Each of 20 persons who are domiciled throughout Texas, Oklahoma, and Nebraska, asserted a claim of $25,000 against XYZ Corporation, a Maryland corporation. Their joinder of claims is based upon the assertion that fumes from XYZ's plant in Arkansas caused them minor respiratory problems. XYZ's principal place of business is in Maryland. May the twenty persons sue XYZ Corporation in a U.S. district court?

A. Yes, but only if their claim is based upon a federal statute.

B. Yes, because plaintiffs suing on related claims can aggregate their claims to satisfy the amount in controversy requirement.

C. Yes, because diversity of citizenship exists between each plaintiff and XYZ.

D. Yes, but only if there is diversity of citizenship between all the plaintiff's and XYZ.

62. P was injured when he attempted to rescue X from a burning car. X and Y had collided at an intersection. P sued Y in the appropriate U.S. district court, but not X. Y claims that X's conduct was the exclusive cause of the accident, which resulted in injury to P, and moves to join X in the action. Under applicable state law, if X is not named as a defendant and X and Y were joint and several tortfeasors, Y would have no right of contribution from X.

P is a citizen of Minnesota, Y is a citizen of Vermont, and X is a citizen of Minnesota. Y's motion should be

A. granted, because there is a common nucleus of operative facts.

B. granted, because X is or may be liable to Y if Y is found liable to X.

C. denied, because X is not an indispensable party.

D. denied, because joinder of X would destroy subject matter juris-diction.

63. Arnold borrowed $76,000 from Bill and signed a promissory note in which he promised to repay that sum, plus interest, in six months. Chuck guaranteed the note and promised to pay the sum due to Bill in the event Arnold defaulted. Arnold became delinquent under the note, and Bill sued Arnold. Arnold asserted a usury defense to Bill's claim. Which of the following statements is correct?

A. A judgment in favor of Bill is *res judicata* as to Chuck.

B. A judgment in favor of Bill would result in issue preclusion against Chuck as to those issues that had been fully litigated in *Bill v. Arnold*.

C. If Arnold won on the issue of usury, Chuck probably could assert collateral estoppel in an action brought by Bill against Chuck on the guaranty.

D. None of the above.

64. Paul loaned $77,000 to Jim. Ralph guaranteed the loan. Subsequently, Jim became delinquent in his payments. Paul sued Jim in the appropriate U.S. district court. Paul is a citizen of State X, Jim is a citizen of State Y, and Ralph is a citizen of State X. Which of the following statements is correct?

A. Ralph is an indispensable party because Jim could otherwise be liable for the full amount of Paul's judgment.

B. The court probably would permit Ralph to intervene on Jim's side, if Ralph chose to do so.

C. Ralph may intervene on Jim's side as of right since otherwise he could be precluded from raising any issues that were fully and fairly litigated in Paul's action against Jim (if Paul subsequently sued Ralph on the guarantee).

D. None of the above.

65. Polly, a citizen of Nevada, purchased $7,000 of ABC Corporation securities from her broker, Don, also a citizen of Nevada. However, because ABC was insolvent, the securities were later shown to be worthless. Polly sued Don in the appropriate U.S. district court for violation of federal securities law. Which of the following claims or actions may be joined or occur in Polly's suit against Don?

I.   *Polly v. Don* for injuries caused when Don's car rear-ended Polly's car following a party that they had both attended.

II. *Don v. ABC Corporation*, a Nevada corporation, if, as part of their contract, the latter entity warranted its solvency to Don.

A. I only

B. II only

C. I and II

D. Neither I nor II

66. P sues D for trespass at her Los Angeles residence. The action was properly commenced in a U.S. district court. D defends by claiming that he was in New York at the time when the incident allegedly took place. D intends to call Wanda as a witness to testify that she saw him in New York on the day in question. P believes Wanda is hopelessly nearsighted and could easily have mistaken someone else for D.

    To impeach Wanda's testimony, P sends Wanda a Notice to Appear for Medical Examination before a licensed ophthalmologist selected by P. Which of the following statements is correct?

    A. W must appear, but D is entitled to a copy of the ophthalmologist's findings.

    B. W must appear since her eyesight is in issue.

    C. W need not appear because she is not a party to the action.

    D. W need not appear because physicians making medical examinations must be selected by the judge.

67. Denny, a citizen of Texas, leased an apartment from Polly, a citizen of California, under a one-year rental agreement at $500 per month. The rental agreement states that Denny may not sublet the premises to any person of Asian ancestry. With six months remaining on the lease, Denny sublet the apartment to an individual of Chinese ancestry.

    Polly sued Denny in the appropriate U.S. district court for breach of contract, seeking to evict Denny and recover the remaining six months' rent. The complaint states that Denny violated the terms of the rental agreement and asserts that the clause concerning subletting does **not** violate the U.S. Constitution. Denny moves to dismiss the case for lack of subject matter jurisdiction.

    With respect to Denny's motion:

    A. Denny will win because subject matter jurisdiction based upon a federal claim is lacking.

B. Denny will win because subject matter jurisdiction based upon diversity is lacking.

C. Both (A) and (B).

D. Denny will lose.

68. Mel is an investment banker. He handles the accounts of Ms. Wine and Ms. Ball. Mel decided to invest some of their money in a new entrepreneurial enterprise he had just started. Unfortunately, things did not go well. In a period of months, all of Wine's and Ball's money was gone.

    Ball sued Mel for breach of fiduciary duty. She recovered a default judgment for the full amount of her claim. Which of the following statements is correct?

    A. Ball's judgment is *res judicata* with respect to a subsequent lawsuit by Wine against Mel.

    B. Assuming the mutuality doctrine is inapplicable, a court may permit Wine to assert collateral estoppel in a subsequent lawsuit by Wine against Mel.

    C. Ball's judgment should have no effect on a subsequent lawsuit by Wine against Mel.

    D. None of the above.

69. P sues as the sole representative of a class of persons who had brought limited partnership interests in worthless oil producing property from D. P alleges that all purchasers received identical written sales materials (which contained numerous misrepresentations), and that many members of the class also received verbal "pitches" that were also fraudulent.

    P commenced an FRCP 23(b)(3) class action based upon diversity subject matter jurisdiction against D in the appropriate U.S. district court. The aggregate damages of the class total $2.5 million. Which of the following statements is correct?

    A. If the court refuses to certify the proposed class, P may appeal the decision immediately.

    B. Assuming the class is certified, P may enter into a settlement agreement with D, as long as notice is given to all members of the class and a majority approve of the compromise.

    C. Assuming the class is certified, if P prevails in the suit, he is not entitled to recover attorney fees, unless a federal statute explicitly provides for such an award.

    D. None of the above.

70. Art and Bob were riding in a car driven by Art when they were suddenly rear-ended by Oscar. Art is a citizen of Illinois, and Oscar is a citizen of Ohio. Art commenced a lawsuit in the appropriate U.S. district court in Ohio (where the accident had occurred), claiming $80,000 in injuries and damages as a result of the occurrence. Bob (a citizen of Ohio) seeks to intervene as a plaintiff. However, his injuries were far less severe than those suffered by Art. Bob has been informed by his attorney that he probably would not be able to recover more than $11,000.

    Bob's motion to intervene should be

    A. granted, because there is supplemental jurisdiction.
    B. granted, because he is an indispensable party.
    C. denied, because there is no subject matter jurisdiction over his claim against Oscar.
    D. denied, unless Bob believes in good faith that his attorney's calculation of potential damages is incorrect.

71. Bill and Jane were riding in a car owned by Ellwood. Bill is a citizen of Georgia, and Jane is a citizen of Arkansas. They were involved in an accident in Tennessee with Carl (a citizen of Alabama). Ellwood's insurer, Insurco, is a Georgia corporation, which has its principal place of business in Alabama. Ellwood is a citizen of Texas. Melvin, a citizen of Alabama, who was visiting his aunt in Tennessee when the accident occurred, was injured while extricating Bill and Jane from their vehicle.

    Melvin and Carl have threatened to sue Ellwood, contending that he is vicariously liable for the alleged negligence of Jane (who was driving the car). Insurco contends that it is not liable for Jane's driving, but commences an interpleader action against Bill, Jane, Carl, Ellwood, and Melvin in the U.S. district court in Alabama. The policy limit of Ellwood's insurance is $75,000. Carl and Melvin claim personal injuries in excess of that amount.

    Which of the following statements is correct?

    A. The action is appropriate under "statutory" interpleader.
    B. The action is appropriate under "rule" interpleader.
    C. Under statutory or rule interpleader, the U.S. district court would be obliged to refer to the long-arm statute enacted in Tennessee to determine if personal jurisdiction could be asserted over the defendants.

D. Interpleader is inappropriate since Insurco is contending that it is not liable under the policy.

Questions 72–74 are based on the following facts:

Joan visited Dr. Brown. After examining her, he put some drops in her left ear. She then left. However, she continued to have difficulties with her balance. Three weeks after her visit to Dr. Brown, Joan fell and sustained serious injuries. Joan sued Dr. Brown and requested a jury trial. The action was properly commenced in a U.S. district court.

At trial, Joan testified to the foregoing, and then called Dr. Edward to the stand. He testified that, in his opinion, (1) he had examined Joan and found substantial damage to her inner ear, and (2) the damage was caused by a fluid containing acid. Joan rested her case. Dr. Brown took the stand and testified that (1) Joan had been suffering from an infection that affected the inner ear, and (2) he had put some drops of perforium (an innocuous, nonacidic substance) into her ear. He further stated on cross-examination that the bottle containing perforium stood in the vicinity of a bottle containing an acidic substance. He then rested his case. In rebuttal, Joan called Dr. Edward, who stated that the injury to Joan's inner ear is totally inconsistent with Dr. Brown's assertion of an infection. All sides then rested.

72. If Joan moves for judgment as a matter of law:
    A. Her motion should be granted because Dr. Brown admitted that the perforium bottle stood near a bottle containing an acidic substance.
    B. Her motion should be granted, but not for the reason set forth in (A).
    C. Her motion should be denied.
    D. None of the above.

73. Assume that Dr. Brown (rather than Joan) moved for a judgment as a matter of law, and that the motion was granted. Joan then appeals. The court of appeals should
    A. reverse the judgment and order a new trial.
    B. reverse the judgment and direct that judgment be entered for Joan.
    C. affirm the judgment.
    D. None of the above.

74. Assume neither party moved for a judgment as a matter of law. The case goes to the jury, which returns a verdict for Joan. Dr. Brown then moves for a judgment notwithstanding the verdict ("JNOV") and, in the alternative, for a new trial. The trial judge grants the motion for a JNOV, but denies the motion for a new trial. Joan then

appeals the JNOV granted by the trial court. The court of appeals should

A. reverse the judgment since a motion for a new trial cannot be joined with a JNOV.

B. affirm the judgment.

C. reverse the judgment, but order a new trial.

D. reverse the judgment and reinstate the verdict for Joan.

75. X, a citizen of Kentucky, entered into a contract to sell a car to Z, also a citizen of Kentucky. However, when Z was late in tendering a prepayment, X advised Z that he was no longer bound to complete the transaction. Z unequivocally informed X that the contract was still binding. Prior to the due date for delivery of the automobile under the original agreement, X entered into a new transaction with Y, whereby X agreed to sell the vehicle to Y for a higher amount than had been agreed to by Z.

Y is a citizen of Ohio. Y was aware of the outstanding contract that X had with Z, but was assured by the former that Z's right in the automobile had been lawfully terminated. X subsequently repudiated his contract with Y, contending it was entered into under coercive circumstances. Y commenced an action against X in the appropriate U.S. district court for specific performance and breach of contract. X moved to dismiss upon the ground that Z was an indispensable party. The court will probably

A. grant the motion, because Z has an interest in the vehicle.

B. grant the motion, because Z entered into an agreement with X for purchase of the car prior to Y.

C. deny the motion, because Z ought to be joined and Z's joinder will be within the court's subject matter jurisdiction.

D. deny the motion, because Z is not a party who should be joined.

Questions 76–78 are based on the following facts:

Paul was a citizen of South Dakota. He was an employee of Construction Company ("CC"), a Colorado corporation. Paul was killed when some scaffolding collapsed on a CC project in Colorado. The scaffolding had been provided by a subcontractor for the job, Big Builders (a U.S. corporation). Paul's wife, Mary, as the executrix of his estate, sued CC in an appropriate U.S. district court in Colorado. She claimed that CC had been negligent in failing to inspect the defective scaffolding supplied by Big Builders. Colorado law provides that a general contractor is presumed to have not inspected materials supplied to it by a subcontractor. This presumption is rebuttable. At the time of his death, Paul owed CC $7,000 in advanced wages. The amount claimed by Mary is $1 million.

76. Which of the following statements is correct?

  A. Big Builders may intervene as of right.

  B. CC can implead Big Builders, if personal jurisdiction requirements are satisfied.

  C. CC could assert a counterclaim for the advance in wages that it made to Paul.

  D. None of the above.

77. At the trial, CC introduced evidence showing that Paul had been warned by his supervisor not to work near the scaffolding until it had been thoroughly checked since it looked unsafe. Paul had disregarded the supervisor's instruction. Mary then produced a witness who testified that Paul had always objected to working close to scaffolding. If no further evidence was introduced by either side:

  A. CC's motion for a judgment as a matter of law would have to be granted.

  B. CC's motion for a judgment as a matter of law would have to be denied.

  C. Mary's motion for a judgment as a matter of law would have to be granted.

  D. If the jury rendered a verdict for CC, Mary's motion for a JNOV must be granted.

78. Assume that (1) each side introduced substantial evidence pertaining to whether CC had adequately inspected the scaffolding, and (2) the case was tried by the judge. Following the trial, the judge entered findings of fact and conclusions of law. The judge found that CC had adequately inspected the scaffolding and that, therefore, Mary was entitled to nothing. Based upon the foregoing:

  A. the judgment must be set aside because it is clearly erroneous.

  B. the judgment must be set aside because it is inconsistent with the applicable presumption.

  C. the finding of fact must be set aside because there was substantial evidence that controverted it.

  D. None of the above.

79. Paul was rear-ended by John, a 17-year-old. The car that John was driving was owned by Mary. Paul is a citizen of Vermont. John and

Mary (who is John's mother) are citizens of Maine. The accident occurred in Vermont. Paul sued Mary and John in the U.S. district court in Maine pursuant to a Vermont statute that made parents liable for the negligent driving of their minor children. The suit demanded $90,000 in damages. Which of the following statements is correct?

A. Mary may assert a cross-claim against John.

B. If Mary fails to assert a cross-claim against John, any claim by her against him will be barred.

C. Mary may not assert a cross-claim against John.

D. Mary may assert a counterclaim against John.

Questions 80–81 are based on the following fact situation:

Albert wrote a best-selling book called *The Trials and Tribulations of a First-Year Law Student* . He began to suspect that the book's publisher, Beacon House, a Virginia corporation whose principal place of business is in that state, was not giving him an accurate accounting of his royalties.

Albert invaded a meeting of the nine-member board of directors of Beacon House, where he found Don (a member of the board of directors and the president of Beacon House). When Albert verbally accused Don of cheating him by underreporting the number of sales for Albert's books, Don grabbed Albert by the shoulders and shouted, "Shut up, you idiot!" Albert then punched Don in the face and left. Albert went to the local newspaper, the *Star* , and advised reporters there that he had been cheated out of thousands of dollars by Don.

Star printed a story reiterating Don's accusations and warning writers about publishers. The story mentioned that Don was the president of Beacon House. Albert is a citizen of Arizona, Don is a citizen of Massachusetts, and *Star* is incorporated in New York and has its principal place of business in Arizona.

80. Assume that *Star* was sued by Beacon House for defamation in the U.S. district court in Arizona. The lawsuit alleged damages of $500,000. Which of the following statements is correct?

A. Principles of subject matter jurisdiction would prevent *Star* from impleading Albert.

B. Albert can intervene as of right on the side of *Star*.

C. *Star* may implead Albert on the ground that he is solely liable to Beacon House.

D. *Star* may implead Albert, but only if the applicable substantive law creates a basis for indemnification of *Star* by Albert.

81. Assume that (1) Beacon House sued both *Star* and Albert for defamation in the only U.S. district court in Arizona, claiming damages in the amount of $100,000; (2) the "mutuality rule" for collateral estoppel has been abandoned in this jurisdiction; and (3) a verdict was returned in favor of Beacon House in the amount of $50,000. Which of the following statements is correct?

    A. *Star* could not file a cross-claim against Albert because they are citizens of the same state.

    B. If Albert counterclaimed against Beacon House for an accounting on his royalties, he would not be entitled to a jury trial.

    C. Don might be able to assert collateral estoppel offensively against *Star* in a subsequent action for defamation against that entity.

    D. Don would be barred from commencing an action against *Star* or Albert since he could have intervened in the present action (*Beacon House v. Star & Albert*) without destroying diversity.

82. X left a will creating a trust for the benefit of A, B, C and D, with T as trustee. A owns 25 percent of the trust, B owns 25 percent, C owns 25 percent, and D owns 25 percent. A, B, and C are citizens of California; D and T are citizens of Ohio. A, B, and C sue T in the U.S. district court in Ohio, based on diversity, for distribution of the $10 million trust, claiming that the terms of the trust require immediate distribution of the rest. T interprets the provisions of the trust to permit distribution only after three additional years. For tax purposes, D is content to have the trust continue for three more years.

T moves to dismiss the action for failure to join D as an indispensable party. The motion should be

    A. denied, because diversity is not defeated as long as any defendant is diverse from any plaintiff and the amount in controversy exceeds $75,000.

    B. denied, because D's interests are more consistent with T's.

    C. granted, because there will be a lack of diversity if D is joined as a plaintiff.

    D. granted, because D is an indispensable party.

83. Plaintiff sued Defendant in a State X court. The FRCP are followed in State X. Plaintiff seeks to recover for personal injuries suffered as a result of a battery inflicted upon him by Defendant. Defendant simply denied Plaintiff's allegations. Plaintiff demanded a trial by jury. Along with the forms for a general verdict, the court submitted written interrogatories to the jury. In answering these interrogatories, the jury found that (1) Defendant had hit Plaintiff with a vase; (2) that Defendant intended to so hit Plaintiff; and (3) that Defendant caused Plaintiff damages as alleged in the complaint. The jury also returned a judgment against Plaintiff.

The judge then ordered a new trial. Plaintiff then filed a stipulation of voluntary dismissal, which was also signed by Defendant. Which of the following statements is correct?

A. Plaintiff may later bring an action against Defendant on the same facts.

B. Where the jury's answers to interrogatories conflict with a general verdict, the judge must enter a verdict in conformity with such answers.

C. Where a jury's answer to interrogatories conflict with a general verdict, the judge must (1) enter the general verdict, or (2) order a new trial.

D. None of the above.

84. Don, while traveling to a nearby relative's house, is injured by a vehicle negligently operated by an Acme employee who was using her car for an Acme business purpose. After initiating an action against Acme (but prior to trial), Don seeks to discover if Acme has insurance. Assuming this jurisdiction follows the FRCP, which of the following are correct regarding discovery of the insurance policy covering the Acme vehicle?

A. If the insurance policy is not admissible at trial, the insurance policy is not discoverable.

B. Insurance maintained by a party is never discoverable.

C. An insured party must disclose an insurance policy if the insurer may be liable for all or part of a judgment entered against the insured.

D. Insurance is discoverable only where it is relevant to the *prima facie* issues of the case.

85. Andy Attorney is a new associate at a prestigious downtown law firm. He is involved in a major federal securities fraud case in the local U.S. district court. Andy has noticed and taken many depositions in the case, but is now confronted with all of the following allegations:

   I.   Andy's examination of a witness was conducted in a manner designed to embarrass the deponent.

II. Andy failed to attend a deposition that he had scheduled for another party.

III. Although a party who was deposed by Andy was not represented by counsel, Andy nevertheless insisted upon carrying out the deposition.

IV. Andy objected to almost every question asked his client at a deposition, and all answers were made subject to Andy's objections.

Which of the foregoing assertions could result in sanctions against Andy and his client?

A. I and II

B. II, III, and IV

C. II and IV

D. II only

86. Ripoff Corporation has engaged in price fixing, causing persons who purchased their stereo equipment to pay $50 per item more than required. Marcia Music sues Ripoff in an appropriate U.S. district court for a federal antitrust violation as representative of the class of persons who have brought Ripoff stereo equipment within the applicable statute of limitations. The class is certified under FRCP 23(b)(3).

The following notice is prepared for mailing to all class members (approximately 125,000 persons):

You are hereby notified that a class action has been brought in U.S. district court under Rule 23(b)(3) of the Federal Rules of Civil Procedure by Ms. Marcia Music on behalf of all persons who have purchased Ripoff stereo equipment. You may opt out of the class within one month of this notice. If you choose to remain in the action, you may appear through an attorney.

Which of the following is correct?

A. If Marcia is unable to pay the costs of mailing notice to all 125,000 class members, the court may, in its discretion and for good cause shown, order Ripoff to pay these costs.

B. If a class member opts out and Ripoff prevails at trial, Ripoff can assert collateral estoppel against that individual in a subsequent lawsuit.

C. The notice to class members is not adequate.

D. None of the above.

87. Counselor Carlos Clark has been retained to defend WDM Corporation, an international microchip kingpin, in a federal antitrust action commenced by Plaintiff, a corporation, in the appropriate U.S. district court. After Clark sought discovery of a large volume of documents from Plaintiff, Plaintiff advised Clark that it objected to his discovery requests on all of the following grounds:

   I.   The documents sought are privileged.

   II. The information is factual in nature and relates to the Plaintiff's claims.

   III. The documents sought were not calculated to lead to the discovery of admissible evidence.

   IV. The evidence sought is obtainable from a less expensive source.

   Which, if any, of the foregoing objections might be valid?

   A. I, III, and IV
   B. I and II
   C. I and III
   D. II and IV

88. P filed an action against D Corporation for material breach of contract and misrepresentation in the sale of a home located in a subdivision. An agent of D allegedly represented to P that the property was in excellent condition and ready for occupancy. Actually, P found that (1) the plumbing was defective, and (2) there were termites in the basement. Prior to filing the action, P's attorney consulted with an economist concerning P's damages. Which of the following statements is correct?

   A. The economist's opinion is discoverable.
   B. The opinion of the economist is not discoverable absent exceptional circumstances.
   C. The opinion of an expert is discoverable only if it is solicited or obtained prior to the commencement of litigation.
   D. Discovery of an expert's opinion is privileged.

89. Plaintiff sued Defendant in a State X court of general jurisdiction for injuries suffered in an auto accident in State X. Plaintiff is a citizen of State X, and Defendant is a citizen of State Y. State X is a comparative negligence state. The jury finds Defendant 80 percent at fault and Plaintiff 20 percent at fault, and rules that Defendant must pay

Plaintiff $16,000 for the latter's injuries.

Since all of Defendant's assets are in State Y, Plaintiff sued Defendant on the State X judgment in a State Y court. State Y is a contributory negligence state. Assuming the State X decision is final, which of the following statements is correct?

A. *Res judicata* precludes Plaintiff from suing on the State X judgment in State Y because the two actions involve the same parties and the same occurrence.

B. Full faith and credit need not be granted to the State X judgment.

C. The State Y court may hold a trial *de novo* because that jurisdiction does not recognize comparative negligence.

D. State Y must grant full faith and credit to the State X Court judgment, if Defendant had a full and fair opportunity to litigate on the merits.

90. A sued B, seeking personal injuries and property damage in the amount of $100,000 for B's negligence in causing a collision with a car driven by A. A lost, with the jury expressly finding that B was not negligent. C (a pedestrian walking along the street when he saw the accident) suffered back injuries when he attempted to extricate A from the latter's vehicle. C sued B, claiming B negligently caused the accident with A's car and was therefore responsible for C's personal injuries. In the latter action, B made a motion to dismiss based upon the decision rendered in A's earlier lawsuit. The court

A. may grant B's motion because it has discretion to determine if it will apply collateral estoppel principles.

B. must grant B's motion because C's action is barred under *res judicata* principles.

C. should deny B's motion because it may not apply collateral estoppel in the context of the facts presented.

D. should deny B's motion only if the concept of mutuality of estoppel is not applied in this jurisdiction.

Questions 91–93 are based on the following facts:

Dodo is a State X partnership composed of Jim Do and Bob Do. They manufacture and lease large ovens that are used in restaurants. Dodo's only plant and business office is in State X. Three months ago, the president of Dominic's (a fashionable eating spot in State Z) made a trip to State X and leased an oven from Dodo. Dominic's is incorporated in State Z, where its restaurant is located. The stock of Dominic's is held by Carl, Fred, and Alice. The Do brothers are domiciled in State X.

Two weeks ago, Paul (an employee of Dominic's) was hurt when the door of the leased oven suddenly fell open on him. Paul sued both Dodo and Dominic's in the U.S. district court in State Z. Jim and Bob Do were personally served in State X. Dominic's was served pursuant to a State Z statute that permits notice of the lawsuit to be (1) left with someone of "suitable discretion" at the defendant's home or main business premises; or (2) if no such person is available, posted on the door that is most often used by the occupants of the defendant's home or main business premises. Paul's process server used the latter method. The president of Dominic's saw the notice and delivered the summons and service of process to the corporation's attorney.

91. To determine if subject matter jurisdiction is proper, it would be helpful to know which of the following?

I.   The domicile of the shareholders of Dominic's

II. The domicile of Paul

III. If State Z has a long-arm statute

IV. The extent of Paul's injuries

A. I and III
B. II and IV
C. III and IV
D. II and III

92. With respect to the notice given to Dominic's, which of the following statements is probably the most accurate?

A. Under these circumstances, it is constitutionally invalid.
B. It is invalid because it failed to comply with the FRCP.
C. It is valid because the corporation received actual notice of Paul's action.
D. It is valid because the FRCP authorizes service of process in accordance with the law of the state in which it is located.

93. In determining if the assertion of personal jurisdiction over Dodo is proper, which of the following factors are pertinent?

I.   The State Z long-arm statute

II. Whether Dodo was aware where the leased range would be used

III. Whether Dodo presently does any other business in State Z (whether or not that business is unrelated to the Dominic's lease)

IV. The physical health of Jim and Bob Do

A. I, II, and III

B. II, III, and IV

C. I, II, and IV

D. I and II

Questions 94–96 are based upon the following facts:

Paul sued his employer, Acme corporation, in the proper U.S. district court in State X, claiming that (1) Dan (an Acme supervisor) had defamed him by informing the president of Acme that Dan was an ineffectual employee, and that this statement was within the scope of Dan's employment at Acme; and (2) Acme owed Dan $5,000 in unused vacation pay. As a consequence of both harms, Paul claimed damages in the aggregate amount of $80,000.

Acme responded to Paul's complaint with an FRCP 12(b) motion to dismiss Paul's complaint on the grounds that Dan was an indispensable party and that subject matter jurisdiction was lacking since the two claims aggregated by Paul to satisfy the "in excess of $75,000" requirement did not arise out of the same transaction or occurrence. The court could not obtain personal jurisdiction over Dan. Acme's motion was denied.

Acme then filed an answer that admitted Dan's statement, but denied that it was made within the scope of Dan's employment and asserted the affirmative defense of truth. Paul then filed a summary judgment motion, with his personal supporting affidavit describing facts that demonstrated that he had performed his job competently. Acme failed to respond to Paul's summary judgment motion.

94. Which of the following statements is correct?

   A. Dan is an indispensable party.

   B. Paul may not aggregate unrelated claims to meet the jurisdictional amount.

   C. Dan is probably not an indispensable party.

   D. (B) and (C), but not (A).

95. Paul's motion for a summary judgment should be

   A. granted, because Acme failed to respond with an affidavit that disputed Paul's assertions.

   B. granted, because there is no genuine issue of fact.

   C. denied, because the affidavit was made by a party to the action.

   D. denied, because material issues of fact remain.

96. Assume for purposes of this question that (1) Paul never made a motion for summary judgment, (2) the jury rendered a general verdict in favor of Acme, and (3) the mutuality rule has been

repudiated in this jurisdiction. If Paul now sued Dan for defamation, which of the following is correct?

A. Dan probably could assert *res judicata* to avoid liability.

B. Dan probably could assert collateral estoppel to avoid liability.

C. Dan probably could not assert collateral estoppel principles to avoid liability.

D. (A) and (B), but not (C).

97. Paul is a citizen of Idaho. He recently sued Deeter Corporation (which is incorporated in Delaware and has its principal place of business in Iowa) for $75,042.37. Paul's lawsuit, filed in a U.S. district court in Idaho, claims that Deeter's president, Jack, recently caused Paul losses of $75,000 for defamation, and $42.37 for a dinner that the latter had promised to buy. The action emanates from a business dinner at a restaurant in Idaho. At that meeting, negotiations deteriorated to the point where Jack loudly called Paul a "con artist" and abruptly left without paying the bill. If Deeter Corporation contests the assertion of **subject matter jurisdiction** over it, will Paul prevail? (You may assume that personal jurisdiction requirements are satisfied.)

A. Yes, because diversity jurisdiction is present.

B. Yes, because (based upon the defamation) a federal question is present.

C. No, because neither of Paul's claims exceeds $75,000.

D. No, because the facts fail to indicate that Deeter Corporation has sufficient "minimum contacts" with Idaho.

98. Babco Publishing Company is a New York corporation that prints and sells law school outlines. Babco's major sales are in New England, but it annually sells outlines in California via its exclusive distributor, Armco, a New Jersey corporation. Babco noticed that Dumbco, a Texas corporation, had recently published a series of outlines that closely resembled those of Babco. Dumbco also sells its outlines in State X. State X's long-arm statute permits its courts to exercise personal jurisdiction over nonpersonal injury defendant-tortfeasors, who are **not** domiciled in that state, if their business within the jurisdiction exceeds $80,000. Neither Babco's nor Dumbco's business in State X exceeds $15,000. Can a U.S. district court in State X successfully exercise personal jurisdiction over Dumbco for copyright infringement if Babco sues Dumbco?

A. Yes, if Dumbco has sufficient minimum contacts in State X.

B. Yes, despite the state statute, because diversity requirements are satisfied.

C. No, because State X requires that the defendant's business exceed $80,000, and federal courts ordinarily "borrow" the long-arm statute of the jurisdiction in which they reside.

D. No, because the aggregate amount in controversy fails to exceed $75,000.

99. Arthur was a partner in the XYZ Public Relations Group, a Massachusetts general partnership, with offices in Boston, New York City, and Los Angeles. XYZ was recently sued by KABD radio station. The suit alleged that XYZ had charged KABD $250,000 without disclosing that XYZ also represented a competitor of KABD, and that this resulted in a less than competent effort by XYZ. Arthur, who four months before this lawsuit had relocated from Boston to Los Angeles, was subpoenaed to have his deposition taken in New York City (at the offices of KABD's legal counsel). While in New York, Arthur was personally served by Clarence, who owns the apartment that Arthur had lived in while in Boston. Clarence lives in New York City. Clarence's lawsuit was commenced in a U.S. district court sitting in New York. The action, based upon diversity of citizenship, claims that Arthur had (1) held "wild parties" at the premises, which damaged the rental unit (a private home); and (2) failed to pay rent, in an aggregate amount exceeding $75,000. Under these circumstances, is Arthur subject to personal jurisdiction in New York?

A. Yes, because the requirements for diversity jurisdiction appear to be satisfied.

B. Yes, because Arthur was personally served in New York.

C. No, if Clarence subsequently fails to prove at trial that his damages, in fact, exceeded $75,000.

D. No, because Arthur was in New York in response to a subpoena.

100. ABC Corporation, a relatively new Illinois entity, manufactures high-powered motors that are installed in yachts manufactured by Defendant, an Ohio corporation. ABC knew that Defendant sold most of its yachts in California and Florida, which abut major water bodies. A yacht was sold by Defendant to Bonzo Watercraft Sales (a Florida corporation), which then sold it to Paul. Due to a defect in the motor, the yacht capsized during its first "run." Paul was seriously injured. Paul sued Bonzo in the appropriate U.S. district

court in Florida. Four months later, after discovery, Paul sought to add ABC as an additional defendant. Florida's long-arm statute permits jurisdiction over nonresidents when the person or entity involved has done business in Florida or sold personal property to a Florida domiciliary or entity. Under these circumstances, can the U.S. district court assume personal jurisdiction over ABC? (Assume that ABC has never sold any of its motors directly to a Florida citizen or entity.)

A. Yes, if ABC could reasonably foresee that its motors might eventually be used in Florida.

B. Yes, because ABC did business with Defendant, who sold the yacht in question to a Florida entity.

C. No, because ABC never did any business in Florida or sold personal property to a Florida citizen or entity.

D. No, because ABC clearly lacks sufficient minimum contacts with Florida.

Questions 101–102 are based upon the following facts:

Pat is domiciled in Los Angeles. While driving her car in Chicago, Pat collided with Dan, a Bar Review lecturer who lived in Chicago. Settlement discussions took place, but were not successful. Four months later, while Dan was giving a lecture in Los Angeles, he was personally served by Pat's process server. The lawsuit, filed in a U.S. district court, alleges that Dan's negligence caused the accident and claims damages exceeding $75,000.

101. Assuming Dan has no contacts with California other than lecturing there four days each year for the Bar Review course that employs him, can Pat successfully assert jurisdiction over Dan in California?

A. Yes, because Dan was personally served within California.

B. Yes, because Dan had adequate minimum contacts with California.

C. No, because Dan lacked sufficient minimum contacts with California.

D. No, because diversity of citizenship is lacking (Dan was served in California and Pat lives there).

102. Assume that Dan does not object initially to personal jurisdiction. He answers (denying liability) and counterclaims against Pat for the injuries he sustained in the accident. After some discovery, however, it appeared that Pat would probably prevail. Can Dan now contest personal jurisdiction?

A. Yes, because a lack of personal jurisdiction can be raised at any stage of a federal litigation matter.

B. Yes, because a lack of personal jurisdiction can be raised at any time prior to trial.

C. No, because an objection to personal jurisdiction must be raised at the first available opportunity.

D. No, because Pat, as the domiciliary-plaintiff, has the right to choose the forum.

103. Wanda brought an action in the applicable U.S. district court in Idaho against XYZ Insurance Company. She was the sole beneficiary under a policy under which her ex-husband, Arthur, was the insured. XYZ answered that the policy was fraudulently procured because Arthur misrepresented the condition of his health at the time the policy was issued. XYZ deposed both Wanda and Dr. Belton (who was Arthur's family doctor). At the trial, it is most likely that XYZ may:

A. use Wanda's deposition for any purpose.

B. use Wanda's deposition solely to impeach her own or Dr. Belton's credibility, if either testifies.

C. not use Wanda's deposition because a deposition is merely a discovery tool.

D. not use Wanda's deposition, unless her attorney deposed one or more officers or employees of XYZ.

104. Pete commenced a lawsuit in U.S. district court against Doe. The action alleged that Pete had been injured on Doe's premises about one month ago and that Doe's negligence caused the injury. Doe filed an answer, and also claimed that Pete had breached a contract with Doe about nine months ago. The action was tried, and both Pete and Doe successfully prevailed upon their claims. About one month after these judgments, Pete commenced a breach of contract action against Doe, filed in U.S. district court, alleging that the latter party had breached the contract upon which Doe's earlier judgment against Pete was based. (Assume that all of the aforementioned actions were properly filed.) Under these circumstances, it is most likely that

A. Pete's action will be dismissed because he should have counter-claimed against Doe in the earlier action.

B. Pete's action will be dismissed because the question of Doe's liability to Pete is settled under collateral estoppel principles.

C. Pete's action will not be dismissed because the question of Doe's
liability to Pete under the contract is a distinct, new claim that is
unrelated to Pete's initial lawsuit.

D. Pete's action will not be dismissed because, even though Pete's
claim is related to the earlier action, it is not barred by collateral
estoppel principles.

Questions 105–107 are based on the following facts:

P, seeking damages from D Inc., for patent infringement, sues D in an appropriate
U.S. district court. P's complaint alleges in part that D's agents knowingly copied P's
patented electric generator and purposely made meaningless cosmetic changes to
cover up the infringement. D answered by generally denying all of P's allegations.

105. D's research and development department keeps detailed records as
well as models of all of its research projects. Must D disclose the
existence of these items?

A. No, these documents are privileged.

B. No, a party need not perform discovery for its opponent.

C. Yes, a party may discover any relevant, nonprivileged material.

D. Yes, a party must disclose the existence of documents and tangible
things relevant to the disputed facts.

106. D retained five experts in anticipation of litigation. D procured
reports from each expert, but does not plan to call the experts at
trial. Instead, D plans to call two of its employees as experts. Can P
obtain the identities and opinions of the nonemployee experts?

A. Yes, a party must disclose the identity and opinions of an expert
it retains in anticipation of litigation.

B. Yes, a party, through interrogatories, may discover the opinions
of any expert the opposing party retains in anticipation of litigation.

C. No, since the opinions are not admissible at trial they are not
discoverable.

D. No, unless the moving party can show exceptional circumstances
that warrant discovery of the expert's opinions.

107. Twenty days before trial, D learns that a retired employee developed
the first sketches of its new generator. Must D divulge this
information to P?

A. Yes, since a party has a duty to supplement its initial mandatory disclosures.

B. No, since the adverse party could find this person through its own discovery devices.

C. No, unless D intends to use the employee as a witness.

D. No, since a party is not obligated to supplement its initial mandatory disclosures.

108. On March 21, 1996, Goldie Miner enlisted the services of the renowned law firm of Weare Phulla Bull & Associates. She claims that pesticides produced by Toxin, Inc., were sprayed next to her home and that these insecticides have turned her skin deep purple. Bull looks at Ms. Miner, and her skin is indeed a revolting deep purple hue. Bull helps his new client on with her coat and spots a box of dye hanging out of one of the pockets. He assures her that he can probably get Toxin to settle out of court to avoid adverse publicity for at least $10 million.

On April 1, Bull files a complaint in the district court alleging $100 million in damages. Toxin answers and deposes Goldie on April 17, 1996. During the deposition, Toxin's attorney becomes disgusted with Goldie and throws a glass of water at her. Remarkably, her skin pigment washes right off. The next day, Toxin files several motions with the court including a motion to impose sanctions against Bull for filing a frivolous pleading. Bull withdraws his pleading 15 days after being served with the motion. May the court impose sanctions against Bull?

A. Yes, because an attorney has a duty to conduct a reasonable inquiry to ensure the claim is not baseless.

B. Yes, because the purpose of the claim was clearly to harass the defendant.

C. No, because Bull withdrew the complaint before the court is allowed to impose sanctions.

D. No, because an attorney cannot be punished for misrepresentations made by his client.

109. Gipetto, a famous cosmetic surgeon domiciled in California, develops a hair growth formula to cure baldness. His initial tests on rats and wooden puppets show promise, so he test-markets his new product in the small town of Wannalie, Wyoming. Forty bald men try Gipetto's new tonic, and all experience miraculous hair

growth. Unfortunately, they all, to varying degrees, also experience terribly disfiguring nasal protrusions. The men join as plaintiffs in a suit against Gipetto in a district court in California. Their claims vary in value between $100,000 and $1.5 million.

Gipetto's attorney determines that it would be tactically advantageous to question the men before the effect of the tonic wears off. She serves the plaintiff with notice of the depositions. The plaintiffs move to prevent Gipetto from deposing all of them. The plaintiff's motion should be

A. granted, since a party ordinarily may not take this many depositions.

B. granted, since parties to an action may not be deposed.

C. denied, because the information sought is relevant and not privileged.

D. denied, unless the court finds Gipetto's only intent is to harass the plaintiffs.

Multiple-Choice
Answers

1. **A**   ***U.S. district courts are competent*** to hear cases involving a federal claim (i.e., one arising under the Constitution, a treaty, or the laws of the United States). Paul's claim is based upon violation of a state statute. It does ***not*** arise under the U.S. Constitution, a treaty, or a federal law. Thus, Denton's motion should be granted. Choice **B** is incorrect because, while Denton is asserting a defense based upon the U.S. Constitution, competency based upon a "federal question" is analyzed only from the viewpoint of the claim being asserted by the plaintiff. Choice **C** is incorrect because no federal claim has been asserted by Paul. Finally, choice **D** is incorrect because Paul's claim does not arise under the U.S. Constitution.

2. **C**   For ***diversity subject matter jurisdiction*** to exist, (1) no plaintiff and no defendant may be citizens of the ***same state,*** and (2) the amount in controversy ***must exceed $75,000,*** exclusive of interest and costs. Since (1) the plaintiffs are citizens of Florida, and D is a citizen of Michigan and Delaware (a corporation is deemed to be a citizen of the states in which it is incorporated or has its principal place of business), and (2) each plaintiff is claiming damages in excess of $75,000, diversity subject matter jurisdiction is satisfied. Choice **D** is incorrect because D is also a citizen of Michigan. Choice **A** is incorrect because diversity subject matter jurisdiction is not dependent on the place of plaintiff's injury. Finally, choice **B** is incorrect because a corporation is a citizen of the states in which it is incorporated or has its principal place of business. The fact that D was headquartered in Florida would not deprive the court of diversity subject matter jurisdiction.

3. **B**   Cases based upon "federal question" subject matter jurisdiction must be commenced in the judicial district in which (1) any defendant resides, if all defendants reside in the same state; (2) a substantial part of the events or omissions on which the claim is based occurred or a substantial part of the property is located; or (3) any defendant may be found, if there is no district in which the action may otherwise be brought. 28 U.S.C. §1391(b). When venue is improper, a U.S. district court may, on its own motion or on the motion of any defendant, transfer the action to another U.S. district court in which the matter could have originally been commenced, or dismiss the lawsuit. 28 U.S.C. §1406(a). Since the action could have been commenced in either California (where the defendant resides) or Texas (where the discrimination took place), it may be transferred to the proper federal judicial district in either of those

states. Choice **D** is incorrect because the court may not retain the action since the (1) defendant does not reside in Nevada, and (2) the cause of action did not arise in Nevada. Choice **A** is incorrect because the action may be transferred to either California or Texas. Finally, choice **C** is incorrect because the action may be transferred to any U.S. district court where the litigation may have originally been commenced.

4. **C** Lack of subject matter jurisdiction may ordinarily be raised *at any time* throughout a legal proceeding. In state courts, an objection to personal jurisdiction is ordinarily deemed to be waived by a general appearance. Since federal courts have exclusive subject matter jurisdiction with respect to *admiralty claims*, the State A court was not competent to render a valid judgment (despite being a court of general jurisdiction). Choice **B** is incorrect because a lack of personal jurisdiction is ordinarily waived by a general appearance. Choice **A** is incorrect because Derek is likely to prevail only on the lack of subject matter jurisdiction issue. Finally, Choice **D** is incorrect because the State A court was not competent to render a judgment in this matter, even though any possible objection to personal jurisdiction was probably waived by Derek's general appearance.

5. **B** Where a suit is properly commenced in a state court and "federal claim" subject matter jurisdiction is satisfied, the action *may be removed* to the U.S. district court that is in the judicial district that encompasses the state court, if (1) *all* of the defendants join in the petition for removal, and (2) removal is sought *within 30 days* from the time the moving party received service of process. Since the action involves a federal claim, Defendant is *entitled* to have the litigation removed to the appropriate U.S. district court. Choice **A** is incorrect because where removal is otherwise proper, the fact that the action could not have originally been commenced in the U.S. district court to which it is removed is irrelevant. Choice **C** is incorrect because state courts of general jurisdiction are ordinarily competent to hear federal claims. Finally, Choice **D** is incorrect because citizenship is not pertinent where removal is based upon a federal claim.

6. **C** U.S. district courts are competent to hear cases involving a *federal claim* (i.e., one arising under the Constitution, a treaty, or the laws of the United States). Since Acme is asserting a federal claim against Union, subject matter jurisdiction exists — even though the

amount in controversy does not exceed $75,000. Choices **A** and **B** are true in that (1) there is no diversity since an unincorporated association is deemed to be a citizen of each state in which *any* of its members are domiciled (Acme and Union are therefore each citizens of Indiana), and (2) the amount in controversy does not *exceed* $75,000. *However,* subject matter jurisdiction still exists because a federal claim is involved (i.e., one arising under a U.S. statute). Finally, Choice **D** is incorrect because a federal, rather than state, claim has been asserted.

7. **C** Under *statutory* interpleader, a U.S. district court is competent where (1) any two of the defendant-claimants are citizens of *different* states, and (2) the amount involved is $500 or more. In a *statutory* interpleader action, venue is proper in any judicial district in which any of the claimants reside. Since venue is proper only in a judicial district in which a defendant-claimant resides, a U.S. district court would be *obliged to dismiss the action or transfer it* to a U.S. district court where the lawsuit could have been commenced. The citizenship of the plaintiff-stakeholder is *irrelevant* for purposes of determining subject matter jurisdiction in a statutory interpleader case. Choice **A** is incorrect because Sam's citizenship would not be imputed to Harvey. However, even if it were, diversity of citizenship for a statutory interpleader action would still exist. Choice **B** is incorrect because the jurisdictional amount for statutory interpleader cases is only $500 or more. Finally, Choice **D** is incorrect because choices **A** and **B** are erroneous, as discussed above.

8. **C** A summons and complaint ordinarily may not be delivered by a person who is *a party to the action.* FRCP 4(c)(2). Since Pete is the plaintiff and personally delivered the summons and complaint to Doris, service *should be quashed.* Choice **A** is incorrect because Big Time did receive actual notice of the pending lawsuit through the service upon Doris (service upon a corporate president is deemed to constitute notice). Choice **B** is incorrect because the fact that Doris was not an officer at the time at which the answer was due is irrelevant. Choice **D** is incorrect because service of the summons and complaint was made by Pete.

9. **A** A person who is not a party *should be joined* where failure to do so will leave any party to the action subject to a *substantial risk of incurring multiple liability* for a single obligation. If the court determines that in equity and in good conscience the action should

be dismissed in the nonparty's absence, he is regarded as being *indispensable*. Where the joinder of an indispensable party will destroy subject matter jurisdiction, a federal court *must dismiss the action*. FRCP 19. Where an action is dismissed because of the failure to join an indispensable party, the court's decision is *not* deemed to be on the merits. Thus, dismissal of an action upon this ground would have no *res judicata* effect, and statement I is correct. Statement II is also correct (hence choice **A** is correct) since the court could avoid the finding of indispensability by shaping the relief to avoid any prejudice to the Bank. The court could accomplish this end by ordering the Bank to interplead Plaintiff & Krooke under FRCP 22. There would be complete diversity between the stakeholder Bank (Nevada) and both claimants (California), and the amount in controversy would also be satisfied. The interpleader would also satisfy the court's supplemental jurisdiction under 28 U.S.C. §1367. Through this technique, the court would eliminate any prejudice to the Bank and obviate the necessity of dismissing the case. Statement III is incorrect since the interpleader alternative avoids the finding of indispensability. Finally, statement IV is incorrect because it presents an incomplete description of the problem.

10. **C** There *must* be subject matter jurisdiction with respect to a claim filed by the plaintiff against a *third-party defendant* (i.e., the impleaded party). Since P and T are both citizens of Idaho, diversity subject matter jurisdiction is lacking. Choice **D** is incorrect because the fact that diversity exists between P and D is irrelevant to the plaintiff's action against T. Choice **A** is incorrect because the pendent jurisdiction doctrine is applicable only to situations where the plaintiff is attempting to attach a state cause of action to a federal claim. Here, P is attempting to assert an action against an additional party (rather than seeking to add a state cause of action to a federal claim). Choice **B** is incorrect because the U.S. Supreme Court has specifically rejected the application of supplemental jurisdiction to this type of situation. *Owen Equipment Co. v. Kroger*.

11. **B** Under the federal concept of *supplemental jurisdiction*, if a federal claim exists, a U.S. district court may permit the plaintiff to append any state claims so related to the federal claim that they constitute the same "case or controversy" under Article III of the Constitution. 28 U.S.C. §1367. (Note: This section essentially codifies the judge-made pendent jurisdiction standard, allowing a district court

to hear state claims arising out of "a common nucleus of operative facts" with claim that rests on an independent basis of jurisdiction. *United Mineworkers v. Gibbs*). Choice **A** is incorrect because there is no amount in controversy requirement with respect to federal claims. 28 U.S.C. §1331. Choice **C** is incorrect because the U.S. district court would not have subject matter jurisdiction based upon diversity since the amount in controversy does not exceed $75,000. Finally, choice **D** is incorrect because choice **B** is true.

12. **A** Full faith and credit *must be given* to an out-of-state default judgment obtained in a procedurally and constitutionally valid manner. The court in California, even though one of general jurisdiction, was *not* competent to hear this matter (patent infringement cases are within the exclusive jurisdiction of federal courts). Thus, the California judgment is not procedurally sound and would not be entitled to full faith and credit by a New York court. Choice **B** is incorrect because service of process within a jurisdiction has traditionally been recognized as a valid means of obtaining personal jurisdiction over an out-of-state defendant. Choice **C** is incorrect because a defendant who fails to appear in an out-of-state action does not waive his right to later collaterally attack the constitutional and procedural aspects of that default judgment. Finally, choice **D** is incorrect because choice **A**, as discussed above, is true.

13. **D** Where (1) no plaintiff and no defendant are citizens of the same state, and (2) the amount in controversy *exceeds* $75,000, exclusive of interest and costs, *diversity subject matter jurisdiction exists*. The "amount in controversy" is usually satisfied if the benefit or cost to the plaintiff is *not*, to a "legal certainty," $75,000 or less. Since P has not alleged damages in *excess* of $75,000, the amount in controversy requirement is *not* satisfied. Also, *venue is not proper* because Arizona has *no connection* with the accident, the defendant does not reside there, nor is he subject to personal jurisdiction there. Choice **A** is incorrect because, while venue is *not* proper, statement II is also correct. Choice **B** is incorrect because, while statement II is correct, statement I is also true. Choice **C** is incorrect because P's claim does not satisfy the "amount in controversy" requirement.

14. **A** In all averments of fraud or mistake, the circumstances constituting fraud or mistake shall be stated with particularity. FRCP 9(b). While the FRCP ordinarily require only "a short and plain statement of the claim showing that the pleader is entitled to relief,"

FRCP 8, *fraud claims must be stated with specificity.* Choice **B** is incorrect because the assertion of a fraud constitutes an exception to the general rules for pleading in federal court. Choice **C** is incorrect because the manner of pleading prescribed by the FRCP would be controlling in the event of conflict with an otherwise applicable state rule of pleading. ***Hanna v. Plumer.*** Finally, choice **D** is incorrect because choice **A** is true.

15. **D** The fact that two or more plaintiffs, or two or more defendants, are citizens of the same state does ***not*** destroy diversity. Choice **A** is incorrect because diversity requires that no plaintiff and no defendant be citizens of the same state. Choice **B** is incorrect because plaintiffs are not "compelled" to join their actions simply because their claims arise out of the same transaction or series of transactions. Their joinder is permissive. Finally, **choice C** is incorrect because D's motion probably would be denied (rather than granted) if the conditions described in C are satisfied.

16. **C** Under the Class Action Fairness Act of 2005, 28 U.S.C. §1332(d)(2), federal courts may exercise diversity jurisdiction over a class action in which the aggregate amount in controversy exceeds $5 million, exclusive of interests and costs, and in which any member of the class is a citizen of a state different from any defendant. Choice **C** is therefore correct since the aggregate amount in controversy exceeds $5 million and since some of the class members are domiciled in states other than New York or Illinois. Choice **A** is incorrect because complete diversity is not required under these circumstances. Choice **B** is incorrect because aggregation is specifically allowed in class actions so long as the aggregated amount exceeds $5 million. Choice **D** is incorrect because it combines two incorrect answers.

17. **D** Where a suit is properly commenced in a state court and federal diversity requirements would be satisfied, the action can be removed to the U.S. district court that is in the judicial district that encompasses the state court, if (1) ***no defendant*** is a citizen of the state in which the action was brought, (2) ***all of the defendants*** join in the petition for removal, and (3) ***removal*** is sought within ***30 days*** of the time the party seeking removal received service of process. Statement I is not correct because the ***D v. P*** action is not removable since P is a citizen of the state (New York) in which the action has been commenced. Statement II is incorrect because, even if the state court was competent to hear this matter, P (being

a citizen of New York) could not remove the action to the applicable U.S. district court. Finally, statement III is correct because D's action against P does not appear to have arisen "out of the transaction or occurrence" that is the subject of P's lawsuit against D (the latter litigation involving the failure to manufacture and deliver restaurant equipment). Thus, it was not a compulsory counterclaim.

18. **D** A defendant *may implead* a person, not a party to the action, who is or may be liable to her for all or part of the plaintiff's claim against the defendant/impleading party. FRCP 14(a). An *impleaded party may assert against the impleading party* any counterclaims permitted under FRCP 13. FRCP 14(a). Statement I is correct (a third-party action is *not* proper) since Baker is not asserting an indemnity-type claim against Chance. Statement II is correct because, pursuant to FRCP 13(b), a defending party may assert as a counterclaim "any claim against an opposing party." FRCP 13(b). Of course, as the answer suggests, assertion of permissive counterclaim must have an independent basis for subject matter jurisdiction. Finally, statement III is incorrect because (1) diversity in an impleader action is not analyzed from the viewpoint of the original plaintiff and the impleaded party (rather, it is examined from the perspective of the impleading and impleaded parties); and (2) supplemental jurisdiction ordinarily extends to third-party claims.

19. **A** A party asserting a claim against a single defendant *may join any independent causes* of action which he has against the latter. FRCP 18(a). Persons may be joined as defendants if (1) there is asserted against them jointly, severally, or in the alternative, *any right* arising out of the same transaction, occurrence, or series of transactions or occurrences; and (2) any question of law or fact common to *all defendants* will arise in the action. FRCP 20(a). A court, however, may order separate trials of any claim (or cross-claim) to (1) avoid prejudice, and (2) promote judicial economy. FRCP 42(b). Subject to FRCP 42(b), Paul could assert an unrelated breach of contract action against Mary. Statement II is incorrect because Peter's cross-claim must arise out of the transaction or occurrence for ancillary jurisdiction to apply. Thus, subject matter jurisdiction is lacking with respect to Peter's counterclaim since the "amount in controversy" requirement is not satisfied. Finally, statement III is incorrect because a plaintiff may aggregate personal injury and property

claims to satisfy the "in excess of $75,000" requirement necessary for diversity subject matter jurisdiction.

20. **D** Under the Class Action Fairness Act of 2005, 28 U.S.C. §1332(d)(2), a federal district court would have jurisdiction over this controversy since the aggregate damages exceed $5 million and the requisite minimal diversity requirement has been satisfied. Choice **A** is wrong since venue would be proper in Pennsylvania where substantial events giving rise to the controversy occurred. Choices **B** and **C** are wrong for the same reasons that choice **D** is correct.

21. **C** Where there has been *a prior, valid judgment* on the merits between the parties (or their privies) with respect to the cause of action being asserted in a subsequent lawsuit, the doctrine of *res judicata* precludes the latter action. The fact that Joan obtained a judgment against Bill would not preclude Matt from subsequently contesting Joan's claim since Matt is *not* in privity with Bill. Choice **A** is incorrect because Bill could sue Matt for indemnity. Choice **B** is incorrect because a plaintiff is not required to sue every possible defendant in one action. Finally, choice **D** is incorrect because Joan's claim against Bill for personal injuries is barred, in most jurisdictions, by *res judicata* because this action arose out of the same transaction as Joan's property loss.

22. **A** A *compulsory counterclaim* arises out of the transaction or occurrence that is the subject matter of the opposing party's claim and does not require for its adjudication the presence of third parties over whom the court cannot acquire jurisdiction. FRCP 13(a). There is *ancillary jurisdiction with respect to compulsory counterclaims*. If Union's counterclaim is deemed to be compulsory (as opposed to merely permissive) in nature, ancillary jurisdiction would apply to avoid an assertion by Acme that subject matter jurisdiction is lacking. Choice **B** is incorrect because, if Union's claim is merely permissive in nature, there would have to be an independent basis of subject matter jurisdiction for it to be assertable in a federal court. Since there is no diversity and Union's cause of action is not based on a federal statute, the U.S. Constitution, or a treaty, the counterclaim could *not* be asserted in a U.S. district court. Choice **C** is incorrect because the fact that a state claim is being asserted is irrelevant to determine if federal subject matter jurisdiction is satisfied. Finally, choice **D** is incorrect because a lack of diversity would (but for supplemental jurisdiction) result in Acme prevailing on its motion.

23. B A party may ordinarily obtain discovery of documents and other tangible items prepared in anticipation of litigation or for trial, (1) by or for another party, or (2) by or for that other party's representative (including her attorney), only upon a showing that (1) the party seeking such discovery has a **substantial need** for the items, and (2) she is **unable, without undue hardship**, to obtain the equivalent thereof by other means. FRCP 26(b)(3). In effect, B restates the applicable provision of the FRCP. Choice **A** is incorrect because, even if the report had been prepared by Brown in anticipation of litigation or trial, it would still be discoverable if Paul could show a substantial need for the document and that he was unable to otherwise obtain it (or its equivalent) without undue hardship. Choice **C** is incorrect because the work product privilege extends to tangible items created by another party (not just to items prepared by that party's representative). Finally, choice **D** is incorrect because the fact that Manco had obtained the report at the suggestion of counsel would not, by itself, make the item nondiscoverable. It could still be obtained if Paul could persuade the court that (1) there was a substantial need for it, and (2) he was otherwise unable to acquire it without undue hardship (i.e., the machine was destroyed and Brown cannot be deposed).

24. C In U.S. district courts, the judge **may** conduct the **voir dire** examination. FRCP 47(a). **Bias or prejudice** of a potential juror against one of the parties is usually a **proper subject for inquiry** at the **voir dire**. The defendant's question with respect to prejudice against corporations was probably an appropriate inquiry upon **voir dire**, and therefore the judge's refusal to ask potential members of the jury that question was probably **erroneous**. Choice **B** is incorrect because the fact that a party may exercise peremptory challenges does not detract from the court's failure to inquire about a general prejudice against corporations. Choice **A** is incorrect because any question regarding a juror's ability to reach a fair and impartial verdict is appropriate at the **voir dire**. Questions in this context need bear no relationship to the factual issues that will be contested at trial. Finally, choice **D** is incorrect because the judge may use her discretion in determining whether questions that counsel requests are appropriate.

25. C A plaintiff who **accepts a remittitur** in federal court **may not** challenge the trial court's ruling on appeal. By accepting the remittitur, and thereby avoiding the delay and cost of a new trial, the plaintiff is deemed to have *relinquished* her *right to appeal* the court's order. If Paul was dissatisfied with the remittitur, he should have appealed the court's order on the basis that the judge had abused his discretion (i.e., there was no good faith basis for reducing the verdict of $75,000 to $25,000). The fact that Paul agreed to the reduction "under protest" is irrelevant. Choice **A** is incorrect because the Seventh Amendment argument is overcome by the fact that the plaintiff is considered to have agreed to the remittitur (i.e., the plaintiff was free to have rejected the remittitur and to have had the case retried by a jury). Choice **B** is incorrect because, whether the trial court abused its discretion or not in ordering a new trial, Paul waived his right to review the court's order by accepting the decreased sum. Finally, choice **D** is incorrect because, where a legal claim is involved, the Seventh Amendment is applicable to damage issues.

26. **A** A U.S. district court is competent to hear federal claims (i.e., claims arising under the Constitution, a treaty, or the laws of the United States). 28 U.S.C. §1331. Since the plaintiffs are *asserting a right under the U.S. Constitution,* "federal claim" subject matter jurisdiction *exists* (regardless of diversity or the amount in controversy). Choice **B** is incorrect because the court would have subject matter jurisdiction whether or not (1) there is diversity of citizenship between the plaintiff's representative and the defendants, and (2) the "amount in controversy" requirement was satisfied. Choice **C** is incorrect because where a federal claim is involved, there ordinarily is no "amount in controversy" requirement. Finally, choice **D** is incorrect because (1) for purposes of a class action, diversity of citizenship is analyzed from the viewpoint of the class representatives, on the one hand, and the opposing party or parties, on the other hand; and (2) even if diversity was lacking, the motion would still be denied because competency in this instance is predicated upon a federal claim.

27. **C** There are *four prerequisites* to a class action: (1) the class must be so large that *joinder* of all members is *not feasible,* (2) the claims or defenses of the representatives must be *typical* of the class they seek to represent, (3) there must be *common questions* of law and fact to the class, and (4) the representative must fairly and adequately represent the *interests of the class.* FRCP 23(a). Since there is the possibility that many potential members of the class (all college students in State X) would not be desirous of challenging the flag

desecration statute, the defendants' strongest argument for denying certification of the class probably would be on this ground. Choice **A** is incorrect because the class probably would be sufficiently numerous (there are ordinarily thousands of college students within each state). Choice **B** is incorrect because there ordinarily is no amount in controversy requisite with respect to the assertion of a federal claim. Finally, choice **D** is incorrect because plaintiffs' claim probably would be characterized as a FRCP 23(b)(2) class action, and notice is expressly mandated only with respect to a FRCP 23(b)(3) action. Additionally, even if due process considerations mandated reasonable notice, it probably would not be impossible to notify the class because persons matriculating at a college presumably disclose their names and addresses to the institution. Finally, acceptable notice might be possible through college newspapers.

28. **B** If a trial court **refuses to certify the class**, its finding is not a final order, and therefore, an immediate appeal may not be taken. The case must be tried as a **nonclass action**, and only after a judgment is rendered can the correctness of the trial court's refusal to grant certification be reviewed. The result in B is required as a consequence of the holding in *Coopers & Lybrand v. Livesay*. Choice **A** is incorrect because the "death knell" doctrine was specifically rejected in the *Coopers* decision. Choice **C** is incorrect because the opposite is true (the party seeking class certification must try the case on the merits before he can appeal the trial judge's refusal to permit the class action). Finally, choice **D** is incorrect because the existing parties may litigate the case, even though certification of the class has been refused.

29. **A** Where a state attempts to exercise personal jurisdiction over an out-of-state defendant, and no traditional basis of personal jurisdiction exists, there (1) must be an **appropriate long-arm statute** that permits service of process, and (2) the assertion of such personal jurisdiction must be **consistent with due process**. Since Manco was served outside of State X and is not present in that forum, service of process must be within the purview of the applicable long-arm statute, and the assertion of personal jurisdiction must comport with due process. The latter element is arguably satisfied because (1) it was reasonably foreseeable that Manco's machinery would ultimately reach State X (since Roe distributed Manco's products in that state), and (2) the impact of the contact

(i.e., the injuries to Arnold and Bates) was significant. Choice **B** is incorrect because U.S. district courts ordinarily "borrow" (i.e., apply) the long-arm statute of the jurisdiction in which they are located. Thus, with rare exceptions (i.e., statutory interpleader), U.S. district courts do not have nationwide service of process. Choice **C** is incorrect because, even if the "amount in controversy" element is satisfied, that would merely establish the court's competency. Subject matter jurisdiction is irrelevant with respect to determining if the assertion of personal jurisdiction is appropriate. Finally, choice **D** is incorrect because, where an action is brought in federal court, service of process may be accomplished in accordance with either the FRCP or the applicable state procedural rules. FRCP 4(e)(1).

30. **C** A *compulsory counterclaim* arises out of the transaction or occurrence that is the subject matter of the opposing party's claim and does not require for its adjudication the presence of third parties over whom the court cannot acquire jurisdiction. FRCP 13(a). ***There is supplemental jurisdiction with respect to compulsory counterclaims.*** Storeco's counterclaim against Arnold is totally unrelated to the occurrence upon which Arnold is contending that Storeco is liable. Since the amount involved does not exceed $75,000, the U.S. district court does not have subject matter jurisdiction over Storeco's counterclaim. Choice **D** is incorrect because Storeco's counterclaim is permissive (rather than compulsory) in nature. Choice **A** is incorrect because there is no supplemental jurisdiction with respect to permissive counterclaims. Finally, choice **B** is incorrect because the fact that Arnold may have consented to personal jurisdiction in State X by commencing the action does not cure the lack of subject matter jurisdiction with respect to Storeco's counterclaim.

31. **A** A cross-claim arising out of the transaction or occurrence that is the subject matter of (1) the original action, or (2) a counterclaim therein, may be made by one party against another. FRCP 13(g). There is supplemental jurisdiction with respect to such cross-claims. Since Manco's cross-claim against Storeco is **unrelated** to the plaintiffs' action, it is ***not permissible*** (even if there is an independent basis of subject matter jurisdiction over that cross claim). Choice **B** is incorrect because there is no such "adversity" rule. Choice **C** is incorrect because Manco's cross-claim is not permissible, regardless of whether or not it might confuse the jury's

determination of the original claim. Finally, choice **D** is incorrect because, even though there is "diversity" subject matter jurisdiction between Manco and Storeco, this action is unrelated to the underlying claim and may not be asserted.

32. **B** Where the precise issue was actually litigated in a prior lawsuit by the party (or her privy) against whom issue preclusion is being asserted in a subsequent action, and that issue was essential to the decision that was rendered in the earlier lawsuit, *issue preclusion* ordinarily will be applied. Federal courts ordinarily must follow the issue preclusion rules of an earlier, valid state court decision. *Marrese v. American Academy of Orthopedic Surgeons.* Since mutuality is not required in this jurisdiction, collateral estoppel may be asserted by Bank against Paul. This is because in the latter's action against Doris, it was decided that Carol had made a gift to Doris of the funds in question. This fact (Carol's gift) would also serve as a defense to Paul's action against Bank for unauthorized withdrawals (if Carol had consented to the transfer, it cannot be said that the disbursement to Doris was not authorized). Choice **A** is incorrect because federal courts must give *res judicata* and collateral estoppel affect to an earlier, valid state court decision. Choice **C** is incorrect because Bank and Carol are *not* in privity. Finally, choice **D** is incorrect because choice **B** is true.

33. **C** A *judgment* in an FRCP 23(b)(2) *class action is binding on the entire class.* X would be bound by the determination that there was insufficient proof that D had not read the exams. FRCP 23(c)(3). This issue is critical for both injunctive relief and monetary damages. Choice **A** is incorrect because a judgment rendered by a court that lacked subject matter is generally entitled to full faith and credit. Choice **B** is incorrect because there was diversity. P and D are citizens of different states. Finally, choice **D** is incorrect because choice **C** is true.

34. **D** The *assertion of personal jurisdiction* pursuant to an applicable *long-arm statute* must be consistent with *due process* (i.e., the defendant must have such "minimum contacts" with the forum as not to offend "traditional notions of fair play and substantial justice"). *International Shoe Co. v. Washington.* Neither statement is correct. Even if State Y had a nonresident motorist statute that asserted personal jurisdiction over a nonresident who was involved in a motor vehicle accident *within the state,* such fact alone would *not* be an adequate basis for obtaining personal jurisdiction

over D in State Y because the accident occurred in State X. Also, regardless of the language of a long-arm statute, the exercise of personal jurisdiction must still conform to due process. Choice **B** is incorrect because mere ownership of a vacant parcel of land, without any connection of that realty to the cause of action, is probably insufficient to constitute the defendant's "presence" within that state. The fact that D was personally served in State X is irrelevant to the determination of whether he has sufficient contacts with State Y for personal jurisdiction to be exercised over him in that state.

35. **B** *Persons may join* in an action as plaintiffs if (1) they assert *any right* to relief jointly, severally, or in the alternative in respect of any claim arising out of the same transaction, occurrence, or series of transactions or occurrences; and (2) *any question of law or fact* common to all plaintiffs will arise in the action. FRCP 20(a). Choice **B** is correct because the court may exercise supplemental jurisdiction over Q's claim. Section 1367(a) permits a federal court to exercise "supplemental party" jurisdiction over claims brought by additional parties so long as those claims arise out of the same transaction or common nucleus of operatives as the claim over which the court has an independent basis of jurisdiction. Section 1367(b), which limits the exercise of such "supplemental party" jurisdiction in diversity cases, would not apply here because the text of that subsection does not limit claims filed by supplemental parties against the original defendant when the supplemental party did not enter the case via FRCP 19 or 24 and when the party against whom the claim was filed was not joined pursuant to FRCP 14, 19, 20, or 24. None of those limits apply here. Choice **A** is incorrect because joinder of claims would be appropriate since there is a common issue of fact (i.e., whether P's termination from his employment was wrongful). Choice **C** is incorrect because P's claim for damages to his car is unrelated to dismissal from his job. Thus, no claim-splitting would result from P's failure to assert the damage to his car in the present action, and *res judicata* is not applicable. If P had not asserted the claim for damage to his car, subject matter jurisdiction based upon diversity would not exist for that claim (i.e., P's claim would not exceed $75,000). Choice **D** is incorrect because choice **B** is correct.

36. **D** In an impleader action, the third-party defendant (the impleaded party) may assert *any claim* against the plaintiff that arises out of

the transaction or occurrence that is the subject matter of the plaintiff's claim against the third-party plaintiff (the impleading party). Choice **A** is correct. The U.S. district court did **not** have subject matter jurisdiction in the initial action since P and D were citizens of the same state (State X) and no federal claim appears to have been involved. Choice **B** is correct because it conforms to the operative rule of law found in FRCP 14. Finally, choice **C** is correct because under *res judicata* principles, (1) P could not split his claim against D (i.e., P was required to bring all causes of action arising out of the accident against D in the original lawsuit), and (2) D was required to file a counterclaim against P in the original lawsuit with respect to any claims arising out of the accident, or thereafter be barred therefrom. Even though P and D are citizens of the same state, ancillary subject matter jurisdiction would have permitted D to counterclaim against P. In any event, choice **C** specifically directs the reader to disregard subject matter jurisdiction problems in the initial lawsuit.

37. **A** Where a claim over which the *federal courts would have original jurisdiction* is brought in a state court, the action may be *removed to the U.S. district court* that sits in the judicial district that encompasses the state court, if (1) *all the defendants* join in the petition for removal, and (2) removal is sought *within 30 days* from the time the moving party receives service of process. 28 U.S.C. §1446(b). Since federal courts have exclusive jurisdiction over copyright claims, the action is removable; the state court's lack of jurisdiction is *irrelevant* for removal purposes. 28 U.S.C. §1441(e). Choice **B** is incorrect since subject matter jurisdiction is not lacking because the action is premised on a federal claim. Choice **C** is incorrect because a judgment by a court that was not competent can ordinarily be challenged on appeal. Finally, choice **D** is incorrect because choice **A** is true.

38. **C** In a *statutory interpleader* action (1) only *minimal diversity* (i.e., diversity between any two claimants) is required, and (2) the obligation or property involved *must exceed $500 in value only*. 28 U.S.C. §1335. Venue is proper in any judicial district in which any claimant resides. Since venue in a statutory interpleader action is proper where any claimant-defendant resides, choice **C** is correct. Choice **A** is incorrect (a U.S. district court is competent to hear this matter) since (1) there is diversity between D and E, and (2) the amount involved exceeds $500. Choice **B** is incorrect because

the court would not be competent to hear E's claim against F (diversity and a claim in excess of $75,000 are lacking). E's claim against F is not an impleader action (in which event, there would be supplemental jurisdiction) since E is *not* asserting an indemnity-type of claim against F. Finally, choice **D** is incorrect because choice **C** is true.

39. B The parties in a *federal civil case* may stipulate to a jury of *less than 12* persons, but unless the parties otherwise agree, the verdict in a federal civil trial must be unanimous. FRCP 48. Since one of the jurors voted in favor of Defendant, the ruling was defective. Choice **A** is incorrect because the parties stipulated to a jury of less than 12 persons. Choice **C** is incorrect because the fact that a verdict fails to exceed $75,000 is irrelevant (the "amount in controversy" requirement is measured only at the time the action is filed). Finally, choice **D** is incorrect because any lack of personal jurisdiction over Defendant appears to have been waived when the defendant failed to assert this alleged defect. FRCP 12(h)(1).

40. B Transfer would be appropriate since the case could have originally been brought in State Y and since State W has no connection to the controversy. Indeed, venue was improper in State W. That being the case, the transfer would be pursuant to §1406(a). In a §1406(a) transfer, the substantive law does not travel with the transfer. Rather, the law of the transferee court must be followed. Hence a U.S. district court in State Y would apply the law a State Y court would apply to the controversy. Choice **A** is incorrect because D is a citizen of State Y since its principal place of business is there. Thus, removal is *not* possible. Choice **C** is incorrect because, where a *joint* claim is involved, each plaintiff is viewed as asserting the entire sum requested. Finally, choice **D** is incorrect because choice **B** is true, as discussed above.

41. B Under the FRCP, a pleading must contain a short and plain *statement* of the claim showing the pleader is entitled to *relief.* FRCP 8(a). Phil's complaint is certainly minimal, but there is enough there to give Dowd notice that Phil believes Dowd is liable for the injuries Phil incurred in the accident. Notice pleading requires no more than this. Choice **A** is incorrect because a complaint will not be dismissed without leave to amend "unless it appears beyond doubt that the plaintiff can prove no set of facts in support of his claim which would entitle him to relief." *Conley v. Gibson.* Choice **D** is incorrect because expiration of the statute of limitations *subsequent* to the lawsuit is irrelevant (commencement of the action tolls the statute of limitations). Finally, choice **C** is incorrect because under the FRCP it is **not** necessary for a plaintiff to articulate the precise legal theory upon which relief is sought.

42. **C** A party **may set forth two or more claims alternatively**. FRCP 8(e)(2). Since the FRCP specifically authorizes separate claims, regardless of consistency, a complaint setting forth two different theories for recovery is permissible. In this instance, the inconsistency may be explainable by Phil's inability to recollect the exact circumstances of the accident. Choice **B** is incorrect because a federal pleading is not subject to dismissal for containing a legal conclusion. Finally, choices **A** and **D** are incorrect because federal pleadings may contain inconsistent claims or defenses.

43. **A** In the absence of a traditional basis for obtaining personal jurisdiction, the assertion of personal jurisdiction over an out-of-state citizen must (1) conform to the applicable **long-arm statute**, and (2) be consistent with due process (i.e., the defendant must have sufficient minimum contacts with the forum as not to offend traditional **notions of fair play and substantial justice**). Since E (1) could not foresee being haled into New York (D had misrepresented to E that this trip would terminate in New Jersey), and (2) apparently has no other contacts with New York, the assertion of personal jurisdiction over E probably would violate due process. Choice **D** is incorrect because expiration of the applicable statute of limitations *after* the lawsuit had commenced is irrelevant (the filing of the action tolls the statute of limitations). Thus, expiration of the statute of limitations after the action was commenced would not be a basis for granting D's motion. Finally, choice **C** is incorrect because of the fact that the U.S. States federal courts do not have the power of nationwide service of process.

44. **C** In a **diversity** case, the proper judicial district to commence an action is one in which (1) any defendant resides, if all defendants reside in the same state; (2) a substantial part of the events or omissions on which the claim is based occurred or a substantial part of the property is located; or (3) if there is no jurisdiction where the suit may otherwise be brought, any defendant is subject to personal jurisdiction when the case is commenced. 28 U.S.C. §1391(a). Statement I is correct because there is diversity subject matter jurisdiction (i.e., P is deemed to be a citizen of States X and Z, while D is a citizen of State Y) and there is alienage jurisdiction

with respect to E. U.S. Constitution, art. III, §2. Additionally, venue is proper because (1) D "resides" in State Y (where it has its principal place of business), and (2) an alien who does *not* permanently reside in the United States may be sued in any judicial district. 28 U.S.C. §1391(d). Statement II is correct because a "diversity" action may be removed to the applicable U.S. district court when (1) no defendant is a citizen of the jurisdiction in which the action was commenced, and (2) all of the defendants join in the petition for removal. Finally, statement III is incorrect because all persons may be joined in one action as defendants if there is asserted against them jointly, severally, or in the alternative (1) any right to relief arising out of the same transaction, occurrence, or series of transactions or occurrences; and (2) any question of law or fact that is common to all defendants will arise in the action. FRCP 20(a). Since P's action arises out of the fire that occurred at its plant and there is at least one common issue of fact (i.e., the exact amount of P's damages), joining D and E as defendants is proper.

45. D Upon timely application, a person *may intervene* in an action as of right when (1) he *claims an interest* relating to the property or transaction that is the subject of the action; (2) he is so situated that disposition of the action *may,* as a practical matter, *impair* his ability to protect that interest; and (3) the applicant's interest is *not adequately represented* by the existing parties. FRCP 24(a)(2). Statement I is incorrect since P is unquestionably the real party-in-interest in that she is seeking damages in excess of the maximum limit of her insurance policy. Statement II is incorrect because D's action cannot be characterized as impleader (D is not asserting an indemnity-type of claim against E). Statement III is incorrect because E cannot intervene into the action as of right. Her interest would not be impaired by a successful judgment by P against D (since D and E are legally unrelated, there would be no collateral estoppel or *res judicata* effect in the event that P's action against D was successful).

46. A Under the Seventh Amendment, *the right to a jury trial exists* as to any issue that pertains to a *legal* remedy. Since an action for trespass existed in 1791 (when the Seventh Amendment to the U.S. Constitution was ratified), it must be characterized as a "legal" claim. Thus, Delbert would be entitled to a jury trial with respect to all issues pertaining to this action. Choice **C** is incorrect because the "clean-up doctrine" (which allows a federal court to determine legal issues that were "incidental" to a primarily equitable claim) has been repudiated. *Dairy Queen, Inc. v. Wood*. Choice **B** is incorrect because in federal court, each party is entitled to a jury trial with respect to any legal issue (regardless of the "primary" relief that the plaintiff is seeking). Finally, choice **D** is incorrect because the tort of trespass existed in 1791 (when the Seventh Amendment was ratified) and therefore would constitute a "suit at common law."

47. **A** In *diversity cases*, the proper judicial district for *venue* purposes is one in which (1) any defendant resides, if all defendants reside in the same state; (2) a substantial part of the events or omissions on which the *claim* is based *occurred* or a substantial part of the *property* is *located*; or (3) if there is no jurisdiction where the suit may otherwise be brought, any defendant is subject to personal jurisdiction when the case is commenced. 28 U.S.C. §1391(a). If venue is improper, a U.S. district court may dismiss the case or transfer the action to another U.S. district court in which the matter could have originally been commenced. 28 U.S.C. §1406(a). Although D was improperly served, he apparently waived this error by not contesting venue and making a motion to transfer the case to State Z. Since the original venue was improper, the court could transfer the action to State Z where the suit could have originally been commenced. Choice **B** is incorrect because it is not a valid basis of dismissal since D waived the right to object to venue. Choice **C** is incorrect because, despite D having been improperly served, his waiver of this defect allowed the court to transfer the action to State Z. Finally, choice **D** is incorrect because choice **A** is true.

48. **C** A party may generally discover *any matter*, not privileged, that is *relevant* to the action. However, documents and tangible items prepared in anticipation of litigation or trial, by or for (1) another party, or (2) that other party's representative (including his attorney), are discoverable *only upon a showing* that the party seeking discovery has a need for the materials and would otherwise be unable to obtain the substantial equivalent without undue hardship. FRCP 26(b)(3). Jones's memorandum to the president of E probably is *not* within the work product privilege because there is no indication that it was "prepared in anticipation of litigation." Rather, it appears to be an internal memorandum by one member of the board of directors to the president of his corporation. Jones was probably attempting to avoid prospective litigation by advising

the president of E as to what Withers had said. Choices **A** and **B** are
incorrect because the work product rule is probably not triggered
(Jones's memorandum probably was not made in anticipation of
trial or litigation). Finally, choice **D** is incorrect because the work
product privilege is assertable whether or not the attorney who
prepared the document in question is actually representing the
party in the current action.

49. **C** A party is entitled to *summary judgment* when, as a consequence of
there being no "genuine issue of material fact," she is entitled to
judgment as a matter of law. FRCP 56. Choice **A** is correct because
even if Builder Corp. had used substandard materials in the construction, this alone would not prove E was negligent. E would be
negligent only if (1) it failed to use reasonable care in overseeing the
activities of Builder Corp., and (2) there was a causal relationship
between the substandard materials and the building's collapse.
Thus, genuine issues of fact would remain even if substandard
materials had been used by Builder Corp. Choice **B** is correct
because for a plaintiff to prevail on a summary judgment motion,
she must address any affirmative defenses raised by the defendant.
Finally, choice D is incorrect because choices **A** and **B** are correct.

50. **C** A party is entitled to a *summary judgment* when, as a consequence
of there being no "genuine issue of material fact," he is entitled to
judgment as a matter of law. FRCP 56. Although a two-year statute
of limitations is applicable, negligence actions ordinarily do not
begin to run until an injury or damages have been sustained.
Thus, E's summary judgment motion was properly denied. Choice
A is incorrect because the fact that the building was constructed six
years ago is irrelevant if the statute of limitations did not begin to
run until the accident. Choice **B** is incorrect because one need not
respond to a summary judgment motion if it, on its face, would be
unsuccessful. Finally, choice **D** is incorrect because the fact that E
has the burden of proof on this issue is irrelevant in determining
whether there is a triable issue of fact. E could have raised the statute
of limitations defense through a motion for failure to state a claim
upon which relief can be granted. FRCP 12. However, since E supported its motion with an affidavit, it must be treated as a summary
judgment motion.

51. **B** *Default judgments* that are constitutionally or procedurally defective are subject to *collateral attack*. Under FRCP 4 (which has been
enacted in State X), if no acknowledgment is made to a summons

and complaint that are sent by first-class mail, the defendant must be served as otherwise provided in that Rule. Since P failed to properly effectuate service of process, the State X judgment was subject to collateral attack. Choice **A** is incorrect because, despite actual receipt of the documents by D, he was not served in accordance with applicable law. Choice **C** is incorrect because, while a default judgment is usually deemed to be "on the merits," the State X judgment is *not* entitled to full faith and credit (P having failed to conform to the statute pertaining to service of process). Finally, choice **D** is incorrect for the reasons stated above.

52. **A** *Quasi-in-rem* jurisdiction ordinarily will be tested by the *due process standard* applicable to personal jurisdiction (i.e., the defendant must have had sufficient minimum contacts with the forum as not to offend traditional notions of fair play and substantial justice). *Shaffer v. Heitner.* If D does not have sufficient contacts with State X as would support personal jurisdiction over him, the attachment should be quashed. Choice **B** is incorrect because prejudgment attachments are not *per se* unconstitutional. *Mitchell v. W. T. Grant Co.* Assuming proper due process safeguards exist, a defendant's property can be seized prior to the time a judgment is actually rendered against him. Choice **C** is incorrect because even if the motion to quash was denied and the boat sold, A could retain proceeds only in an amount equal to his obligation. The balance would have to be remitted to D. Finally, choice **D** is incorrect for the reasons described above.

53. **B** Where a suit is commenced in a state court and federal diversity requirements are satisfied, the action can be removed to the U.S. district court where the lawsuit was commenced if (1) no defendant is a citizen of the state in which the action is brought, (2) all of the defendants join in the petition for removal, and (3) the defendants seek removal within 30 days of receiving service of process. Removal here would not be possible for two reasons: (1) P and C are both citizens of Utah, hence complete diversity is lacking; and (2) C is a citizen of the forum in which the action has been commenced (i.e., a corporation is a citizen of the state in which it is incorporated *or* has its principal place of business). Hence, choice B is correct. Choice **A** is incorrect because removal cannot occur when *any* defendant is a citizen of the state in which the action was commenced, and C, a named defendant, is clearly a citizen of Utah. Choice **C** is incorrect because removal could not be granted (C being a citizen of the state

in which the action has been commenced), even if C joined in the petition. Finally, choice D is incorrect because C is a citizen of Utah; hence, the fact that amount in controversy is satisfied is irrelevant.

54. **D** *Permissive counterclaims* may be joined only if there is an independent subject matter basis for such claims. Claims by a plaintiff against a third-party defendant (the impleaded party) must have an independent subject matter basis; *Owen Equipment Co. v. Kroger.* The $3,000 counterclaim by Dumb against Pam is permissive in nature (i.e., not arising out of the transaction or occurrence that is the basis of the plaintiff's claim), and therefore supplemental jurisdiction would not exist. Since Dumb's claim does not satisfy the "amount in controversy" requirement (it is not in excess of $75,000), it could not be joined in this action; therefore, statement I is incorrect. Statement II is also incorrect since Pam's claim against Insurance Company could not be joined — both parties are citizens of State B.

55. **B** Where evidence is objected to at trial on the grounds that it is not within the pleadings, a court *may allow an amendment* when (1) presentation of the merits of the action will be subserved thereby, and (2) the objecting party fails to satisfy the court that admission of such evidence would prejudice her in maintaining her action or defense on the merits. FRCP 15(b). Although B failed to raise anticipatory repudiation as a defense, he could be permitted by the court to amend his pleadings at trial to conform to the evidence that he wishes to introduce. Choice **A** is incorrect because there is no *per se* procedural rule in federal courts that evidence outside of the pleadings is never admissible. Choice **D** is incorrect because the admission of evidence outside the pleadings is discretionary with the court. In fact, FRCP 15(b) instructs a court to adopt a liberal approach in admitting such evidence. Finally, Choice **C** is incorrect because amendments to pleadings may be made after trial has commenced.

56. **C** A party *may amend* his pleadings once, as a matter of right, at any time before a responsive pleading has been served. FRCP 15(a). Since a motion under FRCP 12(b) *does not* constitute a "responsive" pleading, Paul was entitled to amend his complaint without leave of the court. Choice D is incorrect because affidavits in support of a motion for summary judgment must be based upon *personal* knowledge. FRCP 56(e). Here, Bill's affidavit is based upon information related to him by Paul (rather than firsthand

knowledge). Even if P's affidavit was based on personal knowledge, at best the burden of production on summary judgment would have shifted to D. Choice **A** is incorrect because a complaint in federal court need not articulate the particular legal theory being asserted. Finally, Choice **B** is incorrect because alternative claims may be asserted, regardless of consistency. FRCP 8(e)(2).

57. **B** A *contractual provision* stipulating a particular choice of forum in the event of litigation ordinarily will be observed. Where a motion to transfer venue is granted, the law of the transferring state will be applied in the transferee forum. Choice **B** conforms to the applicable principles of law. Choice **A** is incorrect because a plaintiff's choice of forum will rarely be disturbed. The fact that litigation in Oregon is inconvenient to a party's employees is probably insufficient to transfer the action to such party's "home state." Y Corporation's contention is further diminished by the contractual clause stipulating to litigation in Oregon. Choice **C** is incorrect because a "choice of forum" contractual provision would not be disregarded simply because it would otherwise be inconsistent with due process to assert personal jurisdiction over a party in that forum. While a court could refuse to exercise jurisdiction where (1) neither party nor the cause of the action has a nexus with the forum, or (2) the party asserting the clause had a grossly favorable bargaining position, neither of those situations is applicable here because X is a citizen of Oregon and Y Corporation is a "large" corporation. Finally, **D** is incorrect because choice **B** is true.

58. **D** In a class action asserted under FRCP 23(b)(3), the court is *required to give members of the class the best notice practicable under the circumstances*, including individual notice to members who can be identified through reasonable effort. FRCP 23(c)(2). If the names and addresses of purchasers of the Daleon automobile are truly unavailable (except for the buyers who are located in New Mexico and Delaware), notice by publication in major newspapers throughout the country probably will be adequate. However, presumably Daleon would have access to the records of its retailer sellers and, before dispensing with a notice reasonably calculated to succeed, some minimal effort to gather those records would be in order. Therefore, Choice **B** is incorrect. Choice **A** is incorrect because, for diversity purposes, only the citizenship of the class representatives and the other party are analyzed. Choice **C** is incorrect because notice is mandated by FRCP 23(c)(2), which

states that "the court ***shall***" require notification to the class. Thus, a court cannot dispense with the notice requirement in a FRCP 23(b)(3) class action.

59. B A party may ordinarily obtain discovery of documents and tangible items prepared in anticipation of litigation or trial by or for another party, or that party's representative (including her attorneys), only by showing that the party seeking discovery (1) ***has a need*** for the materials, and (2) is ***otherwise unable*** to obtain them (or the substantial equivalent) without undue hardship. FRCP 26(b)(3). However, FRCP 26(a)(2) mandates that an expert, whose opinions may be presented at trial, prepare a report containing his opinions and the basis for them (as well as other specified information). This report must be disclosed to the opposing party. In addition, since the lock was repaired prior to the time that Amusement Company's attorney had an opportunity to examine it, the pictures taken by P's boyfriend are likely discoverable (even though they are arguably prepared in anticipation of litigation and thus "work product"). Accordingly, choice **B** is the correct selection.

60. C Where a suit is commenced in a state court and federal subject matter jurisdiction would be satisfied based upon a federal claim, the action is removable to the U.S. district court which is in the judicial district that encompasses the state court if (1) all of the defendants join in the petition for removal, and (2) removal is sought within 30 days from the date the moving party received service of process. 28 U.S.C. §1441(b). Since Polly's claim is based on a federal claim, Acme may remove the case to the appropriate U.S. district court. ***Diversity is not pertinent where a federal claim is involved.*** Choice **D** is incorrect because there is no diversity of citizenship because Polly and Acme are both citizens of Georgia. Choice **B** is incorrect because, while there is a lack of diversity, removal is appropriate since Polly is asserting a substantial federal claim. Finally, Choice **A** is incorrect because (1) becoming a citizen of a different state for litigational purposes is usually permissible, and (2) in any event, the citizenship of Polly is irrelevant for purposes of removal since she is asserting a federal case.

61. A This action cannot be maintained under the court's diversity jurisdiction because no single plaintiff has satisfied the amount in controversy requirement. FRCP would allow this joinder, but the only possible basis for subject matter jurisdiction would be federal question. Choice **A**, therefore, is the only correct choice. Choices **B, C,**

and **D** all misstate the law. As to choice **B**, aggregation is not allowed under such circumstances. Choices **C** and **D** ignore the problem with the amount in controversy requirement.

62. **B** Although Y claims that the accident was X's fault, given the standards of Minnesota law regarding contribution between joint tortfeasors, Y should be allowed to implead X under FRCP 14(a). Choice **A** is incorrect because "a common nucleus of operative facts" is not the standard used in determining whether a defendant can join a third party to the proceeding. Choice **B** is incorrect because the question of indispensability is not relevant to an impleader. Choice **D** is incorrect because the citizenship of the third-party defendant is relevant for purposes of establishing diversity; jurisdiction over that claim is supplemental within the terms of 28 U.S.C. §1367.

63. **C** Where the precise issue was actually litigated in a prior action by the party against whom issue preclusion is asserted, and that issue was essential to the decision rendered in the prior lawsuit, *issue preclusion may be permitted*. If Arnold prevailed, Chuck would probably be able to assert collateral estoppel against Bill. Choice **A** is incorrect because the action against Chuck (based upon the guarantee) is different from that asserted against Bill (based upon nonpayment of the promissory note). Choice **B** is incorrect because Chuck was not a party to the *Bill v. Arnold* action. Finally, choice **D** is incorrect because choice **C** is true.

64. **D** Upon *timely* application, a person *may* intervene in an action as of right when he (1) *claims an interest* relating to the property or transaction that is the subject of the action; (2) he is so situated that disposition of the action may, as a practical matter, *impair* his ability to protect that interest; and (3) the applicant's interest is *not adequately represented* by the existing parties. FRCP 24(a)(2). Choice **A** is incorrect because Paul should be able to obtain full relief against Jim as prime obligor. Choice **B** is incorrect because, while Ralph has an interest in the action, permitting him to intervene would destroy diversity. It is therefore unlikely that permissive intervention would be permitted in this instance. Finally, choice **C** is incorrect because Ralph's ability to protect his interest would not be impaired or impeded by a judgment in the outstanding action. Any judgment against Jim probably *would not* have a *res judicata* or collateral estoppel effect on Ralph if Paul subsequently sued him under the guarantee.

65. B A party *may implead another person*, not a party to the action, who is or may be liable to him for all or part of the plaintiff's claim against the impleading party. FRCP 14(a). An impleaded party may assert against the impleading party any counterclaims permitted under FRCP 13. FRCP 14(a). Statement II is correct because Don has an indemnity-type claim against ABC. Since there is supplemental jurisdiction for impleader actions, Don's claim against ABC is proper (even though diversity and "amount in controversy" requisites would otherwise not be satisfied). Statement I is not correct. Polly's personal injury action against Don does not arise from the same nucleus of operative facts that constitutes the basis of her federal claim against him. Thus, supplemental jurisdiction is *not* applicable. "Diversity jurisdiction" is lacking for the car accident claim, since (1) Polly and Don are both citizens of the same state, and (2) the amount in controversy does not exceed $75,000.

66. C When the mental or physical condition of a *party* is in controversy, the *court may order* that party to *submit* to a physical or mental examination by a physician. Such an order will be made only upon motion, for good cause shown, and prior notice to the person to be examined and all other parties. FRCP 35. Since Wanda is *not* a party to the action, an eye examination of her by P cannot be ordered. Choice **D** is incorrect because, while the order requiring the examination must be issued by the court, it is not necessary that the judge actually select the physician (i.e., she might approve a physician recommended by one of the parties). Choice **A** is incorrect because Wanda, who is not a party, cannot be ordered to submit to a physical examination. Finally, choice **B** is incorrect because, although Wanda's vision is important to the question of whether D's alibi can be sustained, an eye examination cannot be ordered since she is not a party.

67. C *U.S. district courts are competent* to hear cases involving a federal claim (i.e., one arising under the Constitution, a treaty, or the laws of the United States). There is no "federal question" because Polly has alluded to a violation of the U.S. Constitution only in the context of anticipating a possible defense that might be raised by Denny. However, a defense based upon the U.S. Constitution or a federal statute cannot serve as the basis for subject matter jurisdiction in federal court. Additionally, there is no "diversity" because Polly's claim is for only $3,000 (six months' rent at $500 per month). Thus, choice **C** represents the only correct selection.

68. C Where the precise issue was actually litigated in a prior action by the party against whom *issue preclusion* is being asserted, and that issue was essential to the decision rendered in the prior lawsuit, issue preclusion *may be* permitted. Since Ball recovered a default judgment against Mel in the initial lawsuit, it would have no collateral estoppel effect (i.e., obviously, the issues were not actually litigated). Also, since Wine and Ball are not in privity, the initial judgment would have no *res judicata* effect. Choice **A** is incorrect because Wine and Ball are not in privity with each other; they are complete strangers. Choice **B** is incorrect because the issues in Ball's action against Mel were not actually litigated. Finally, choice **D** is incorrect because choice **C** is true.

69. D *Notice* of a proposed settlement of a class action *must be* approved by the court. FRCP 23(e). Choice **A** is incorrect because a decision to refuse to certify a class action is *not* a final order, and consequently an immediate appeal therefrom may *not* be taken. *Coopers & Lybrand v. Livesay.* Choice **B** is incorrect because a class action settlement must be approved by the court. FRCP 23(e). Finally, choice **C** is incorrect because where a class action is successful (or a favorable settlement is arranged), federal courts often award the class representative reasonable attorney fees. However, if a class action is predicated on a specific federal statute, attorney fees are awarded only if the enactment explicitly permits them to be recovered. *Alyeska Pipeline Service Co. v. Wilderness Society.*

70. C When diversity is the basis for jurisdiction, intervention does not fall within the federal courts' supplemental jurisdiction. 28 U.S.C. §1367(b). An intervenor must independently satisfy subject matter jurisdiction requirements. Since Bob and Oscar are citizens of the same state (Ohio), competency based upon diversity would not be satisfied. Choice **D** is incorrect because Bob's belief as to the potential damages is irrelevant since diversity does not exist. Choice **A** is incorrect because there is no supplemental jurisdiction, as stated above. Finally, choice **B** is incorrect because Bob is not an indispensable party. Art can obtain complete relief without Bob joining as a party, and Bob's absence would not expose Oscar to a risk of multiple liability for the same obligation. FRCP 19(a). Oscar owes Art a separate and distinct obligation from that owed to Bob.

71. A *Statutory interpleader* is appropriate where (1) there is *diversity* between at least two of the defendant-claimants, and (2) the obligation or property involved *exceeds $500* in value. 28 U.S.C. §1335.

There is nationwide personal jurisdiction for statutory interpleader. 28 U.S.C. §2361. For "rule" interpleader, the ordinary rules of subject matter and personal jurisdiction apply. Since there is minimal diversity amongst the claimant-defendants (i.e., they are not all citizens of the same state) and the amount in controversy exceeds $500, a "statutory" interpleader action is appropriate. **Venue** is proper in any district in which any claimant-defendant resides. There is a federal statute authorizing nationwide personal jurisdiction for statutory interpleader. Choice **B** is incorrect because "rule" interpleader is not appropriate since diversity does not exist (Insurco is a citizen of the same states as Bill, Carl, and Melvin) and the amount in controversy does not exceed $75,000. Choice **C** is incorrect because, under "statutory" interpleader, there is nationwide personal jurisdiction. 28 U.S.C. §2361. Finally, choice **D** is incorrect because the party commencing an interpleader action may claim that he has no liability whatsoever to the claimant-defendants.

72. **C** A *motion for a judgment as a matter of law* should be granted where there is no sufficient legal basis for any other judgment. Since it is entirely possible that a jury could conclude that Joan's physical problems were the consequence of the infection (rather than the inadvertent application of an acidic substance by Dr. Brown), a judgment as a matter of law would not be appropriate. Choice **A** is incorrect because the fact that Dr. Brown admitted that the perforium bottle was located near a container holding an acidic substance would not preclude the jury from reasonably concluding that the wrong bottle had *not* been used. Choice **B** is incorrect because it cannot be said that there was no sufficient legal basis for concluding that Dr. Brown was *not* negligent. Finally, choice **D** is incorrect because choice **C** is true.

73. **A** A *motion for a judgment as a matter of law* should be granted where there is no legally sufficient basis for any other judgment. Since a jury could reasonably conclude that Dr. Brown inadvertently applied an acidic substance to Joan's ear, a judgment as a matter of law in favor of Dr. Brown would be inappropriate. Thus, the trial court's judgment should be reversed and a new trial ordered. If the trial court had withheld its decision upon the motion for a judgment as a matter of law until the jury had rendered its decision, it might not have been necessary to order a new trial (i.e., the jury verdict could be in conformity with the judgment as a matter of law). For this reason, a determination upon a motion for a

judgment as a matter of law *will ordinarily be withheld* until after the jury's verdict has been returned. Choice **B** is incorrect because, as described in the answer to the preceding question, a jury could reasonably find that Dr. Brown was *not* at fault. Choice **C** is incorrect because a jury could reasonably render a verdict for Joan. Finally, choice **D** is incorrect because choice **A** is true.

74. **D** *A motion for a judgment as a matter of law is a prerequisite for a JNOV.* FRCP 50(b). A motion for a new trial may be joined with a motion for a JNOV ("judgment as a matter of law"). FRCP 50(b). Since Dr. Brown did not make a motion for a judgment as a matter of law at the close of the evidence, a JNOV cannot be granted. Since the trial court denied the motion for a new trial and Dr. Brown did not appeal this decision, the jury verdict must be reinstated. Choice **A** is incorrect because a motion for a new trial may be joined with a JNOV motion. Choice **C** is incorrect because no appeal was taken by Dr. Brown from the order denying a new trial. Thus, a new trial cannot be ordered. Finally, choice **B** is incorrect because no motion for a judgment as a matter of law was made, so a JNOV cannot be sustained.

75. **C** A person who is not a party *should be joined* where failure to do so will leave any party to the action subject to a substantial risk of incurring multiple liability for a single obligation. Z should be joined because a judgment in favor of Y could subject X to multiple liability or even inconsistent judgments should Z later sue X. There is a potential problem here, however, since Z and X are from the same state. Hence, if Z is joined as a plaintiff, complete diversity will be destroyed and, under the terms of §1367(b), supplemental jurisdiction would not be available. However, this problem is easily avoided if the court orders X to interplead Y and Z in a counterclaim against Y, combining FRCP 13(a) and (h). Under the standards of §1335, jurisdiction would be established since Z and Y (the claimants) are from different states and the amount in controversy — the value of the vehicle — exceeds the $500 minimum requirement. In addition, since this claim is transactionally related to Y's claim against X, supplemental jurisdiction will be satisfied as well, there being no limit imposed by §1367(b) on this type of joinder by a defendant. Choices **A** and **B** are incorrect because Z ought to be joined and it is feasible to do so. Choice **D** is incorrect since the failure to join Z may subject X to multiple liability or inconsistent judgments.

76. B Upon timely application, a person may intervene in an action as of right when she (1) *claims an interest* relating to the property or transaction that is the subject of the action; (2) she is so situated that disposition of the action may, as a practical matter, *impair her ability to protect that interest*; and (3) the applicant's interest is *not adequately represented* by the existing parties. FRCP 24(a)(2). Since CC might have an indemnity-type claim against Big Builders, impleader would be appropriate if personal jurisdiction requisites were satisfied. Subject matter jurisdiction is *not* a consideration because supplemental jurisdiction extends to the action by CC against Big Builders. Choice **A** is incorrect because, while Big Builders arguably has an interest in the *Mary v. CC* lawsuit, there appears to be no reason to believe that CC could not effectively contest Mary's claim. Additionally, any judgment obtained by Mary would not have a collateral estoppel or *res judicata* effect in a subsequent action by CC against Big Builders. Choice **C** is incorrect because, CC's counterclaim being permissive in nature, the "amount in controversy" requirement would not be satisfied. Finally, choice **D** is incorrect because choice **B** is true.

77. A Where the party against whom a presumption operates has introduced proof sufficient for the fact finder to resolve the factual proposition embodied by the presumption in his favor, *the party in whose favor the presumption operated must carry the burden of proof with respect to such factual proposition.* FRE 301. Since CC has introduced sufficient proof for a fact finder to determine that it had inspected the scaffolding (i.e., the supervisor had told Paul it looked "unsafe"), Mary had to produce proof adequate for a fact finder to conclude that CC had not inspected the scaffolding. However, Mary did not do this; her proof indicated only that Paul was apprehensive about working near the scaffolding. Choice **B** is incorrect because the evidence introduced by Mary does not pertain to CC's alleged failure to inspect the scaffolding. Since Mary (as the plaintiff) would have the burden of proof on this issue, a verdict must be directed for CC. Choice **D** is incorrect because CC introduced enough evidence to rebut the presumption against it (i.e., for a jury to conclude it had inspected the scaffolding). Finally, choice **C** is incorrect because, under these circumstances, the court is obliged to direct a verdict in favor of CC.

78. D Where the party against whom a presumption operates has introduced proof sufficient for the fact finder to resolve the factual proposition embodied by the presumption in her favor, the party in whose favor the presumption operated must carry the burden of proof with respect to such factual proposition. FRE 301. *A verdict cannot be set aside if there is substantial evidence to support it.* Since CC introduced enough evidence to rebut the presumption (i.e., to cause Mary to introduce evidence sufficient to carry her burden of proof on the issue of whether CC was negligent in its inspection of the scaffolding), the court's factual determination and corresponding judgment could *not* be set aside. Choice **A** is incorrect because, since substantial evidence pertaining to the factual proposition embodied by the presumption was introduced by each side, the presumption could be overcome. Thus, the court's judgment should be sustained. Choice **B** is incorrect because the presumption was rebutted when CC introduced proof sufficient for a jury to infer that it had made a reasonable inspection of the scaffolding. Finally, choice **C** is incorrect because a finding of fact may not be set aside when there is substantial evidence to support it.

79. **A** A *cross-claim may be asserted* against a co-party if the cause of action arises out of the transaction or occurrence that is the subject matter of the original action. FRCP 13(g). Since Mary's cross-claim against John (presumably for indemnity) arises from the accident, it may be asserted in this action. Although Mary and John are both citizens of Maine, there is supplemental jurisdiction with respect to cross-claims. Choice **B** is incorrect because cross-claims are not compulsory under the FRCP. Thus, an action is not barred if no cross-claim is made in the original lawsuit. Choice **C** is incorrect because Mary may assert a cross-claim against John under these circumstances. Finally, choice **D** is incorrect because Mary's claim against John is a cross-claim, rather than a counterclaim (John is a co-party and has not commenced an action against Mary).

80. **D** A defendant may implead another person, not a party to the action, who is or may be liable to it for all or part of the plaintiff's claim against the defending/impleading party. FRCP 14(a). *Star* probably would have an indemnity-type claim against Albert if the information that the latter supplied to it was incorrect. The fact that *Star* and Albert are citizens of the same state would *not* prevent the lawsuit since there is supplemental jurisdiction for impleader actions. Choice **C** is incorrect because an impleader action may be instituted for an indemnity-type of claim. If *Star* were asserting that

Albert alone *was* liable to Beacon House, it would *not* satisfy this requisite. Choice **A** is incorrect because courts have supplemental jurisdiction over impleader actions. Finally, choice **B** is incorrect because (1) any judgment by Beacon House against *Star* would not have a collateral estoppel or *res judicata* effect upon Albert in the event of a subsequent action against the latter, and (2) Albert's interests probably will be adequately represented by *Star.* Thus, intervention into the action by Albert would be permissive (rather than "as of right").

81. **C** Where the precise issue was actually litigated in a prior suit by the person against whom issue preclusion is being asserted, and that issue was essential to the decision rendered in that action, *issue preclusion may be permitted.* Since *Star* would have actually litigated the issues pertaining to whether the statements in its article were true, a finding that such statements were untrue presumably would be binding on *Star* in a subsequent action against it by Don. A court, however, could refuse to allow Don to assert collateral estoppel if it felt that he had "hung back" by failing to commence litigation until the initial lawsuit was completed. Choice **D** is incorrect because one is never required to intervene in an action (even if he could have done so as of right). Thus, a party who fails to intervene in an existing action does not forfeit his right to assert an action against a party in the initial lawsuit. Choice **B** is incorrect because, even though an action for an accounting traditionally has been viewed as being equitable in nature, it is now viewed as one for damages. ***Dairy Queen v. Wood.*** Thus, Albert probably would be entitled to a jury trial on this question. Finally, choice **A** is incorrect because courts have supplemental subject matter jurisdiction over cross-claims.

82. **B** *A court may realign parties to reflect their true interests in the litigation for diversity purposes.* Although D has an interest in the action (i.e., D wishes the trust to continue) that might be impaired if the plaintiffs are successful (i.e., D would pay a greater amount of taxes), diversity probably would *not* be destroyed by D's joinder. This is because D should be aligned with T (rather than made an involuntary plaintiff) since, as a practical matter, his interests coincide with those of T; they both desire to maintain the trust. Thus, complete diversity would exist even if D were compelled to join the litigation. Choice **A** is incorrect because for diversity to be satisfied, no plaintiff and no defendant may be citizens of the same state.

Choice **D** is incorrect because, while D may be an indispensable party, he probably would be aligned with T. Thus, diversity would still exist. Finally, choice **C** is incorrect because, even if D was aligned with T, diversity still exists.

83. **A** Where the jury's answer to written interrogatories are inconsistent with a general verdict rendered by the jury, *the judge may* (1) *enter a verdict* in accordance with the answers to the interrogatories, (2) *return the answers* to the jury for further consideration and verdict, or (3) *order a new trial.* FRCP 49(b). A party may ordinarily dismiss a lawsuit after the other side has filed an answer by filing a stipulation of dismissal, which is signed by all the parties who have appeared in the action. Unless otherwise stated in the notice of dismissal or stipulation, a dismissal by consent is without prejudice. FRCP 41(a)(1). Since the dismissal was signed by Defendant, it would be deemed to be without prejudice to Plaintiff's right to subsequently initiate a similar action against Defendant. Choice **B** is incorrect because a court is not obliged to render a judgment in strict conformity with the jury's answers to interrogatories. Choice **C** is incorrect because (1) the court cannot enter a general verdict inconsistent with the jury's answers to interrogatories, and (2) the court may send the interrogatory answers and verdict back to the jury for further consideration. Finally, choice **D** is incorrect because choice **A** is true.

84. **C** Unless the parties or local rules stipulate otherwise, a *party must disclose without waiting for a discovery request any insurance policy under which any person carrying on an insurance business may be liable to satisfy part or all of a judgment.* FRCP 26(a)(1)(D). Thus, the insured party must disclose the insurance policy even if it would not be admissible at trial. Choice **D** is incorrect because the existence of insurance by a party will rarely be relevant to the issues of the case. Choices **A** and **B** are incorrect because choice **C** is true.

85. **A** If a *deposition* is conducted in bad faith or in such a manner as to annoy, embarrass, or oppress the deponent, *the court may order* the officer conducting the *examination to cease* forthwith from taking the deposition or limit the scope and manner of the deposition. In such event, the court may order the party conducting the deposition to pay the attorney fees of the objecting party. FRCP 30(d)(3). If the party who scheduled the deposition fails to attend, the court may order that party to pay the other the reasonable

expenses incurred by the latter, including reasonable attorney fees. FRCP 30(g)(1). If Andy (1) conducted a deposition in a manner designed to embarrass the deponent, or (2) failed to attend a deposition that he had scheduled, the aggrieved party is entitled to obtain his reasonable expenses associated with the depositions, including attorney fees. Statement III would not be a cause for sanctions against Andy. If the deposed person or party can show that she was unable (despite the exercise of diligence) to obtain counsel to represent her at a deposition, the testimony may be precluded from being used against such party at trial. FRCP 32(a)(3). Finally, statement IV does not justify sanctions unless the objections were made in an argumentative or suggestive manner. FRCP 30(b)(1).

86. C In a FRCP 23(b)(3) class action, the notice must advise each class member that (1) any member *may opt out* of the class, (2) any member who does *not* opt out of the class will be bound by the final judgment, and (3) any member who remains in the class *may appear* in the action through an attorney. FRCP 23(c)(2). Since the notice fails to indicate that a final judgment is binding upon all members of the class, it is inadequate. Choice **A** is incorrect because the plaintiff (rather than the defendant) must pay the costs of mailings to class members. If he fails to do so, the action will be dismissed. Choice **B** is incorrect because a class action judgment has no negative collateral estoppel effect with respect to individuals who decided to opt out of the class. Finally, choice **D** is incorrect because choice **C** is true.

87. C Parties may obtain discovery regarding any matter, not privileged, which is relevant to the subject matter of the pending action. It is *not a ground for objection* that the information sought will *not be admissible* at trial, if such information is reasonably calculated to lead to the discovery of admissible evidence. FRCP 26(b)(1). If information sought is (1) privileged, or (2) not reasonably calculated to lead to admissible evidence, it need not be disclosed. Thus, statements I and III embody valid objections. Statement II is incorrect because factual information relating to the claims of a party is discoverable. Finally, statement IV is not a valid objection because, although the evidence might be obtained from a less expensive source, this type of limitation upon the ordinary rights of discovery must be embodied in a court order. FRCP 26(b)(1).

88. B Opinions of experts retained by counsel in anticipation of litigation who are not to be called as witnesses are discoverable only "upon a showing of *exceptional circumstances*" (where the party would otherwise be unable to obtain the same facts or opinions by other means). FRCP 26(b)(4)(B). Thus, the economist's opinion is not discoverable because there are no indications that the other party was unable to access the facts or opinions through other means. Choice **D** is incorrect because no privilege appears to be applicable to the economist's opinion. Choice **C** is incorrect since the time at which an expert forms his opinion is irrelevant to its discoverability. Finally, Choice **A** is incorrect because **B** is true.

89. D Under Article IV, §1, of the U.S. Constitution, each *state must ordinarily give the judgments of other states the same effect* (i.e., full faith and credit) that the earlier judgment would have in the state in which it was rendered. The State Y court would be obliged under full faith and credit principles to recognize the decision rendered in the State X court. Choice **A** is incorrect because, while the earlier judgment would prevent Defendant from *relitigating* the claim, plaintiff is seeking only to enforce the prior judgment. Choice **B** is incorrect because the State Y court cannot constitutionally disregard the State X judgment. Finally, choice **C** is incorrect because the State Y court must give effect to the earlier judgment, even though it was based upon a doctrine that is not adhered to in State Y.

90. C *Where the precise issue was actually litigated* in a prior action by the person against whom issue preclusion is being asserted, and that issue was essential to the decision rendered in that lawsuit, *issue preclusion may be permitted.* Since C was not in privity with A, the judgment against A could not preclude C from litigating the question of B's negligence. The application of collateral estoppel here would violate C's due process rights. Choice **A** is incorrect because the application of collateral estoppel principles would violate C's due process rights. Choice **B** is incorrect because (1) a different action is involved (C's rights of recovery, rather than A's), and (2) A and C are not in privity. Finally, choice **D** is incorrect because collateral estoppel may not constitutionally be applied, whether or not the mutuality rule has been repudiated in this state.

91. B For purposes of diversity, a *partnership is deemed to be a citizen of the states in which any one of its partners is domiciled.* It would be helpful to know where Paul is domiciled to determine if that state is the same one in which (1) either of Dodo's partners is domiciled (State X), or (2) Dominic's is a citizen for diversity purposes (State Z). Thus, statement II is important since, if Paul were a citizen of either State X or State Z, diversity subject matter jurisdiction would not exist. Also, consistent with statement IV, it would also be helpful to know the extent of Paul's injuries to determine if the "in excess of $75,000" requirement is satisfied. Statement I is unimportant because the citizenship of a corporation is determined by its states of incorporation and principal place of business. The place of domicile of its shareholders is irrelevant for diversity purposes. Finally, as to statement III, whether State Z has a long-arm statute is irrelevant to the question of subject matter jurisdiction.

92. **C** Under FRCP 4, notice with respect to actions commenced in a U.S. district court must be accomplished in accordance with the FRCP or the applicable local law. However, as a matter of due process, *notice must always be reasonably calculated* under the circumstances to apprise the defendant of the outstanding action. There is little doubt that a procedure that permits notification by posting in a situation where personal service could probably be effectuated would be unconstitutional. *Schroeder v. City of New York; Walker v. City of Hutchinson.* Since the names of the officers or directors of Dominic's presumably could be ascertained from the State Z corporate records, the State Z notice statute would be unconstitutional as applied to these circumstances. Choice A, then, appears to be correct. Choice **C**, however, is nonetheless correct, since the process service complied with the State Z statute and since D received actual notice. While receipt of actual notice by a defendant does not cure a statutorily invalid service, *Wuchter v. Pizzutti*, it does cure due process violations. Choice **B** is incorrect because notice in a federal court proceeding may be given in accordance with the applicable state service of process statute (provided, of course, it is valid). Finally, choice **D** is factually true but incorrect because the state notice statute must be constitutional as applied to the existing circumstances.

93. **A** Unless a traditional basis of personal jurisdiction exists, *personal jurisdiction may not be taken over an out-of-state defendant unless it is statutorily and constitutionally permissible.* Since Dodo's is not physically present in State Z (i.e., it has no personnel in the jurisdiction), the existence of a long-arm statute that empowered State Z courts to assert personal jurisdiction over a defendant in

circumstances such as these would be a very significant question. Thus, statement I is pertinent. Statement II is pertinent because Dodo's awareness that the oven would be used in State Z would certainly make it more likely that Dodo should have reasonably foreseen being haled into court in the state. *World-Wide Volkswagen Corp. v. Woodson.* Statement III is pertinent because the greater volume of business by Dodo in State Z, the less likely it is that "traditional notions of fair play and substantial justice" would be "offended" by making the defendant stand trial in that state. *International Shoe Co. v. Washington.* Finally, the physical health of the parties involved in litigation has never been cited as a relevant factor in the determination of whether personal jurisdiction exists (it could presumably be considered in the context of a *forum non conveniens* motion). Statement IV, therefore, is not relevant.

94. **C** *A person who is not a party should be joined* where failure to do so will leave any party to the action subject to a substantial risk of incurring multiple liability for a single obligation. If the court determines that in equity and in good conscience the action should be dismissed in the nonparty's absence, he is regarded as being indispensable. Where the joinder of an indispensable party will destroy subject matter jurisdiction, a federal court must dismiss the action. FRCP 19. Paul can obtain complete relief (a judgment for the full amount of his damages) without the necessity of joining Dan. Additionally, Acme will not be exposed to multiple liability for the same obligation since (1) Paul can obtain only one recovery for his injuries; and (2) where the potential defendants are joint tortfeasors, neither is prejudiced by a plaintiff's decision to refrain from suing every person who could possibly be liable. The risk that a particular defendant could have to bear the entire amount of the plaintiff's recovery always exists where there are joint tortfeasors. Choice **B** is incorrect because a plaintiff in a U.S. district court suing a single defendant may aggregate totally unrelated claims to meet the jurisdictional amount. It is only where plaintiff asserts actions against more than one defendant that the plaintiff must show that at least one of his claims (1) arises from a common transaction or occurrence, and (2) possesses a common question of law or fact. Choice **A** is incorrect because, as explained above, Dan is not an indispensable party. Finally, choice **D** is incorrect because choice **B** is not true.

95. D A party is *entitled to summary judgment* where, as a consequence
of there being no "genuine issue of material fact," he is *entitled to
judgment as a matter of law*. FRCP 56. Even though Acme neglected to respond to Paul's affidavit, Paul would be entitled to a
partial summary judgment only on the issue of his job competency.
His affidavit does not address the issues of (1) whether Dan's statement about Paul was within the scope of Dan's employment, and
(2) whether Paul was entitled to recover for the unused vacation
pay. Choice **C** is incorrect because the affidavit necessary to support
a summary judgment motion may be made by the moving party,
personally. Although choice **A** is factually accurate, it is incorrect
because it would entitle Paul only to a summary judgment on the
issue of his competence. Finally, choice **B** is incorrect because, as
explained above, genuine issues of fact still exist.

96. C Where the precise issue was actually litigated and decided in a prior
lawsuit by the party (or his privy) against whom issue preclusion is
being asserted in a subsequent action, and that issue was essential to
the decision that was rendered in the earlier lawsuit, *issue preclusion ordinarily will be applied*. The general verdict in favor of
Acme does not disclose which issue was decided — whether
Dan's statement was true or whether it was within the scope of
Dan's employment. Either one, if decided unfavorably to Paul,
would have been sufficient to sustain the verdict. But since we
do not know which was decided, even though one of them must
have been, neither is binding. Choice **B** is incorrect because, as
explained above, collateral estoppel is not applicable. Choice **A** is
incorrect because (1) a different cause of action is involved (*Paul v.
Dan*), and (2) Dan is probably *not* in privity with Acme. Finally,
choice **D** is incorrect because choices **A** and **B** are incorrect.

97. A A federal district court is competent to hear matters that (1) involve
a federal question, or (2) satisfy diversity requirements (i.e., no
plaintiff and no defendant are citizens of the same state and the
plaintiff's claim exceeds $75,000). The correct answer is choice **A**.
Because Paul and Deeter Corporation are citizens of different states
and the aggregate amount of the plaintiff's claim exceeds $75,000,
diversity requirements are met and the district court may properly
exercise subject matter jurisdiction. Choice **B** is incorrect because
no federal question exists (i.e., the plaintiff is not suing pursuant to
a federal statute). Choice **C**, while factually true, is incorrect because
the plaintiff's claims must only *aggregate* "in excess of $75,000." It

is not necessary for each claim to exceed $75,000. Finally, choice **D** is incorrect because the sufficiency of minimum contacts relates to personal jurisdiction, and the facts stipulate that personal jurisdiction requirements are satisfied.

98. C   In the absence of a specialized jurisdictional statute, federal courts borrow the jurisdictional statute of the state in which they sit. This is true in both federal question and diversity cases. Hence, given that State X's jurisdictional statute cannot be satisfied here, jurisdiction cannot be asserted. Choice **A** is, therefore, incorrect. The satisfaction of minimum contacts in not sufficient. Choice **B** is incorrect. Even if the elements of diversity subject matter jurisdiction are satisfied, the State X long-arm statute would not permit its courts to assume personal jurisdiction over Dumbco (the out-of-state defendant). Finally, choice **D** is incorrect because the basis of competency (i.e., subject matter jurisdiction) is a federal claim, not diversity of citizenship; the requirement that claims exceed $75,000 (exclusive of interest and costs) applies only in diversity cases.

99. D   In federal cases, the amount in controversy stated by the pleader in diversity cases controls, unless it appears to a legal certainty that the claim fails to exceed $75,000. Where an out-of-state defendant is personally served while in the jurisdiction to assist in the administration of justice, courts often quash a service of process upon that person. This action is discretionary with the court. The correct answer is choice **D**. Because Arthur was in New York to assist in the administration of justice (i.e., complying with a subpoena), he will probably be able to quash the service of process made upon him. Choice **C** is incorrect because the damages actually established (even if proven to not exceed $75,000) would not result in the failure of Clarence's lawsuit. A plaintiff in diversity cases must demonstrate at the commencement of the litigation (if challenged) only that there is no "legal certainty" that his damages will not exceed $75,000. Choice **A** is incorrect because (although diversity requirements appear to be satisfied) the service of process upon Arthur will probably be quashed. Finally, choice **B** is incorrect because the service of process will probably be quashed.

100. C   *Under FRCP 4(k)(1), federal courts generally borrow* the long-arm statute of the jurisdiction in which the federal court is located. The correct answer is choice **C**. Although ABC *arguably* had minimum contacts with Florida as a consequence of its knowledge that its motors were integrated into yachts that were sold in that state, the Florida long-arm statute precludes personal jurisdiction in this situation because ABC neither sells products in Florida nor to Florida domicilliaries. Choice **D** is incorrect because ABC's knowledge that its motors might be operated in Florida could constitute "sufficient minimum contacts" with Florida if this were a federal question rather than a diversity situation. Choice **A** is incorrect since Florida's long-arm statute precludes the assertion of personal jurisdiction in this instance. Finally, choice **B** is incorrect because the fact that ABC did business with the party that sold the item in question to a Florida domicilliary does not permit a court of that state to assume personal jurisdiction over ABC.

101. A Courts may exercise personal jurisdiction over a defendant who is served while physically present in the jurisdiction. The correct answer is choice **A**. Because Dan was personally served while within California, he can be required to stand trial in that jurisdiction. The fact that he was served while performing an activity completely different from the one during which Pat was injured is irrelevant. Choice **B** is incorrect because Dan probably lacks adequate minimum contacts with California; he is there only four days per year and at the discretion of his employers. Choice **C** is incorrect because, although Dan probably lacked minimum contacts with California, he was personally served in the jurisdiction. As explained above, personal service within the jurisdiction can be sufficient. Finally, choice **D** is incorrect because diversity of citizenship does exist (Pat is a California citizen and Dan is a citizen of Illinois, and the amount claimed exceeds $75,000).

102. C Under FRCP 12(b), "[e]very defense ... to a claim for relief in any pleading shall be asserted in the responsive pleading ... except that the following defenses may at the option of the pleader be made by motion: ... (2) lack of jurisdiction over the person. ... A motion making any of these defenses shall be made before pleading if a further pleading is permitted." Since Dan failed to object to personal jurisdiction in his first pleading (his answer and counterclaim), he has waived this defense, and thus the correct answer is choice **C**. Choice **D** is incorrect because a plaintiff's choice of forum remains subject to the proper exercise of personal jurisdiction over the defendant. Choices **A** and **B** are incorrect since a lack of personal jurisdiction must by raised in the initial response of the objecting party; otherwise, it is waived.

103. **A** Under FRCP 32(a)(2), "[t]he deposition of a *party* . . . may be used by an adverse party for any purpose." Thus, the correct answer is choice **A**. XYZ can use Wanda's deposition for any purpose (i.e., as direct evidence or to impeach her). Choice **B** is incorrect because the deposition *of a party* to the action can be used for purposes other than impeachment. Choice **C** is incorrect since Wanda's deposition may be used for substantive purposes by XYZ. Finally, choice **D** is incorrect because XYZ can use Wanda's deposition whether or not her attorney deposed any of XYZ's officers or employees.

104. **A** A pleading shall state as a counterclaim any claim which, at the time of serving the pleading, the pleader has against any opposing party, if it (1) arises out of the transaction that is the subject matter of the opposing party's claim, and (2) does not require for its adjudication the presence of third parties of whom the court cannot acquire jurisdiction. FRCP 13(a). The correct answer is choice **A**. Doe's action against Pete for breach of contract required Pete to assert any counterclaim that he (Pete) might have against Doe under the specific agreement in question. When Pete failed to assert a counterclaim, any action against Doe under that contract was forfeited. Choice **B** is incorrect because collateral estoppel is not applicable. Collateral estoppel comes into play when an issue has arguably been decided in an earlier action. The specific issue of Doe's possible liability to Pete under the contract was presumably *not* litigated in the earlier case. Choice **C** is incorrect because Pete was required to counterclaim against Doe when he (Pete) was sued by Doe under the agreement. Finally, choice **D** is incorrect because, even though Pete's claim is not barred under collateral estoppel principles, it can no longer be asserted. Pete was obliged to file a counterclaim against Doe when the latter asserted a breach of contract action under that agreement against Pete.

105. **D** Before discovery begins, a party must disclose the following information if relevant to the disputed facts *pleaded with particularity:* (1) the name, address, and telephone number of every person likely to have discoverable information; and (2) a copy or a description of all tangible things and documents. FRCP 26(a)(1) Since the documents and model would be relevant to P's allegation as stated in her complaint, D was required to disclose these

documents to P by copying them or describing them by category and location (unless the court had opted out of the mandatory prediscovery disclosure). Choice **C** is a correct statement of the law. However, this alone would not require a party to **voluntarily disclose** known sources of discoverable information. There is no indication of any privilege here, so choice **A** is wrong. Finally, choice **B** is incorrect because **D** is true.

106. D A party may discover experts retained by counsel who will not be called at trial only upon a showing of **exceptional circumstances** (that it, is impossible for the moving party to obtain these facts or opinions by another means). FRCP 26(b)(4)(B). Since there is no indication of such circumstances here, P may not discover the identities and opinions of D's retained experts. Thus choice **A** is false. Choice **B** is incorrect because it states the law prior to the 1993 amendments to the FRCP. Choice **C** is a misstatement of the law since evidence need only be relevant, not admissible, to be discoverable. FRCP 26(b)(1).

107. A A party must supplement its initial mandatory disclosure if it discovers they are no longer complete or accurate. FRCP 26(e)(1). Thus, the existence of a new witness who may have discoverable information regarding disputed facts pleaded with particularity would have to be disclosed by D. Choices **B**, **C**, and **D** are all incorrect because they fail to recognize this mandatory requirement to supplement initial disclosure.

108. C FRCP 11 provides that attorneys who file frivolous or harassing pleadings may be sanctioned by the court. However, the rule allows attorneys a **"safe harbor"** of 21 days from the date the adverse party serves a motion on him to withdraw or correct the offending pleading. FRCP 11(c)(1)(A). Thus, no matter how outrageous the pleading, Bull cannot be sanctioned because he withdrew the complaint within the safe harbor period. An attorney must make a reasonable inquiry before signing the pleading. Bull's failure to ask about the dye probably fails this standard. However, choice **A** is incorrect because Bull withdrew the complaint in a timely fashion. Similarly, choice **B** is incorrect because the outrageousness of the attorney's conduct is irrelevant as long as the pleading is withdrawn within the 21-day period. Choice **D** is not true. Since an attorney swears to the pleading, he is responsible to make reasonable inquiries to determine the veracity of the complaint. If he fails to do this, he is open to sanctions under FRCP 11.

109. A FRCP 30(a)(2)(A) sets a presumptive limit of *10 depositions* for each party. However, the parties can agree to more depositions, or the court can order more. Since there is no evidence that this limit has been lifted, P's motion should be granted. Choice **B** is incorrect because parties may be deposed. Since the limit is imposed irrespective of whether added depositions are likely to lead to relevant information, choice **C** is not correct (but a court might consider this in deciding whether to issue an order permitting more depositions). Choice **D** is incorrect because choice **A** is true.

Table of References to the
Federal Rules of Civil Procedure

Table of References to
Title 28, United States Code

Index

References are to the number of the question raising the issue. "E" indicates an Essay Question; "M" indicates a Multiple-Choice Question.